Are There Laws of Innovation?

Other World Scientific Titles by the Author

The COVID-19 Epidemic in China
ISBN: 978-981-122-250-4
ISBN: 978-981-122-419-5 (pbk)

Are There Laws of Innovation?

Lawrence J Lau
The Chinese University of Hong Kong, Hong Kong

Yanyan Xiong
Zhejiang University, China

World Scientific

NEW JERSEY • LONDON • SINGAPORE • BEIJING • SHANGHAI • HONG KONG • TAIPEI • CHENNAI • TOKYO

Published by

World Scientific Publishing Co. Pte. Ltd.
5 Toh Tuck Link, Singapore 596224
USA office: 27 Warren Street, Suite 401-402, Hackensack, NJ 07601
UK office: 57 Shelton Street, Covent Garden, London WC2H 9HE

Library of Congress Cataloging-in-Publication Data
Names: Lau, Lawrence J., 1944– author. | Xiong, Yanyan, author.
Title: Are there laws of innovation? / Lawrence J. Lau, Chinese University of Hong Kong, Hong Kong, Yanyan Xiong, Zhejiang University, China.
Description: New Jersey : World Scientific, [2022] | Includes bibliographical references and index.
Identifiers: LCCN 2021051574 | ISBN 9789811251177 (hardcover) | ISBN 9789811251184 (ebook) | ISBN 9789811251191 (ebook other)
Subjects: LCSH: Technological innovations--Group of Seven countries. | Research and development projects--Group of Seven countries.
Classification: LCC HC79.T4 L374 2022 | DDC 338/.064--dc23/eng/20211021
LC record available at https://lccn.loc.gov/2021051574

British Library Cataloguing-in-Publication Data
A catalogue record for this book is available from the British Library.

For any available supplementary material, please visit
https://www.worldscientific.com/worldscibooks/10.1142/12692#t=suppl

Desk Editor: Ong Shi Min Nicole

Typeset by Stallion Press
Email: enquiries@stallionpress.com

To Ayesha, my muse, my love and my life, LJL

To my beloved grandparents who enlightened me with endless love, YX

Foreword

One month has passed since I received the manuscript of the new book of Lawrence J. Lau and Yanyan Xiong. Each time I read it, I can see their unique insight and incisive analysis. Lawrence Lau is a world-renowned economist with outstanding achievements and profound knowledge in econometrics. From the perspectives of economics and natural sciences, Lau and Xiong research into the laws of innovation and development through tightly-knit arguments and extensive citations, basing the core argument on a large quantity of data and logical thinking, which fully reflects the rigorous academic attitude of leading economists.

Since the Industrial Revolution, mankind has been exploring the laws of scientific and technological innovation. From the macro to the micro, from the single field to multi-disciplinary fields, knowledge has been accumulating and its boundary has been extended continuously, contributing to the scientific, technological and industrial revolutions of human society. The continuous investment in science and technology, the constant improvement of the intellectual property system, and the legacy of scientific culture and spirit have provided strong support for innovation and accelerated the advancement of mankind as well as the progress of civilisation.

All the achievements in science, technology and innovation are the common wealth of mankind. Although different nations have been developing at different paces, the differences among them are actually quite small on a historical scale. These nations have been constantly interacting with and learning from one another, and eventually, they will reach the same destination. In order to promote the common development of diverse economies, the scientific and economic circles should join hands to research into these differences and their causes so as to find corresponding counter-measures.

I am delighted to see that the authors have done systematic thinking on methodology when researching into these differences. Most studies examine the relationship between the output and input of R&D by either analysing the data collected from enterprises in a single economy or estimating the relative efficiency of research and development (R&D) processes among different economies from economy-level data. But Lau and Xiong carry out research from the perspective of a global market economy, comparing the scientific and technological activities of the Group-of-Seven (G-7) developed economies, the four East Asian Newly Industrialised Economies (EANIEs) (Hong Kong, South Korea, Singapore and Taiwan), and the Chinese Mainland, at both macro and micro levels. They believe that, with the passage of time, the centre of global innovation has gradually shifted from developed economies to developing ones, and from the economies in Europe and North America to those in East Asia. This new and illuminating research approach will promote further studies regarding innovation and economic development activities under globalisation.

Lau and Xiong propose that innovation is the result of long-term research and development activities of an economy, and regard it as an important "law behind innovation". They take the accumulative effect and depreciation of R&D investment into account when studying the above-mentioned economies and use the real R&D capital stock as an indicator to measure the economic innovation input of an economy. They also explore the relationship and efficiency deviation between the innovation output and input, and develop indicators of relative success in innovation across different economies through an econometric analysis of the data on real R&D capital stock, patent applications and patent grants.

They believe that the fundamental reason for the different levels of innovation and efficiency in different countries is the variation in their long-term research and development (R&D) investments. In 2019, the United States, China and Japan were the three countries with the largest real R&D capital stock in the world. Although China ranked second in overall real R&D capital stock, it still lags far behind the United States and Japan in terms of real basic research capital stock. Lau and Xiong find that the higher the real basic research capital stock in an economy is, the higher its cumulative number of Nobel Laureates will be, which shows that basic research is an important determinant of breakthrough scientific discoveries. In the long run, innovation leadership can only be achieved with significant investment in basic research. At present, the proportion of basic research capital stock in total R&D capital stock in China is still low compared with those of other major economies. Thus, China needs to provide stronger support for, accelerate the reform of, and increase investment in basic research.

I believe that these research findings will be a source of inspiration for the decision-makers in macroeconomic and science and technology management, and they also have important reference value for decision makers in science and technology innovation in China.

First, innovation does not come by accident, but is a result of the long-term accumulation of R&D efforts. More R&D investment of an economy will result in more innovation and technical progress, which depend not only on current R&D investment, but more importantly, on long-term commitment and planning when carrying out R&D and other innovation activities. Basic research is an important source of innovation output as it can bring breakthroughs in science and technology in the long run, creating numerous patents and other key intellectual property rights in the process. In terms of the proportion of basic research expenditure in total R&D expenditure, during the 20 years from 1999 to 2018, the average proportion in the United States was 17.3%, while that of China was only between 4.5% and 6%. In the book, the authors show, through a large amount of data and cases, that only by carrying out long-term R&D investment, especially investment in basic research, can an economy develop in science and technology, and innovate continuously, so as to bring the economic and social development to a higher level.

Second, enterprises are the main carriers of technological innovation activities. From the perspective of historical experience, enterprises are the cradle of major innovations. Under the conditions of a market economy, the size of the scientific and technological personnel and the quantity of the R&D capital investment of an enterprise are the two basic determinants of its technological innovation. We need to adhere to the policies that regard enterprises as an important source of innovation, provide strong support for enterprises in their technological innovation activities, protect their intellectual property rights, and maintain the vitality and motivation of enterprise innovation. Only in this way can the innovation vitality of the entire society be maintained, and this will ultimately contribute to economic and social progress.

Third, the modern intellectual property system protects and boosts enterprise innovation. After nearly 40 years of development, China has transformed from a large intellectual property importing country to a large intellectual property creating country. However, it should be clear that there is still significant room for China to improve the quality of its patent applications, different from the United States and other developed economies of the West. In the next step, China should shift its focus from pursuing the quantity to improving the quality of its intellectual property in making relevant policies. At the same time, the intellectual property system should be improved to make the whole society realise that "innovation is the primary driving force for development, and protection of intellectual property contributes to innovation".

Fourth, equal and win-win international cooperation is an important way of scientific and technological innovation. It is important for developing economies to import technology in the process of improving their own innovation capabilities, but "introducing technology" does not mean "introducing technological innovation capabilities." The authors reveal an important fact in their research: "New equipment and technology imported by developing economies from developed economies are often already fully priced, so that the importing economy cannot expect to derive additional benefits over or above the cost of the imported equipment and technology paid." Experience has proved that technological innovation capability is endogenous and can only be acquired through organised learning and actual practice. Simple introduction of technology from abroad does not necessarily lead to improved innovation capability. In the National Medium- and Long-Term Plan for the Development of Science and Technology (2006–2020) of China formulated in 2004, it was proposed to strengthen the three aspects of home-grown innovation: (1) original innovation; (2) integrated innovation; and (3) introduction of foreign innovation and its digestion, absorption and re-innovation (Ministry of Science and Technology, 2006). Home-grown innovation is by no means self-innovation, nor is it innovation behind closed doors. Thus, in international cooperation and technology introduction, China should strive to improve its own innovation capacity continuously so that it can achieve higher-level and more open international collaboration and cooperation.

Fifth, talent is an important and integral component of R&D input, and top-notch personnel is the key to scientific and technological innovation. I agree with the authors' judgment that even though the total number of educated people in China has seen significant increase in recent decades and the total number of scientists and engineers ranks second in the world, there is still a serious shortage of world-class scientific and technological experts and strategic scientists, the quantity of human capital per capita is still relatively low, and it will take a long time for China to catch up to the level of the G-7 economies. To this end, we must make arduous efforts.

Paul Romer, 2018 Nobel Laureate in Economic Sciences, believes that the huge increase in growth and productivity is the outcome of meta ideas. The British Empire was built on the meta idea of patents and copyrights in the 17th century, and the United States thrived on the meta ideas of the modern research universities in the 19th century and the peer-reviewed competitive research grant system in the 20th century. He said to the effect that we don't know what the next meta idea will be or where it will appear, but the meta idea of this century will definitely appear.

In the 21st century, all countries are faced with the challenge of how to make scientific and technological innovations and achieve social and economic progress, and they are also faced with the challenge of how to become a factory of ideas. China needs to create new ideas and utilize the ideas from all over the world if it wants to be a contributor to global development in the future. China should strive to become one of the most important factories of ideas in the world and the fountain of meta ideas. What will be the meta idea of this century? We believe that it might be a result of the integration of the cultures of the East and the West as they have many similarities as well as differences, and it is precisely because of their differences that their integration will bring great possibilities. In the new era of scientific and technological innovation, we should explore new ideas and new approaches that combine the strengths of both Eastern and Western cultures, promote more efficient development of innovation, carry forward the economic value and social responsibility of science and technology, and lead the community of shared destiny for mankind to a more glorious future.

Xu Guanhua
Beijing, China
May 2021

Preface

The objectives of this book are threefold: (1) to identify the determinants of innovation at the economy-wide level; (2) to ascertain whether they are the same across different economies; and (3) to find suitable metrics for comparing the relative success in innovation across different economies. In other words, we try to discover whether there is a common law of innovation that applies across different economies. We also try to develop indicators of relative success in innovation across different economies.

An important innovation input is Research and Development (R&D). While discoveries and inventions are brought about by R&D activities, they are not brought about by only R&D activities in the current period. They can result from R&D activities initiated a long time ago. We therefore measure the innovation input of an economy by the quantity of its real R&D capital stock, defined as the cumulative past real expenditures on R&D, less a depreciation of 10% per annum. Important innovation outputs are patent applications submitted to and patent grants awarded by different official patent authorities, such as the United States Patent and Trademark Office (USPTO), the European Patent Office (EPO), and the China National Intellectual Property Administration (CNIPA), and other domestic patent authorities. We try to establish systematically the positive relationship between innovation outputs and innovation inputs of different economies.

The economies included in our study consist of the Group-of-Seven (G-7) countries (Canada, France, Germany, Italy, Japan, the United Kingdom (UK), and the United States (US)), the four East Asian Newly Industrialised

Economies (EANIEs) (Hong Kong, China, South Korea, Singapore and Taiwan, China), and the Mainland of China.

We wish to express our deepest gratitude to Professor Xu Guanhua, who served as Minister of Science and Technology of the People's Republic of China from 2001 to 2007, for writing a Foreword for our book. We are most grateful to Mrs. Ayesha Macpherson Lau and Prof. Jungsoo Park for their helpful comments and suggestions on earlier drafts. The authors also wish to thank Dr. Paul Aiello, Prof. Michael J. Boskin, Prof. Cyrus Chu, Prof. Dale W. Jorgenson, Prof. Lang Kao, Prof. Chung-Ming Kuan, Prof. Masahiro Kuroda, Prof. Jiadong Shea, Mr. Kenny Shui, Mr. Junjie Tang, and the late Prof. John Wong of the National University of Singapore for their advice and assistance. We also wish to thank the Lau Chor Tak Institute of Global Economics and Finance of The Chinese University of Hong Kong for its financial support of this research project. Finally, Ms. Nicole Ong and her colleagues at the World Scientific Publishing Company deserve our special thanks for their advice and assistance. Responsibility for any errors remains with the authors.

Lawrence J. Lau, Hong Kong, China
and
Yanyan Xiong, Hangzhou, Zhejiang, China
31 May 2021

About the Authors

Lawrence J. Lau is Ralph and Claire Landau Professor of Economics, Lau Chor Tak Institute of Global Economics and Finance, The Chinese University of Hong Kong, and Kwoh-Ting Li Professor in Economic Development, Emeritus, Stanford University.

Yanyan Xiong is ZJU100 Young Professor, School of Economics, and Research Fellow, Center of Social Welfare and Governance, Zhejiang University, Hangzhou, China, and Research Fellow (Honorary), Lau Chor Tak Institute of Global Economics and Finance, The Chinese University of Hong Kong.

Contents

Part One
Introduction

Chapter 1
Introduction

An important indicator of the economic strength of a country, in addition to its real Gross Domestic Product (GDP), is its innovative capacity. Innovative capacity eventually translates into technical progress (or equivalently, growth in total factor productivity), that is, the ability of an economy to increase the quantity of its output without increasing the quantities of its conventional inputs of tangible capital, labour and human capital. However, innovation or technical progress is not manna from heaven. Sustained investments in Research and Development (R&D) are essential for innovation to occur in an economy. The objectives of this study are threefold: first, to identify the determinants of innovation at the economy-wide level; second, to ascertain whether they are the same across different economies; and third, to find suitable metrics for comparing the relative success in innovation across different economies. In other words, we try to discover whether there is a common law of innovation that applies across different economies, and if not, to identify the similarities and differences. We also try to develop indicators of relative success in innovation across different economies.

Initially, we measure the annual innovation output of an economy by using the following: (1) the annual number of patent applications filed with respectively its home patent office and the United States Patent and Trademark Office (USPTO); and (2) the annual number of patents granted to it by respectively its home patent office and the USPTO. Subsequently, we also look at the patent grants of the European Patent Office (EPO) and the China National Intellectual Property Administration

(CNIPA).[1] We associate a patent application or patent grant with the primary residence of the listed applicant, whether an individual or an organisation (the first listed applicant if there is more than one listed applicant).[2]

Of course, a patent application is not equivalent to a patent grant. However, we believe that a patent application must have been based on some supposed discovery or invention that has resulted from R&D activities. Thus, it should also be considered an innovation output similar to (but of course not quite as good as) a patent grant. We use data on patent applications and grants from the USPTO in addition to those from the individual national and regional patent offices to ensure the comparability of the qualities of the patent grants across different economies, as every USPTO patent application, regardless of national or geographical origin, would have been evaluated by the USPTO using the same procedures and standards. While it is in principle possible that United States (US) nationals may have a "home-court" advantage with the USPTO,[3] the historical data on USPTO patent grants indicate that applications from other economies have in general been treated without bias, with no evidence that applications from US residents have received special preference. Moreover, the United States is such a large and important market that almost all important discoveries and inventions, regardless of national or geographical origin, will want to apply for patent protection there.

While discoveries and inventions are brought about by R&D activities, they are not brought about by only the current-period R&D activities. They can result from R&D activities initiated a long time ago. We, therefore, use as our measure of the innovation input of an economy the quantity of its real R&D capital stock, defined as the cumulative past real expenditures on R&D, less a depreciation of 10% per annum. A 10% annual depreciation implies a useful life of approximately ten years on average for R&D investments, which seems reasonable, since R&D,

---

[1] CNIPA's name in Chinese is "Guojia Zhishi Chanquanju (国家知识产权局)". It was formerly known as the State Intellectual Property Office (SIPO).

[2] There may, however, be a discrepancy between this classification, by the nationality of the inventor or discoverer, and a classification by the ownership of the patent. The patent of an invention of a Singaporean employee of a US firm in Singapore is classified as Singaporean origin in our study but may in fact be owned by the US firm.

[3] However, an analysis of the actual historical data shows that there is in fact no evidence of a "home-court" advantage for US nationals (see Chapter 5).

especially basic research, has a relatively long gestation period. In the following, we examine some prima facie empirical evidence that one of the innovation outputs, the number of patent grants, is positively related to the quantity of the innovation input, that is, the real R&D capital stock.

The sample of economies included in our study consists of the Group-of-Seven (G-7) countries (Canada, France, Germany, Italy, Japan, the United Kingdom and the United States), the four East Asian Newly Industrialised Economies (EANIEs) (Hong Kong, China, South Korea, Singapore and Taiwan, China), and the Mainland of China. In 2019, this group of economies includes the top nine of the top ten USPTO patent applicants and grantees,[4] the top six of the top seven EPO applicants and grantees,[5] and the top seven of the top seven CNIPA applicants and grantees.[6] Thus, they are quite representative of innovative economies. (See Appendix Table A1.1.)

In Figure 1.1, a scatter diagram of the number of patents granted by the USPTO to an economy each year versus the quantity of its real R&D capital stock at the beginning of that year for all the economies included in our study is presented.[7] Because of the vast differences in the magnitudes of the number of patents and the quantity of the real R&D capital stock, both the vertical and horizontal axes of Figure 1.1 are in logarithmic scales. A positive relationship between the number of USPTO patent grants received and the quantity of real R&D capital stock is clearly apparent — the higher the quantity of real R&D capital stock of an economy, the higher is the number of USPTO patents granted to it — even though significant differences in the relationship across the different economies can also be discerned.

We shall employ a meta-production function model[8] to estimate econometrically the relationship between the innovation outputs, in this case, the numbers of patent applications and patent grants of each economy, and the

---

[4]The 10th economy was India.

[5]The seventh economy was Switzerland.

[6]The eighth economy was also Switzerland.

[7]In this book, we have adopted the data practice that the longest available time series will be used for any variable of any economy, except in the econometric analyses of Chapters 10 and 11, which demand comparability and consistency of data over time and across economies.

[8]The meta-production function model was first introduced by Hayami and Ruttan (1970) and extended by Lau and Yotopoulos (1989). See also Boskin and Lau (1992).

Figure 1.1: A scatter diagram between the annual number of USPTO patents granted and the quantity of real R&D capital stock, G-7 countries, Mainland China, and four EANIES

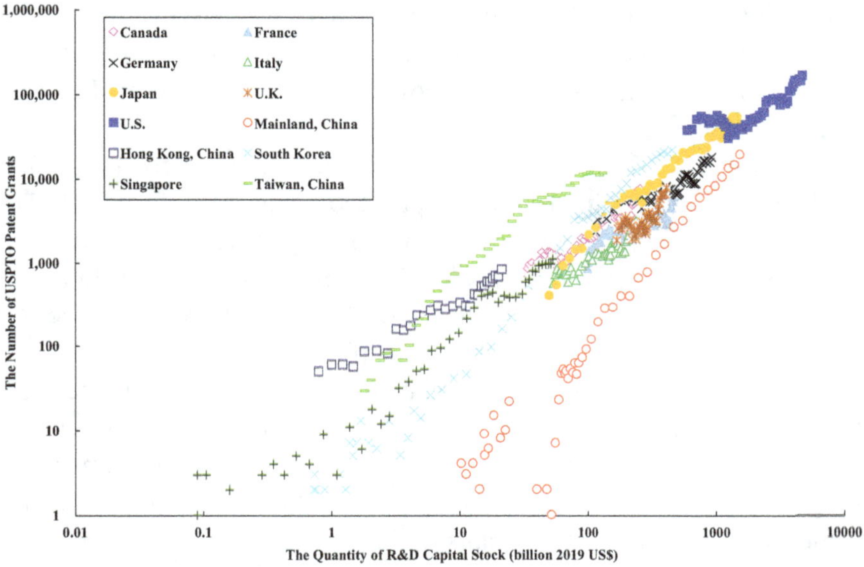

Source: Data on the number of USPTO patent grants are taken from Table A5.2. Data on the quantity of R&D capital stocks are taken from Tables A3.2 and A3.3.

innovation input, the quantity of its real R&D capital stock. In the case of applications to and grants by the USPTO, we further control for the annual total patent grant rate of the USPTO. We shall also test statistically the hypothesis that there is a common meta-production function relating the numbers of patent applications and grants respectively to the quantities of the real R&D capital stocks across the different economies.

One intriguing question is whether technical progress, or the ability of an economy to increase the quantity of its output without increasing the quantities of any of its conventional inputs, can only be brought about with indigenous innovation. Can technical progress, or equivalently the growth of total factor productivity, be imported? Past empirical research findings of Kim and Lau (1994, 1995, 1996) and Young (1992)[9] indicate

[9] See also Krugman (1994).

that very little technical progress could be found in the EANIEs before they began investing in R&D, especially if the growth of the human capital input is also taken into account. Essentially new equipment and technology imported by developing economies from developed economies are often already fully priced, so that the importing economy cannot expect to derive additional benefits over and above the cost of the imported equipment and technology paid.

In Chapter 2, there is a brief review of the relevant literature on the relationship between innovation output and input, specifically R&D, using different methodologies. In Chapter 3, a systematic comparison of R&D investments across our sample of economies is presented. In addition, time series of the quantities of real R&D capital stocks are explicitly estimated for all the economies in our sample.[10]

In Chapter 4, we analyse the relationship between the numbers of domestic patent applications and grants on the one hand and the quantities of real R&D capital stocks on the other in our sample of economies. In Chapter 5, we examine the relationship between the numbers of US patent applications from and patent grants to the different economies and their respective quantities of real R&D capital stocks. In Chapter 6, we examine the data on EPO patent grants and compare them to those on the USPTO patent grants. We also explore the relationship between the numbers of EPO patent grants to specific economies and their respective quantities of real R&D capital stocks. In Chapter 7, we study the data on CNIPA patent grants and compare them to those on the domestic, USPTO and EPO patent grants. In Chapter 8, we develop indicators of relative success in innovation across different economies. In Chapter 9, we explore innovation activities at the microeconomic level, that is, at the level of the individual firm, and see how the firm-specific patent grants relate to firm-specific R&D investments. Specifically, we examine the relationship between the number of patent grants and the quantity of the real R&D capital stock for selected Chinese and US enterprises.

In Chapter 10, our full econometric model, based on the concept of the meta-production function, is derived and estimated for the USPTO patent applications and grants of the six economies in our study whose

[10] It is necessary to estimate an initial quantity of real R&D capital stock for each economy.

number of domestic patent applications is greater than or equal to its number of USPTO patent applications.[11] Chapter 10 is quite technical in nature; the non-technical reader may wish to read only the summary sections at the end of Chapter 10. The estimation results are analysed and interpreted in Chapter 11.

In Chapter 12, we look beyond R&D to other innovation inputs that are complementary to R&D. In Chapter 13, we explore other possible measures of innovation success and outputs from R&D activities in addition to patent applications and grants.

Finally, in Chapter 14, we summarise our research findings and indicate some possible directions for further research on innovation in the future.

[11] The other economies are excluded because when the number of foreign patent applications of an economy exceeds the number of domestic applications, the application decision must have been based on considerations other than the quality of the discovery or invention, since foreign patent application and continued maintenance are much more costly for foreign patents than for domestic patents.

Appendix

Table A1.1: Top 10 economies by patent applications and grants, USPTO, EPO, and CNIPA, in 2019

USPTO Applications		USPTO Grants		EPO Applications		EPO Grants		CNIPA Applications		CNIPA Grants	
1 US	285,113	1 US	167,115	1 US	46,201	1 US	34,614	1 Mainland, China	1,231,093	1 Mainland, China	354,111
2 Japan	84,435	2 Japan	53,542	2 Germany	26,805	2 Japan	22,423	2 Japan	48,867	2 Japan	30,401
3 Mainland, China	**39,055**	**3 South Korea**	**21,684**	**3 Japan**	**22,066**	**3 Germany**	**21,198**	**3 US**	**39,450**	**3 US**	**23,114**
4 South Korea	**36,424**	**4 Mainland, China**	**19,209**	**4 Mainland, China**	**12,247**	**4 France**	**8,800**	**4 Germany**	**16,421**	**4 Germany**	**9,989**
5 Germany	30,290	5 Germany	18,293	5 France	10,163	5 South Korea	7,247	5 South Korea	16,019	5 South Korea	9,437
6 Taiwan, China	19,599	6 Taiwan, China	11,489	6 South Korea	8,287	6 Mainland, China	6,229	6 Taiwan, China	11,152	6 Taiwan, China	6,197
7 UK	14,124	7 UK	7,791	7 Switzerland	8,249	7 Switzerland	4,770	7 France	4,826	7 France	2,997
8 Canada	13,432	8 Canada	7,595	8 Netherlands	6,954	8 Netherlands	4,326	8 Switzerland	3,820	8 Switzerland	2,329
9 France	11,690	9 France	7,233	9 UK	6,156	9 UK	4,119	9 Netherlands	3,348	9 Netherlands	2,033
10 India	10,478	10 India	5,378	10 Italy	4,456	10 Sweden	3,838	10 UK	2,957	10 Sweden	1,484

Source: USPTO, EPO, and chinese statistical yearbook, 2020.

Chapter 2

Review of the Literature

Previous studies on Research and Development (R&D) show that the elasticities of innovation outputs with respect to innovation inputs range from 0.3 to 1.9 for developed countries and much lower for developing countries. Most of them use firm-level data. Studies that use cross-sectional national data focus primarily on estimating the relative efficiency of the R&D processes across different economies.

2.1 Estimating the Relationship between R&D Outputs and Inputs

Some early studies using United States (US) firm-level data have documented a positive relationship between R&D outputs and inputs. An implicit assumption used in these studies is that the R&D processes are essentially identical across firms. Hausman, Hall and Griliches (1984) use data from 128 US manufacturing firms from 1968 to 1974 to estimate the relationship between the number of patent applications and R&D expenditure. By estimating the statistical models of counts (that is, non-negative integers) in the context of panel data, they find that the elasticity of R&D output with respect to contemporaneous R&D input at the firm level is around 0.38, implying that an increase of 10% in the R&D expenditure of a firm increases the number of patent applications by approximately 3.8%. To further understand the role of the stock of knowledge in innovation, Hall *et al.* (1986) go on to test whether R&D

expenditure has lagged effects on patent applications. They assemble data on a panel of 650 US manufacturing firms from 1966 to 1979 and use nonlinear least squares, Poisson, negative binomial, and weighted nonlinear least squares to correct any misspecification in the model. Their results show a strong contemporaneous relationship between patent application and R&D expenditures, controlling for firm size, its propensity to apply for patents, and its R&D history. They also find that the elasticity of patent application with respect to current R&D expenditure is around 0.3 and observed R&D history at most contributes another 0.05.

Analyses of different sets of firm-level data in other developed economies yield similar results. Beneito (2006) uses manufacturing firms in Spain over the period 1990–1996 to estimate the effects of in-house and contracted R&D capital stocks on the number of patents and utility models granted by the domestic patent office, respectively.[1,2] He employs the transcendental production function and addresses the "excess zeroes" problems in count data by using a negative binomial model. This study also controls for detailed firm-level behaviour including the number of workers in the laboratory, scientific and technical services, normalisation and quality control, assimilation of imported technologies, marketing, design, and other informal activities. Results show that the elasticities of patent grants and registered utility models with respect to total R&D capital stocks are 0.309 and 0.173 (for the sample average), respectively. Moreover, significant innovations indicated by patent grants are mainly gestated in-house (the elasticity with respect to in-house R&D stock is 0.233), whereas contracted R&D seems more orientated toward innovations of an incremental nature indicated by models of use (the elasticity is 0.298). Evidence from Generalised Method of Moments (GMM) estimates with 698 manufacturing firms in France from 1984 to 1989 also

[1] The authors derive the quantity of R&D capital stocks from the quantity of R&D expenditure using the perpetual inventory method with an assumed annual depreciation rate of 15%.

[2] In-house R&D expenditure refers to the expenditure incurred when the firm's internal laboratory carries out formal R&D activities. Contracted R&D expenditure refers to the expenditure caused by R&D activities carried out by independent research institutions outside the enterprise.

shows that the elasticity of the number of European patent applications with respect to real R&D capital stocks is around 0.30 (Crépon and Duguet, 1997).[3]

Evidence using national-level data shows a much larger long-run elasticity. Voutsinas *et al.* (2018) estimate the causal relationship between patent applications to the European Patent Office (EPO) and R&D expenditure in Greece. They employ endogenous knowledge-based growth theories and collect time-series data at the national level from 1981 to 2007. By using time-series analysis, they find a relatively large long-run elasticity of patent application with respect to real R&D expenditure of 1.9.

Some evidence from developing economies shows a weak knowledge production function of innovation. An early study using Indian firm-level panel data from 1975 to 1979 finds that there is no impact of R&D expenditure on the probability of patenting, even though the R&D personnel measured by the number of Ph.D. workers has a large and significant effect on it (Deolalikar and Röller, 1989). Kanwar and Singh (2018) estimate the effect of real R&D capital stocks[4] on the number of patent applications using 380 manufacturing firms over the period 2001–2010 in India, controlling for each firm's patenting experience, resource access and knowledge spillovers. They find that the elasticity of the number of patents filed by a firm with respect to real R&D capital stocks is only around 0.02, much lower than those found in developed economies.

Studies based on cross-sectional international data show similar innovation behaviour despite variations in R&D productivity and efficiency among economies. Teitel (1994) uses data from 1976 to 1985 for 68 countries and employs a simple production function model to test the effects of R&D expenditure, the number of scientists and engineers, per capita income and population on the number of patents granted to residents. His results show that a 1% increase in either R&D expenditure or the number

---

[3]The authors use inflation-corrected R&D expenditures to construct real R&D capital stocks, using the perpetual inventory method with an annual depreciation rate of 15%.

[4]The authors derive a time series of the quantity of R&D capital stocks from the quantity of R&D expenditure using the perpetual inventory method with an assumed annual depreciation of 15%.

of scientists and engineers results in a 1% increase in the number of patents granted to residents, that is, the elasticity is unity. Cincera (1997) employs 181 international firms conducting R&D over the years 1983–1991 and finds that the elasticities of EPO patent applications with respect to the real R&D expenditure range from 0.31 to 0.48, controlling for intra-sector spillovers.[5] Griffith *et al.* (2006) collect manufacturing-firm data from four European countries (France, Germany, Spain and the United Kingdom (UK)) and use a structural model to estimate the relationship between innovation output and productivity and R&D expenditure. They conclude that overall, the systems driving innovation and productivity are remarkably similar across the four countries. Doubling R&D intensity measured as R&D expenditure per employee in 2000 increases the probabilities of product innovation (process innovation) by 0.440 (0.303), 0.273 (0.260), 0.296 (0.281), and 0.273 (0.161) percentage points for France, Germany, Spain, and the UK, respectively. Potužáková and Öhm (2018) estimate the relationship between the number of patent applications filed with EPO and R&D expenditure in 18 industries in 19 countries over 1987 to 2005. They employ fixed effects to control for unobserved country-specific and industry-specific characteristics and time effects. They conclude that a one percentage point increase in R&D expenditure generates roughly 100 EPO patent applications. It translates into the elasticities of EPO patent applications with respect to R&D expenditure of between 0.869 and 0.875.

2.2 Estimating the Relative Efficiency of the R&D Process Across Economies

Estimation of the relative efficiency of R&D across different economies is also predicated on the assumption that the R&D processes in the different economies are essentially identical. Rousseau and Rousseau (1997) estimate the relative efficiency of the R&D process across 18 developed countries using Data Envelopment Analysis (DEA). They employ the

[5]The 181 international firms include 28 firms in the European Union, 12 in Japan, 140 in the US, and 1 in the rest of world.

number of publications in the International Scientific Indexing (ISI)'s Science Citation Index (SCI) and the number of patents granted by EPO as the outputs of R&D, and R&D expenditure, GDP and population as the inputs. They conclude that Switzerland and the UK are the most efficient in generating R&D outputs.

Later, Sharma and Thomas (2008) estimate the relative efficiency of the R&D process across 22 developed and developing countries. They also employ the DEA methodology and a production function with patents granted to residents as the output and gross domestic expenditure on R&D and the number of researchers as the inputs. They find that under the assumption of constant returns to scale, Japan, South Korea, and China are found to be efficient; while under the assumption of variable returns to scale, three more economies (India, Slovenia, and Hungary) are efficient.

Recently, Hu *et al.* (2014) compare R&D efficiency across 24 economies in America, Asia, and Europe from 1998 to 2005, applying the distance function approach for stochastic frontier analysis. They estimate the relationship between R&D outputs (the number of patents granted by EPO and United States Patent and Trademark Office (USPTO), the number of scientific journal articles, royalties, and licensing fees) and R&D inputs (R&D expenditure and R&D manpower). Their results show that although Asian economies have a lower overall R&D efficiency compared with American and European economies, it grew much faster and exceeded those of the other two groups of economies after 2002.

2.3 Summary

As aforementioned, the positive relationship between R&D outputs and inputs is well observed in most economies, though the elasticity of R&D outputs with respect to R&D inputs varies across economies and with different measures of R&D outputs and inputs. Developed and newly industrialised economies seem to have higher R&D efficiency than most developing economies, generating more R&D outputs for a given quantity of R&D inputs. However, some developing economies, such as Mainland China, show an increased efficiency in generating R&D outputs from given R&D inputs over time.

The question remains: is there a common law of innovation in the world? First, previous studies using data from a single economy cannot completely answer this question. The R&D efficiency varies significantly across economies. Strong relationships between R&D outputs and inputs have been found in some developed economies and weak relationships have been documented in several developing economies. Moreover, data collected from a single economy may not have sufficient variation in either the R&D outputs or the R&D inputs to allow the precise estimation of the relationship. Second, previous studies using cross-sectional national data primarily focus on comparing the relative R&D efficiency across economies, and cannot fully answer the above question either. These studies are interested in identifying the most efficient economies in a group of sample economies using different measures of R&D outputs and inputs. They find that there are indeed large differences in the innovative capacity across different economies, though their results do not explicitly estimate the elasticity of R&D outputs with respect to R&D inputs. They also do not provide explanations of these efficiency differences across economies.

The purpose of our current study is to ascertain whether there is a common law of innovation in the world. We estimate directly the relationship between innovation output and input across representative economies including the Group-of-Seven (G-7) countries, the four East Asian Newly Industrialised Economies (EANIEs) and Mainland China. However, we do not assume that the relationship between outputs and inputs is identical across all economies. Instead, we employ the flexible meta-production function approach, introduced by Lau and Yotopoulos (1989), Boskin and Lau (1992) and Lau and Park (2002), which enables the transformation of the outputs and inputs of the different economies in our sample so that they are comparable. The meta-production function approach allows each economy to have its own economy-specific and time-varying characteristics and the hypothesis of an identical meta-production function across economies can be explicitly tested. We can therefore provide an unambiguous answer to the question of whether there is a common law of innovation.

Part Two

Research and Development (R&D) Investments

Chapter 3

Comparison of R&D Investments and R&D Capital Stocks across Economies

As mentioned in Chapter 1, an important indicator of the national economic strength of a country, in addition to its real Gross Domestic Product (GDP), is its innovative capacity. Innovation in an economy is not accidental or fortuitous. It is not manna from heaven, but is the return to cumulative long-term investments in Research and Development (R&D). In this chapter, we construct time series of estimates of the quantities of real R&D capital stocks for each economy included in our study using data on their respective real R&D expenditures.

3.1 The Ratio of Research and Development Expenditure to Gross Domestic Product

Sustained investments in R&D (and in human capital) are needed in order to build up the innovative capacity of an economy. However, significant variations in the extent of investment in R&D are observed to exist across economies. In Figure 3.1, the ratios of R&D expenditures to GDP of the Group-of-Seven (G-7) countries (Canada, France, Germany,[1] Italy, Japan,

[1]From 1964 to 1990, R&D expenditure data are only available for West Germany. Thus, the R&D expenditures to GDP ratios of West Germany prior to 1991 are presented separately from those of the unified Germany, data for which are available since 1991.

Figure 3.1: R&D expenditure as a percent of GDP, G-7 countries, Mainland China, and four EANIEs

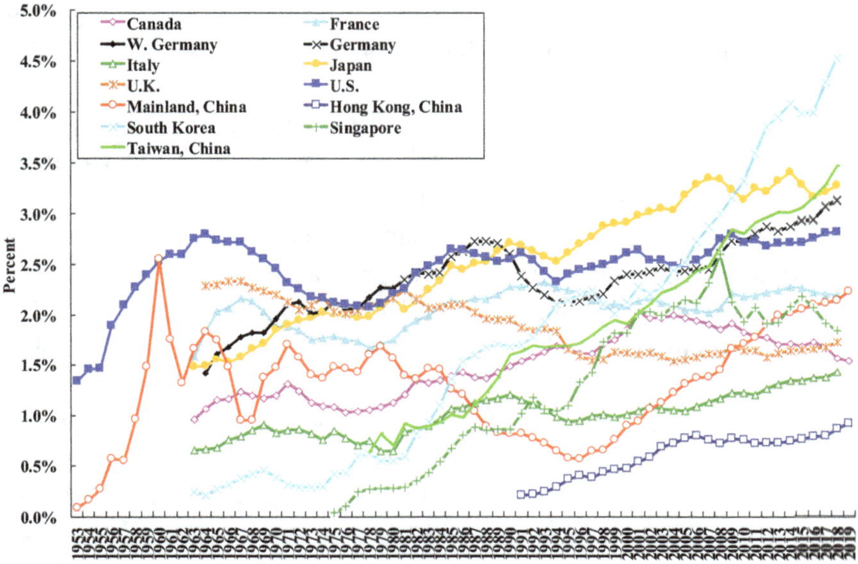

Source: Chinese data were collected from the online statistical database of National Bureau of Statistics, China (https://data.stats.gov.cn/easyquery.htm?cn=C01); data for Hong Kong, China were collected from Census and Statistics Department, Hong Kong (https://www.censtatd.gov.hk/hkstat/sub/sp120.jsp?tableID=207&ID=0&productType=8); US data were collected from the US National Science Foundation (https://ncses.nsf.gov/pubs/nsf20307/#&); data for other economies were collected from Main Science and Technology Indicators (MSTI), OECD Statistical Database (http://stats.oecd.org/Index.aspx?DataSetCode=MSTI_PUB#).

the United Kingdom (UK), and the United States (US)), China (the Mainland),[2] and the four East Asian Newly Industrialised Economies (EANIEs) (Hong Kong, China, South Korea, Singapore and Taiwan, China) are presented.

The United States (US) ratio started with a relatively low percentage, 1.33%, in 1953, but increased rapidly to 2.09% in 1957, partly as a reaction to the unexpected successful launch into space of the Sputnik satellite, the first man-made satellite, by the former Soviet Union. It has since held steady between 2.1% and 2.8% over the past half-a-century (and has

[2] In this study, data for China pertain to only the Mainland of China.

remained above 2.6% since 2007). The Chinese ratio started with less than 0.1% in 1953 but increased rapidly to a peak of 2.55% in 1960, comparable to the US ratio of the same year. Between 1963 and 1984, the Chinese ratio was higher than those of Canada, Italy and the four EANIEs.[3] Then it plummeted below 1%, bottoming in 1996 at 0.56%. Since then, it has recovered steadily to reach 2.23% in 2019,[4] once again surpassing the R&D expenditure to GDP ratios of Canada and Italy, and exceeding those of France, Singapore, and the UK, but still lagging significantly behind not only the developed economies of Germany, Japan and the US but also the newly industrialised economies of South Korea and Taiwan, China. The Chinese ratio was targeted to reach 2.5% in 2020,[5] but only achieved 2.4%.[6] The West German ratio was neck and neck with the US ratio between 1975 and 1990. However, since the German reunification in 1990, the ratio of unified Germany was below the US ratio until 2010, when it finally managed to catch up.[7] The Japanese ratio was 1.47% in 1963 and rose steadily to overtake the US ratio in 1989 and has remained significantly higher than it ever since. Since 2002, the Japanese ratio has consistently stayed above 3%. More recently, the South Korean ratio caught up with the US ratio in 2005 and surpassed the Japanese ratio in 2009. South Korea led the sample of economies in our study with an R&D expenditure to GDP ratio of 4.53% in 2018.[8] The ratio of Taiwan, China also surpassed the US ratio in 2009 and the Japanese ratio in 2017 to become the second highest in our sample in 2018 at 3.46%. Hong Kong, China, at 0.92% in 2019, has the lowest ratio of R&D expenditure to GDP among all the economies in our study.

---

[3] Note that the Chinese ratio was a little bit lower than those of Canada in 1967 and 1968, in part because of the Great Proletarian Cultural Revolution going on there during those years.

[4] The Chinese ratio was supposed to reach 2.2% in 2015 but failed to do so.

[5] "Outline of the National Medium- and Long-Term Scientific and Technological Development Plan (2006–2020) (*Guojia Zhongchangqi Kexue he Jishu Fazhan Guihua Gangyao* (2006–2020))", available at http://www.most.gov.cn/kjgh/kjghzcq/.

[6] http://www.stats.gov.cn/tjsj/zxfb/202102/t20210227_1814154.html.

[7] In 2010, the US ratio was 2.71 compared to Germany's 2.73, almost identical; in 2011, the ratios were respectively 2.74 and 2.81.

[8] However, South Korea does not have the highest ratio of R&D expenditure to GDP in the world. The Israeli ratio was 4.94% in 2018.

3.2 The Quantities of Real R&D Capital Stocks of Selected Economies

The stock of real R&D capital, defined as the cumulative past real expenditures on R&D, less depreciation of 10% per year, is a useful summary measure of the existing capacity of innovation, as it typically takes years of cumulative efforts before investments in R&D, especially basic research, can result in new discoveries and inventions.[9] Given estimates of the quantities of initial real R&D capital stocks and the time series of real R&D expenditures of each economy, the time series of the quantities of real R&D capital stocks can be estimated for all the economies in our study by the perpetual inventory method in a straightforward way. However, the quantities of initial real R&D capital stocks at the beginning of the years for which data on real R&D expenditures are first available are not known and must be separately estimated for each economy.[10] (The estimation procedure is described in detail in Appendix A3.1.)

The estimated quantities of real R&D capital stocks in 2019 US dollars at the beginning of each year are compared across the G-7 Countries, the four East Asian Newly Industrialised Economies (EANIEs) and Mainland China in Figure 3.2 on an aggregate basis and in Figure 3.3 on a per capita basis.[11] Figure 3.2 shows that the US has, since 1953, been clearly the world leader in the quantity of real R&D capital stock. In 2019, the quantity of its real R&D capital stock, estimated at US$4.72 trillion, is more than three times that of China, the country with the second highest quantity of real R&D capital stock (US$1.53 trillion). The quantity of Chinese real R&D capital stock has been growing at double-digit rates since 2001, as both its real GDP and its R&D expenditure to GDP ratio have been growing rapidly. In 2019, the quantity of Chinese real R&D capital stock, at US$1.53 trillion, overtook that of Japan

[9] A rate of depreciation of 15% is used by some scholars (see, for example, the studies cited in Chapter 2).

[10] In particular, we estimated a time series of quantities of real R&D capital stocks for a united Germany beginning in 1964.

[11] We should caution that our estimates of the quantities of the real R&D capital stocks are sensitive to the value of the exchange rates of the local currencies versus the US dollar in 2019.

Figure 3.2: The quantity of real R&D capital stock, G-7 countries, Mainland China, and four EANIEs (billion 2019 US dollars)

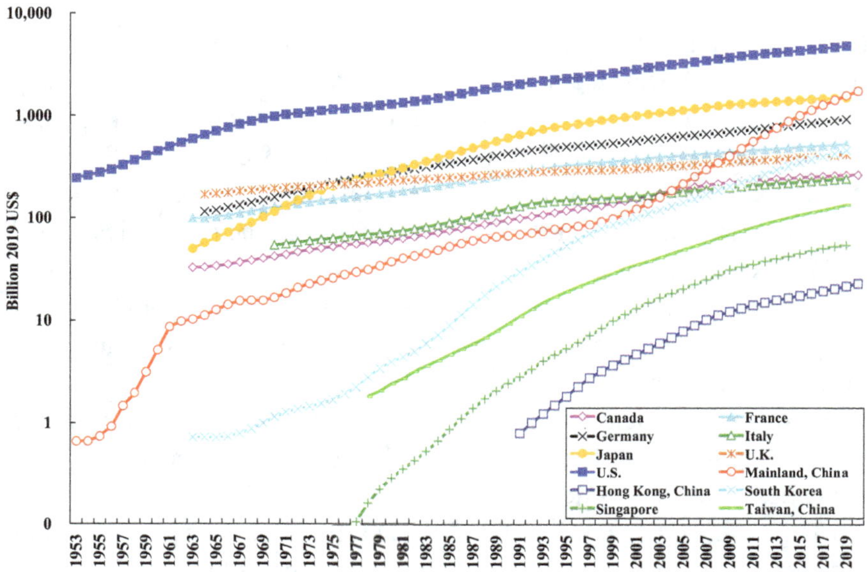

Source: See Table A3.2 and Table A3.3.

(US$1.47 trillion) to become the second highest in the world, but still only less than a third of that of the US. Japan, which had had the second highest quantity of real R&D capital stock since overtaking Germany in 1979, fell to third place in 2019, with Germany in fourth place. Among the EANIEs, the quantity of real R&D capital stock of South Korea has been increasing the fastest to become just behind that of France and ahead of that of the UK. Hong Kong, China has the lowest quantity of real R&D capital stock among all the economies included in this study at US$21.3 billion, in 2019.

In Figure 3.3, we compare the quantities of real R&D capital stock per capita at the beginning of each year across our sample of economies. By this measure, the lead of the US over other economies has also been consistent and large from 1953, the first year for which we have data, to the present time. In 2019, the US quantity of real R&D capital stock per

Figure 3.3: The quantity of real R&D capital stock per capita, G-7 countries, Mainland China, and four EANIEs (thousand 2019 US dollars)

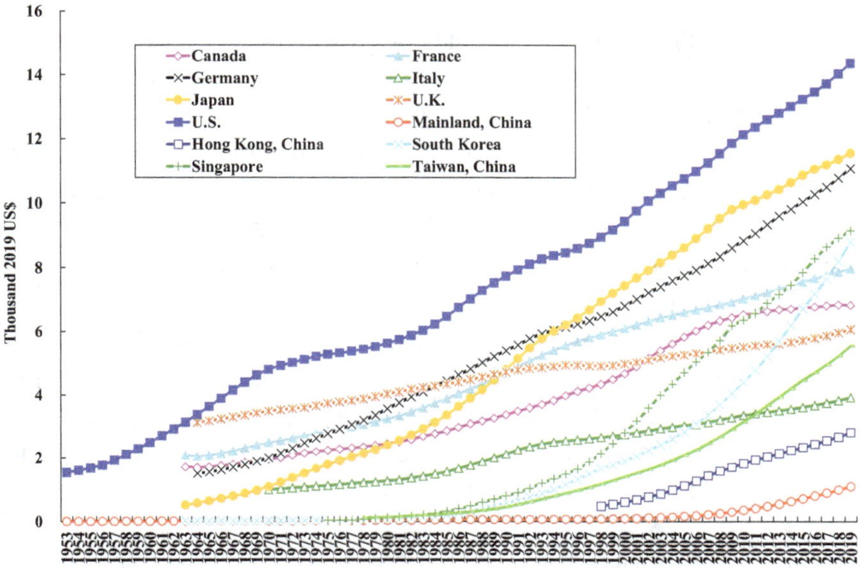

Source: The quantities of real R&D capital stocks are from Table A3.2 and Table A3.3, and the population data are from International Financial Statistics (Canada, France, Germany, Italy, Japan, South Korea, Singapore and UK), World Development Indicators (US) and the local statistical agencies (Mainland China, Hong Kong, China and Taiwan, China).

capita was US$14,400. Japan has been in second place since 1995, with US$11,600 in 2019, followed closely by Germany in third place, with US$11,100. The EANIEs of Singapore and South Korea have had rapidly increasing quantities of real R&D capital stock per capita, and have surpassed France, Canada and the UK, but were still behind Germany in 2019. Taiwan, China overtook Italy in 2012 and is on course to surpass the UK in another couple of years. Mainland China has been and continues to be in the last place among this sample of economies, with only US$1,100 worth of real R&D capital stock per capita in 2019, largely because of its huge population. Even Hong Kong, China has a significantly higher quantity of real R&D capital stock per capita, US$2,800, than the Mainland of China.

3.3 Comparison of the Real R&D Capital Stocks of China, Japan and the U.S.

In Figure 3.4, the quantities and rates of growth of the real R&D capital stocks of China, Japan and the US are compared. In 2019, the US, China and Japan had the three largest real R&D capital stocks in the world. While the US has always been number one, China only overtook Japan to become number two in 2019. The US real R&D capital stock was more than three times those of China and Japan in 2019. In terms of rates of growth, all three countries underwent significant changes over time. The US real R&D capital stock had double-digit annual rates of growth between 1954 and 1961. Then its rate of growth began to decline, reaching a low of 1.8% in 1976 before rebounding to a high of 4.5% in 2001. It has since been fluctuating around 2.5%. China had phenomenally high rates of growth in its real R&D capital stock in the 1950s, but the rate declined to almost zero in the late 1960s. It began growing again at double-digit rates beginning in 2001.

Figure 3.4: The quantities and the rates of growth of the real R&D capital stocks, Mainland China, Japan, and the US

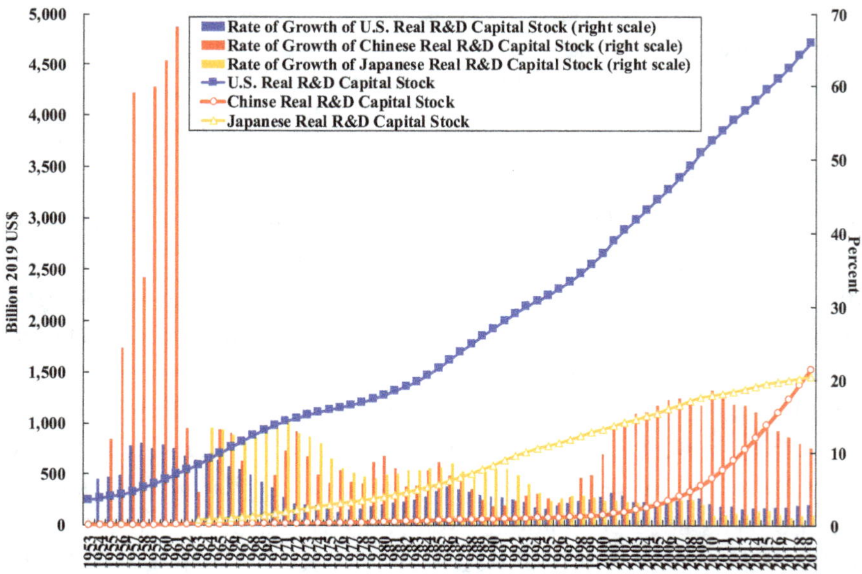

Source: Authors' calculations based on Table A3.2 and Table A3.3.

Japan has had low single-digit rates of growth since 2008. Its rates of growth in recent years have been between 1% and 2% per annum and lagged behind those of both China and the US. However, it will take China at least a couple of decades, even at its higher rates of growth, before the quantity of its real R&D capital stock can catch up with that of the US.

3.4 Investment in Basic Research

Finally, among R&D expenditures, three different categories, basic research, applied research, and development, may be distinguished. It is well known that "breakthrough" discoveries and inventions can occur consistently only in an economy with a strong foundation of basic research. Thus, in the long run, leadership in innovation can only come about with significant investments in basic research. In Figure 3.5, the shares of R&D expenditures

Figure 3.5: The share of basic research expenditure in total R&D expenditure, G-7 countries, Mainland China, and four EANIEs

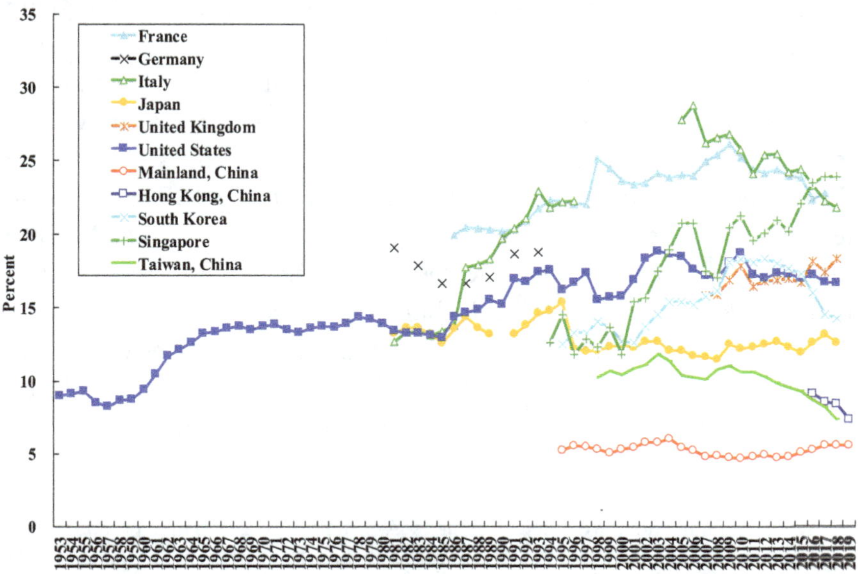

Source: The share of basic research expenditure in total R&D expenditure of each economy is calculated by dividing the share of basic research expenditure in GDP by the share of total R&D expenditure in GDP. Data for the two shares are collected from OECD, Main Science and Technology Indicators. The US data are taken from the US National Science Foundation, Science and Engineering Statistics. Chinese data are collected from the National Bureau of Statistics of China.

devoted to the support of basic research in each of the economies under study are presented. Unfortunately, data on basic research expenditures are not readily available for Canada and Germany. Based on the available data, Italy and France led the group of economies under study with an average basic research ratio of around 25%. In recent years, Singapore managed to achieve a basic research ratio of almost 24%. The US ratio averaged 17.3% in the 20 years between 1999 and 2018, and the UK also had comparable ratios. The South Korean ratio had exceeded the US ratio between 2011 and 2015 but declined to 14.2% in 2018. Japan had a fairly stable ratio in the low teens. The Taiwan, China ratio had been as high as 11.7% at its peak in 2003 but has declined continuously since to 7.3% in 2018. China had the lowest ratio of basic research of between 4.5% and 6%. Official data on basic research expenditures of Hong Kong, China are also not readily available. However, based on private sectoral estimates made by Kenny Shui,[12] we were able to derive estimates of the ratios for Hong Kong for the period of 2016–2019. As basic research typically requires a long gestation period and has little or no immediate commercial or financial returns, investment in basic research will imply a trade-off of short-term gains for long-term rewards.

Using data on the shares of basic research in total R&D expenditures for each economy, we can derive the time series of real basic research expenditures of each economy and estimate from them the quantities of real basic research capital stocks of each economy (see Appendix A3.1). The results are presented in Figure 3.6.[13] Figure 3.6 shows that the US is also the world's leader in the quantity of real basic research capital stock, with US$807 billion in 2019, followed by Japan (US$183 billion) and France (US$122 billion in 2018). As of 2019, China still lagged far behind in terms of the quantity of real basic research capital stock, with only US$79 billion, even though it has been catching up fast, surpassing both South Korea and the UK.[14]

---

[12] Private communication. Mr. Kenny Shui is Assistant Research Director and Head, Economic Development of Our Hong Kong Foundation Limited, a think-tank based in Hong Kong.

[13] The time series of real basic research expenditure data on Hong Kong is too short for a meaningful estimation of its real basic research capital stock.

[14] Unfortunately, basic research expenditure data for Germany are not readily available. Otherwise, it should have a real basic research capital stock that is comparable to France.

Figure 3.6: The quantity of real basic research capital stock, G-7 countries, Mainland China, and three EANIEs

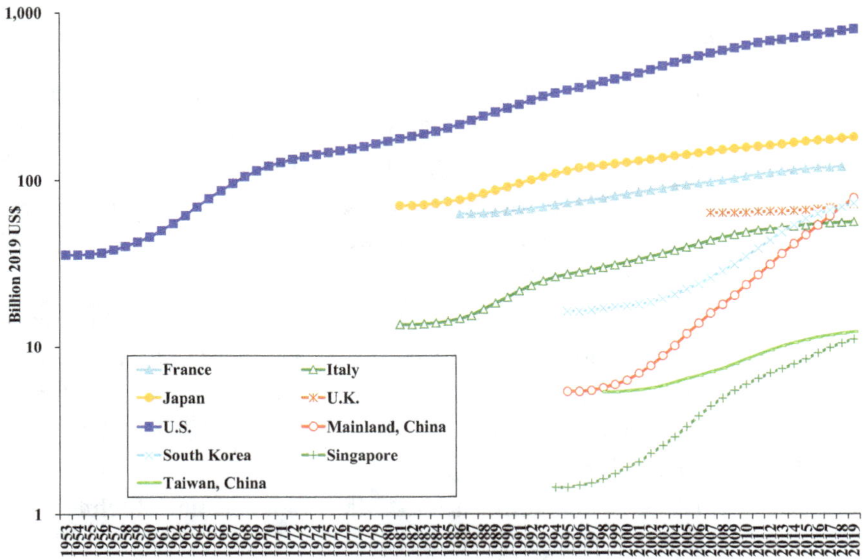

Source: Table A3.4.

Appendices

A3.1 *The construction of time series of quantities of real R&D and real basic research capital stocks*

A3.1.1 *Generating a time series of real R&D expenditures in constant US dollars for each economy*

The first step in the construction of a time series of quantities of real R&D capital stocks for the economies included in our study is to generate time series of annual real R&D expenditures in 2019 prices, converted into 2019 US dollars, for each of the economies. The procedure is as follows:

(A) Data are collected on annual nominal R&D expenditures in national or regional currencies and in current prices. The data sources are as follows:

(I) G-7 countries

(a) The US: from US National Science Foundation http://www.nsf.gov/statistics/nsf14304/content.cfm?pub_id=4326&id=2.

(b) Other countries:

(1) 1981–2019: from Organisation for Economic Cooperation and Development (OECD), Main Science and Technology Indicators (MSTI) (online database);

(2) 1969–1982: from OECD Science and Technology Indicators Unit (OECD/STIU) Data Bank, February 1985 (hard copy), Paris: OECD;

(3) 1963–1968: from OCED Directorate for Science, Technology and Industry (OECD/DSTII), Science and Technology Indicators: Basic Statistical Series — Volume B: Gross National Expenditure on R&D, 1963–1979 (hard copy), Paris: OECD;

(4) 1981–1999: from various Main Science and Technology Indicators (MSTI), hard copies;

(5) For Canada, Japan and the UK, there are slight differences in the R&D expenditure data from 1981 to 1993 between the hard copies and the more updated online database. Thus, data before 1981 are adjusted so that they are consistent with the most updated data in the online databases.

(II) Mainland China

Mainland China, 1953–2019: from Chinese official statistical publications and Statistics of Chinese Technology; China Data Online (http://china-data-online.com).

(III) East Asian Newly Industrialised Economies (EANIEs)

(a) Hong Kong, China, 1998–2019: from Census and Statistics Department, Hong Kong http://www.censtatd.gov.hk/hkstat/sub/sp120.jsp?tableID=207&ID=0&productType=8.

(b) South Korea

(1) 1963–1990: from "Survey of R&D in Korea", Korea Institute of S&T Evaluation and Planning (KISTEP) http://www.ikistep.re.kr/sts/statsMenuList.do.

(2) 1991–2018: from OECD, Main Science and Technology Indicators (online database).

(c) Singapore

1. 1975–1993: from Singapore Yearbook of Statistics;
2. 1994–2019: from OECD, Main Science and Technology Indicators.

(d) Taiwan, China

1. 1978–1980: from Statistical Yearbook of the Republic of China;
2. 1981–1994: from Ministry of Science and Technology, Taiwan
   http://statistics.most.gov.tw/was2/;
3. 1995–2019: from OECD, Main Science and Technology Indicators.

(B) The nominal R&D expenditures are converted into real R&D expenditures in national or regional currencies in 2019 prices using the GDP deflators of the respective economies. Annual GDP deflators are collected from International Financial Statistics (IFS) database and domestic official statistical sources.

(C) The real R&D expenditures in national currencies are converted to US dollars using the 2019 year-end exchange rates collected from the IFS database and from domestic official statistical sources.

A3.1.2 *The estimation of the quantities of initial real R&D capital stocks*

In order to construct time series of the quantities of real R&D capital stocks from time-series data on real R&D expenditures of each economy, we need first of all to estimate the quantities of the initial real R&D capital stocks, K_{i0}'s, for all the economies included in our study. Once an estimate of the quantity of the initial real R&D capital stock is available for an economy, a time series of quantities of real R&D capital stocks can be readily constructed from a time series of real R&D expenditures using the perpetual inventory method and assuming a rate of depreciation of R&D capital of 10% per annum.

We estimate the quantity of the initial real R&D capital stock of each economy by formulating an explicit econometric model relating the annual number of domestic and US patent applications of an economy to the annual quantity of its real R&D capital stock. For domestic applications, there is of course no a priori reason to assume that the same functional relationship applies to all the economies. Thus, in general,

$$YA_{Dit} = F_i(K_{it}), \tag{A3.1}$$

where YA_{Dit} is the number of domestic patent applications in the *i*th economy in year t, K_{it} is the quantity of real R&D capital stock in the *i*th economy in year t, and $F_i(K_{it})$ is the function that relates the number of domestic patent applications to the quantity of real R&D capital stock in the *i*th economy in year t. Note that the function $F_i(.)$ may vary with the economy, indexed by *i*, and may depend on time, but does not vary over time. Thus, it may take the form:

$$YA_{Dit} = F_i(K_{it}, \mathrm{t}). \tag{A3.2}$$

Moreover, it is assumed that the function $F_i(.)$ in Eq. (A3.1) takes the transcendental logarithmic form introduced by Christensen *et al.* (1971), so that

$$\begin{aligned} \ln YA_{Dit} &= \ln A_{0i} + \alpha_{Ki} \ln K_{it} + c_{Di}\mathrm{t} + \mathrm{B}_{Kti} \ln K_{ti}.\mathrm{t} \\ &\quad + \frac{1}{2}\mathrm{B}_{KKi}(\ln K_{it})^2 + \frac{1}{2}\mathrm{B}_{tti}\mathrm{t}^2. \end{aligned} \tag{A3.3}$$

K_{it}, the quantity of real R&D capital stock in the *i*th economy in year t, may be defined as

$$\begin{aligned} K_{it} &= 0.9K_{i(t-1)} + I_{i(t-1)} \\ &= 0.9^t K_{i0} + \sum_{j=1}^{t} 0.9^{j-1} I_{i(t-j)} \end{aligned} \tag{A3.4}$$

where K_{i0} is the quantity of the initial R&D capital stock of the *i*th economy; $I_{i(t-j)}$ is the real R&D expenditure of the *i*th economy in year t–j and 0.9 is the proportion of the undepreciated real R&D capital stock that survives at the end of each year, on the assumption of a depreciation rate of 10%. Substituting Eq. (A3.4) into Eq. (A3.3), we obtain Eq. (A3.5):

$$\begin{aligned}\ln YA_{Dit} &= \ln A_{0i} + \alpha_{Ki} \ln(0.9^t K_{i0} + \sum_{j=1}^{t} 0.9^{j-1} I_{i(t-j)}) + c_{Di}\mathrm{t} \\ &\quad + \mathrm{B}_{Kti} \ln(0.9^t K_{i0} + \sum_{j=1}^{t} 0.9^{j-1} I_{i(t-j)}).\mathrm{t} \\ &\quad + \frac{1}{2}\mathrm{B}_{KKi}(\ln(0.9^t K_{i0} + \sum_{j=1}^{t} 0.9^{j-1} I_{i(t-j)}))^2 + \frac{1}{2}\mathrm{B}_{tti}\mathrm{t}^2. \qquad \text{(A3.5)}\end{aligned}$$

Given time-series data on YA_{Dit} and I_t, Eq. (A3.5) can be estimated by nonlinear methods to yield estimates of K_{i0} and other parameters.

Similarly, since there is also no a priori reason to assume that the same functional relationship applies to the USPTO patent applications of all the economies,[15] an equation for YA_{USit}, the number of patent applications of the *i*th economy submitted in the US in year t, may be derived as follows:

$$\begin{aligned}\ln YA_{USit} &= \ln A_{0USi} + \alpha_{KUSi} \ln(0.9^t K_{i0} + \sum_{j=1}^{t} 0.9^{j-1} I_{i(t-j)}) + c_{USi}\mathrm{t} \\ &\quad + \mathrm{B}_{KtUSi} \ln(0.9^t K_{i0} + \sum_{j=1}^{t} 0.9^{j-1} I_{i(t-j)})\mathrm{t} \\ &\quad + \frac{1}{2}\mathrm{B}_{KKUSi}(\ln(0.9^t K_{i0} + \sum_{j=1}^{t} 0.9^{j-1} I_{i(t-j)}))^2 \\ &\quad + \frac{1}{2}\mathrm{B}_{ttUSi}\mathrm{t}^2. \qquad \text{(A3.6)}\end{aligned}$$

[15]For USPTO patent grants, the functional relationship may be similar across economies because the applications are assessed by the same organisation.

Equation (A3.5) is estimated for France, Japan, the US, China (Mainland), and South Korea, as their numbers of domestic patent applications have consistently exceeded their numbers of US patent applications. Equation (A3.6) is estimated for Canada, Italy, the UK, Hong Kong, China, Singapore and Taiwan, China as their US patent applications have been greater than or equal to their domestic patent applications.[16] Nonlinear methods are used to estimate the two equations to obtain estimates of the parameters including K_{i0}, the quantity of the initial R&D capital stock for each economy. For Germany, Eq. (A3.6) is used to estimate the quantity of its initial real R&D capital stock because the data on its domestic patent applications show unusual fluctuations before and during the reunification process.

The estimation results, including the estimated values of K_{i0} for each of the economies, are presented in Table A3.1.

A3.1.3 *The estimation of the time series of quantities of real R&D capital stocks*

Given the time series of real R&D expenditures and the quantities of initial real capital stocks estimated above, the real R&D capital stocks for each economy can be estimated using Eq. (A3.4):

$$\begin{aligned} K_{it} &= 0.9K_{i(t-1)} + I_{i(t-1)} \\ &= 0.9^t K_{i0} + \sum_{j-1}^{t} 0.9^{j-1} I_{i(t-j)} \end{aligned} \tag{A3.4}$$

where K_{i0} is the quantity of the initial real R&D capital stock of the *i*th economy and $I_{i(t-j)}$ is the real R&D expenditure of the *i*th economy in year t–j.

[16] Of course, for the US the number of domestic patent applications is the same as the number of US patent applications.

Table A3.1: Estimated quantities of the initial real capital stocks and the estimated parameters of Eqs. (A3.5) and (A3.6)

	Panel A: Dependent Variable: ln (the number of domestic applications)				
	France	**Japan**	**US**	**Mainland China**	**South Korea**
A^*_{AiD}	–59.663	28.978***	–92.860**	–2.174	6.521***
	(45.363)	(6.994)	(42.165)	(7.971)	(0.165)
α^*_{Ki}	29.313	–7.797***	34.747**	2.783	–0.252
	(18.891)	(2.840)	(13.700)	(4.804)	(0.373)
K_{i0}	99.304 [b]	49.697***	245.761***	0.665 [c]	0.730 [b]
		(12.021)	(49.428)		
c^*_{Di}	–1.170**	0.583***	–2.200***	0.073	0.081
	(0.561)	(0.159)	(0.520)	(0.493)	(0.051)
B_{kti}	0.238**	–0.096***	0.351***	–0.006	–0.119
	(0.116)	(0.030)	(0.084)	(0.137)	(0.084)
B_{kki}	–6.180	1.647***	–5.773***	–0.101	1.884***
	(3.929)	(0.576)	(2.226)	(1.417)	(0.657)
B_{tti}	–0.014**	0.004	–0.030***	–0.008	0.005
	(0.001)	(0.003)	(0.006)	(0.023)	(0.011)
Adj. R^2	0.834	0.986	0.983	0.996	0.994

	Panel B: Dependent Variable: ln (the number of USPTO applications)						
	Canada	**United Germany**	**Italy**	**UK**	**Hong Kong, China**	**Singapore**	**Taiwan, China**
A^*_{AiUS}	–134.109***	–68.409	–69.529**	867.079	5.000***	2.126	9.511***
	(31.983)	(69.551)	(32.962)	(886.802)	(0.668)	(2.193)	(1.333)

α^*_{Ki}	74.691***	32.046	36.465**	–339.604	–5.000**	2.608**	–0.201***
	(17.907)	(27.651)	(16.039)	(342.642)	(1.955)	(1.301)	(2.274)
K_{i0}	32.527***	114.792***	53.767***	168.727***	0.789***	0.090[b]	1.803***
	(0.752)	(26.433)	(10.506)	(4.922)	(0.159)		(0.180)
c_{Ki}	–2.716***	–0.814	–0.961*	6.915	1.073***	–0.053	0.970***
	(0.706)	(1.119)	(0.554)	(5.241)	(0.229)	(0.277)	(0.236)
B_{kti}	0.712***	0.187	0.233*	–1.365	–0.653***	2.299***	–0.440**
	(0.198)	(0.219)	(0.132)	(1.014)	(0.241)	(0.066)	(0.176)
B_{kki}	–19.611***	–6.670	–8.668**	67.131	5.542**	2.122***	4.943***
	(5.020)	(5.482)	(3.891)	(66.201)	(2.441)	(0.453)	(1.807)
B_{tti}	–0.025***	–0.013	–0.011382	0.056	0.091*	0.023**	0.029*
	(0.008)	(0.016)	(0.008)	(0.056)	(0.047)	(0.012)	(0.017)
$c^*_{USi} \times 1990$[a]		–0.003					
		(0.002)					
Adj. R^2	0.994	0.986	0.986	0.975	0.985	0.992	0.997

Notes: [a]Data for United Germany before 1991 include West Germany only. 1990 is a dummy variable, equal to 1 for the year after 1990 and 0 otherwise.
[b]The estimated quantities of initial real R&D capital stocks for France, South Korea and Singapore are all larger than 10 times the real R&D expenditures of the first year when the data are available (i.e., 144.893, 1.242, and 0.129, respectively). This will result in a decline of the quantity of real R&D capital stock over time, which does not seem reasonable given that all economies have been trying to promote innovation. We therefore use 10 times the real R&D expenditures of the first year as estimates of the quantities of real R&D capital stocks for the first year for these three economies, based on the assumption of an annual depreciation of 10% for real R&D capital stock.
[c]The highest goodness of fit of the nonlinear estimation is achieved for Mainland China when the quantity of the initial real R&D capital stock is set to be 0.6646, equal to 10 times the real R&D expenditures of the first year of data availability.
Numbers in parentheses are estimated standard errors. ***significant at 1% level; **significant at 5% level; *significant at 10% level.

A3.1.4 *Estimated quantities of real R&D capital stocks of selected economies*

Table A3.2: The quantities of real R&D capital stocks of G-7 countries

Economy	Canada	France	United Germany	Italy	Japan	UK	US
	R&D Capital Stocks (Billion 2019 US Dollars)						
1953							245.761
1954							261.292
1955							278.528
1956							297.523
1957							330.123
1958							367.439
1959							406.416
1960							451.269
1961							498.715
1962							546.134
1963	32.527	99.304			49.697		594.766
1964	32.871	99.304	114.792		56.369	168.727	649.657
1965	33.704	101.716	118.612		63.764	172.684	707.485
1966	35.015	105.778	125.031		71.685	176.745	764.585
1967	36.544	110.392	132.186		79.901	181.053	823.615
1968	38.313	116.056	139.826		89.473	185.467	880.562
1969	40.066	121.571	148.403		101.141	189.850	933.724
1970	41.924	126.739	157.801	53.767	114.713	193.730	982.244
1971	43.708	131.336	169.412	55.450	131.111	196.934	1,020.182
1972	46.238	136.322	182.674	57.320	147.760	199.474	1,051.068
1973	48.401	141.357	196.250	59.282	165.694	201.708	1,081.899
1974	50.227	145.951	208.270	61.187	184.495	205.743	1,112.456
1975	51.892	150.852	219.455	62.653	201.501	209.921	1,138.384
1976	53.469	155.262	230.526	64.684	217.407	212.247	1,158.798
1977	54.878	159.733	241.067	66.365	233.138	214.770	1,183.575
1978	56.439	164.256	251.570	68.278	248.740	217.848	1,210.817

Table A3.2: (*Continued*)

Economy	Canada	France	United Germany	Italy	Japan	UK	US
			R&D Capital Stocks (Billion 2019 US Dollars)				
1979	58.217	169.124	263.971	69.799	264.968	221.948	1,242.637
1980	60.012	174.813	279.311	71.644	283.495	226.390	1,278.803
1981	62.103	180.576	293.220	73.689	303.639	229.865	1,318.991
1982	64.699	188.017	306.369	77.148	326.647	234.250	1,362.575
1983	67.754	196.432	318.686	80.635	351.435	237.495	1,411.014
1984	70.533	204.893	330.713	84.507	378.955	240.321	1,467.865
1985	73.860	214.238	344.318	89.082	409.059	243.915	1,538.242
1986	77.647	223.922	359.428	95.069	444.352	248.117	1,620.455
1987	81.597	233.205	374.534	100.961	477.419	252.966	1,701.076
1988	85.223	243.006	391.983	107.511	512.637	257.783	1,779.813
1989	88.853	253.249	409.296	114.465	551.101	262.966	1,856.519
1990	92.999	264.665	426.733	121.553	593.806	268.384	1,930.609
1991	97.285	277.396	443.307	129.069	640.503	273.391	2,005.717
1992	101.395	289.295	462.341	135.154	685.273	276.328	2,079.717
1993	105.614	300.726	477.620	140.111	724.595	278.563	2,147.665
1994	110.287	311.367	488.818	143.537	757.266	281.716	2,203.089
1995	115.701	321.011	498.030	145.808	782.967	285.275	2,252.859
1996	120.708	330.060	507.348	147.498	812.636	285.993	2,314.615
1997	125.003	338.457	516.466	149.452	846.256	286.087	2,386.149
1998	129.644	345.481	526.957	151.153	881.098	286.503	2,467.269
1999	135.555	352.543	538.530	153.501	915.540	288.169	2,557.466
2000	142.306	360.318	553.993	156.305	947.047	292.262	2,661.337
2001	150.760	368.739	571.746	160.055	979.385	296.851	2,780.772
2002	160.795	378.184	588.805	164.538	1,011.910	301.721	2,894.893
2003	169.952	388.016	604.861	169.424	1,043.187	307.131	2,990.635
2004	178.597	396.041	620.048	173.411	1,074.655	312.429	3,088.039
2005	187.566	404.022	633.405	177.123	1,105.358	316.919	3,180.420
2006	196.135	411.021	646.040	180.517	1,142.310	322.554	3,280.415
2007	204.166	418.506	661.460	184.765	1,182.244	329.169	3,390.071

(*Continued*)

Table A3.2: (*Continued*)

Economy	Canada	France	United Germany	Italy	Japan	UK	US
			R&D Capital Stocks (Billion 2019 US Dollars)				
2008	211.394	425.808	677.167	189.859	1,223.658	337.073	3,510.107
2009	217.476	433.415	697.233	194.853	1,259.071	344.067	3,641.395
2010	223.031	442.420	714.333	199.220	1,277.667	350.048	3,753.712
2011	227.521	450.710	732.928	203.561	1,296.065	355.586	3,853.599
2012	231.828	459.707	756.015	207.309	1,317.466	361.295	3,956.193
2013	235.952	468.936	779.721	211.145	1,337.300	365.203	4,047.724
2014	239.245	477.813	799.852	214.888	1,363.283	370.696	4,144.165
2015	243.122	487.311	821.984	218.967	1,391.389	377.350	4,245.116
2016	246.454	496.324	845.006	222.840	1,412.892	384.545	4,350.250
2017	250.314	503.945	868.609	227.204	1,426.992	392.169	4,462.762
2018	253.673	511.710	897.177	231.649	1,445.570	400.469	4,587.506
2019	255.429	519.524	926.003	237.026	1,466.198	409.969	4,718.856
2020	257.102						

Table A3.3: The quantities of real R&D capital stocks of Mainland China and the EANIEs

Economy	Mainland China	Hong Kong, China	South Korea	Singapore	Taiwan, China
		R&D Capital Stocks (Billion 2019 US Dollars)			
1953	0.665				
1954	0.665				
1955	0.743				
1956	0.924				
1957	1.468				
1958	1.965				
1959	3.138				
1960	5.131				
1961	8.627				
1962	9.769				

Table A3.3: (*Continued*)

Economy	Mainland China	Hong Kong, China	South Korea	Singapore	Taiwan, China
	R&D Capital Stocks (Billion 2019 US Dollars)				
1963	10.205		0.730		
1964	11.152		0.730		
1965	12.612		0.723		
1966	14.211		0.744		
1967	15.470		0.794		
1968	15.553		0.880		
1969	15.548		0.995		
1970	16.622		1.156		
1971	18.308		1.283		
1972	20.663		1.377		
1973	22.603		1.454		
1974	24.175		1.557		
1975	25.585		1.682	0.090	
1976	27.530		1.935	0.090	
1977	29.165		2.236	0.105	
1978	30.837		2.782	0.160	1.804
1979	33.527		3.392	0.220	2.027
1980	36.738		3.909	0.285	2.387
1981	39.622		4.353	0.351	2.668
1982	41.768		4.910	0.425	3.130
1983	44.075		5.874	0.526	3.549
1984	47.435		7.173	0.666	4.005
1985	51.555		8.877	0.863	4.540
1986	55.108		11.217	1.099	5.145
1987	58.723		14.149	1.383	5.771
1988	61.632		17.501	1.717	6.654
1989	63.804		21.314	2.060	7.729
1990	65.527		25.226	2.424	9.076
1991	67.312	0.789	29.219	2.809	10.802
1992	69.609	0.998	34.030	3.322	12.630

(*Continued*)

Table A3.3: (*Continued*)

Economy	Mainland China	Hong Kong, China	South Korea	Singapore	Taiwan, China
			R&D Capital Stocks (Billion 2019 US Dollars)		
1993	72.473	1.218	39.234	3.972	14.634
1994	75.642	1.472	45.302	4.573	16.621
1995	78.517	1.801	52.624	5.251	18.713
1996	81.007	2.242	60.604	6.007	20.840
1997	84.167	2.725	69.200	7.061	23.067
1998	89.695	3.176	78.066	8.277	25.540
1999	95.951	3.627	84.317	9.756	28.211
2000	105.357	4.107	90.852	11.330	31.141
2001	119.395	4.618	98.976	12.979	34.048
2002	135.463	5.225	108.427	14.725	36.928
2003	156.294	5.881	117.778	16.451	40.144
2004	180.712	6.714	127.485	18.092	43.715
2005	210.456	7.681	138.975	20.038	47.626
2006	246.752	8.799	151.196	22.201	51.837
2007	289.696	9.993	165.711	24.457	56.582
2008	338.238	11.083	182.260	27.359	61.711
2009	393.915	12.018	199.534	30.721	67.243
2010	467.259	12.958	217.250	32.655	72.760
2011	548.891	13.877	237.920	34.590	78.859
2012	640.142	14.722	261.748	37.060	85.315
2013	745.487	15.542	287.845	39.095	91.668
2014	861.692	16.361	314.398	41.217	97.988
2015	982.912	17.195	341.899	43.890	104.290
2016	1,110.320	18.081	366.825	46.825	110.305
2017	1,245.412	19.039	391.135	49.338	116.559
2018	1,385.944	20.037	419.755	51.345	123.387
2019	1,533.464	21.252	451.133	53.106	131.014
2020	1,697.043	22.508			

A3.1.5 *Estimation of the quantities of real basic research capital stock of selected economies*

As the actual time series of data on the real basic research expenditures are quite short, and the gestation period of basic research can be very long, and the patent applications are not classified as resulting from basic or non-basic research, we cannot use the same method for the estimation of the quantity of the initial capital stock as we did for the real R&D capital stock in Section 2 of Appendix A3.1. Instead, we simply multiply the quantity of the real basic research expenditure in the first year for which such data are available by 10 and use it as the basic research capital stock for that year. This may seem completely arbitrary; however, the multiplication by 10 can be justified by the assumption of an average useful life of 10 years for basic research. In the steady state, this would be a reasonable estimator of the quantity of real basic research capital stock. In any case, given the assumption of an annual depreciation of 10%, the quantity of basic research capital stock is no longer sensitive to the quantity of the initial capital stock after the first 10 years.

Once the quantities of real basic research capital stocks for the first years for which the real basic research expenditure is available are estimated, we can derive a time series of the quantities of real basic research capital stocks for each economy using the perpetual inventory method with an assumed annual depreciation of 10%. The results are presented in Table A3.4 and Figure 3.6. On the whole, these estimates of the real basic research capital stock look quite reasonable.

A3.1.6 *Estimated quantities of real basic research capital stocks of selected economies*

Table A3.4: The quantities of real basic research capital stocks of selected economies

Economy	France	Italy	Japan	UK	US	Mainland China	South Korea	Singapore	Taiwan, China
				Basic Research Capital Stocks (Billion 2019 US Dollars)					
1953					35.791				
1954					35.791				
1955					36.136				
1956					36.844				

(Continued)

Table A3.4: (*Continued*)

Economy	France	Italy	Japan	UK	US	Mainland China	South Korea	Singapore	Taiwan, China
Basic Research Capital Stocks (Billion 2019 US Dollars)									
1957					38.424				
1958					40.350				
1959					42.858				
1960					46.012				
1961					50.095				
1962					55.181				
1963					61.703				
1964					69.335				
1965					77.803				
1966					86.839				
1967					96.147				
1968					105.437				
1969					114.216				
1970					121.842				
1971					128.284				
1972					133.805				
1973					138.628				
1974					143.139				
1975					147.376				
1976					150.987				
1977					155.057				
1978					159.731				
1979					165.596				
1980					171.743				
1981		13.694	70.255		177.814				
1982		13.694	70.255		183.482				
1983		13.805	71.021		189.488				
1984		14.006	72.405		196.680				
1985		14.302	74.103		205.327				
1986	63.044	14.850	76.208		215.156				
1987	63.044	15.480	79.062		228.258				
1988	63.488	16.879	82.987		241.828				

Table A3.4: (*Continued*)

Economy	France	Italy	Japan	UK	US	Mainland China	South Korea	Singapore	Taiwan, China
Basic Research Capital Stocks (Billion 2019 US Dollars)									
1989	64.160	18.356	86.858		255.285				
1990	65.186	19.905	91.004		269.829				
1991	66.555	21.775	95.462		283.479				
1992	67.943	23.453	100.187		301.452				
1993	69.550	24.987	104.960		317.370				
1994	71.426	26.472	109.745		332.487			1.430	
1995	73.344	27.440	113.700		346.561	5.356	16.508	1.430	
1996	75.144	28.291	118.815		358.192	5.356	16.508	1.473	
1997	76.729	29.169	120.903		372.723	5.434	16.796	1.520	
1998	78.063	30.153	123.109		390.861	5.642	17.210	1.615	5.296
1999	80.628	31.240	125.545		403.769	5.878	17.455	1.736	5.296
2000	83.071	32.432	128.066		419.707	6.239	17.750	1.910	5.374
2001	85.255	33.729	130.986		438.218	6.897	18.145	2.046	5.460
2002	87.527	35.132	133.769		460.352	7.701	18.762	2.309	5.593
2003	89.930	36.643	137.144		484.714	8.900	19.652	2.576	5.795
2004	92.214	38.263	140.555		510.847	10.290	20.795	2.891	6.105
2005	94.299	39.996	143.046		534.472	12.110	22.430	3.313	6.427
2006	96.221	41.844	146.440		558.008	13.970	24.195	3.844	6.709
2007	98.208	44.058	149.744	64.243	579.005	16.080	26.266	4.384	7.048
2008	100.625	45.807	153.209	64.243	599.580	18.118	28.844	4.877	7.423
2009	103.283	47.574	155.851	64.269	621.291	20.588	31.657	5.428	7.932
2010	106.609	49.198	158.272	64.634	645.125	23.781	35.294	5.906	8.480
2011	109.137	50.513	160.174	65.392	669.433	27.300	39.489	6.418	9.042
2012	111.381	51.252	162.671	65.610	686.209	31.498	44.143	6.934	9.647
2013	113.557	52.353	165.289	65.765	700.030	36.551	49.300	7.390	10.203
2014	115.762	53.425	168.924	66.254	716.777	41.832	54.323	7.912	10.696
2015	117.875	54.260	172.186	67.022	734.138	47.425	59.288	8.491	11.150
2016	119.812	55.112	174.103	67.804	750.348	54.089	63.542	9.252	11.553
2017	120.600	55.791	176.227	69.363	769.438	61.599	66.931	10.010	11.891
2018	121.766	56.238	179.754	70.674	787.809	70.126	70.030	10.664	12.201
2019		56.818	182.549	72.663	807.200	78.967	73.449	11.241	12.437
2020						90.186			

A3.2 *The detailed definitions of patents in this study*

The detailed definitions of the patents in each of our data sources are listed in the following sections.

A3.2.1 *World Intellectual Property Organization*

A patent is an exclusive right granted for an invention, which is a product or a process that provides, in general, a new way of doing something, or offers a new technical solution to a problem. To obtain a patent, the technical information about the invention must be disclosed to the public in a patent application.

(*Source*: http://www.wipo.int/patents/en/).

A3.2.2 *United States Patent and Trademark Office*

A patent for an invention is the grant of a property right to the inventor, issued by the United States Patent and Trademark Office. Generally, the term of a new patent is 20 years from the date on which the application for the patent was filed in the United States or, in special cases, from the date an earlier related application was filed, subject to the payment of maintenance fees. US patent grants are effective only within the United States, US territories, and US possessions. Under certain circumstances, patent term extensions or adjustments may be available.

The right conferred by the patent grant is, in the language of the statute and of the grant itself, "the right to exclude others from making, using, offering for sale, or selling" the invention in the United States or "importing" the invention into the United States. What is granted is not the right to make, use, offer for sale, sell or import, but the right to exclude others from making, using, offering for sale, selling or importing the invention. Once a patent is issued, the patentee must enforce the patent without the aid of the USPTO.

There are three types of patents:

(1) Utility patents may be granted to anyone who invents or discovers any new and useful process, machine, article of manufacture, or composition of matter, or any new and useful improvement thereof.

(2) Design patents may be granted to anyone who invents a new, original, and ornamental design for an article of manufacture.
(3) Plant patents may be granted to anyone who invents or discovers and asexually reproduces any distinct and new variety of plant (*Source*: http://www.uspto.gov/patents-getting-started/general-information-concerning-patents#heading-2).

A3.2.3 *China National Intellectual Property Administration (CNIPA) of the People's Republic of China*

There are three kinds of intellectual property rights in China, including patent, trademark and copyright. Patents include "patents for invention", "patents for utility model" and "patents for design". Invention means any new technical solution relating to a product, a process or improvement (*Source*: http://english.sipo.gov.cn/FAQ/200904/t20090408_449727.html; http://english.sipo.gov.cn/FAQ/200904/t20090408_449709.html).

A3.2.4 *Intellectual Property Office, Ministry of Economic Affairs, R.O.C. (Taiwan, China)*

A patent is an intellectual property right which is examined and granted by the competent authority (e.g., Patent Office) to an inventor, a utility model creator, or a designer "to exclude others from exploiting the creation without the patentee's consent" for a limited time period in exchange for public disclosure of the creation when the patent is granted (*Source*: http://www.tipo.gov.tw/ct.asp?xItem=522178&ctNode=6818&mp=2).

Part Three

Measuring the Outcomes of R&D — Patent Applications and Grants

Chapter 4

Domestic Patent Applications and Grants

In this chapter, we assemble time-series data on one type of indicator of Research and Development (R&D) success — the annual numbers of domestic patent applications and patent grants, that is, the numbers of applications from and grants to the domestic residents of a country or region, for the Group-of-Seven (G-7) countries, the four East Asian Newly Industrialised Economies (EANIEs), and Mainland China. The patents considered in this study are exclusively what are known as "invention patents", the definitions of which have already been presented in Appendix A3.2.[1] We also explore visually the relationships between the numbers of the domestic patent applications and patent grants of an economy on the one hand and the quantity of its real R&D capital stock on the other. The formal estimation of an econometric model, linking the numbers of patent applications and grants of an economy to the quantity of its real R&D capital stock, will be deferred to Chapter 10.

---

[1] Data on patents used in this study are collected from World Intellectual Property Organization (WIPO), United States Patent and Trademark Office (USPTO), China National Intellectual Property Administration (CNIPA) of the People's Republic of China (for Mainland, China), and the Intellectual Property Office, Ministry of Economic Affairs, Taipei (for Taiwan, China).

4.1 The Quantities of Domestic Patent Applications of Selected Economies

The objective of R&D activities is new discovery and invention, in other words, innovation. How should one assess the effectiveness of the R&D activities in an economy? How should one measure the degree of success in the innovation of an economy? A number of indicators are possible, for example, the numbers of patent applications submitted, both domestically and abroad, each year, as well as the numbers of patents granted, either domestically or in another country or region, each year. The number of patent applications can be used as an indicator of the success of the country or region in innovation because a patent application is filed only if something new (and original) — a new design, a new product, a new procedure, a new process, or a new software — is believed to have been discovered or invented. In Figure 4.1, the number of patent applications

Figure 4.1: The number of domestic patent applications, G-7 countries, Mainland China, and four EANIEs

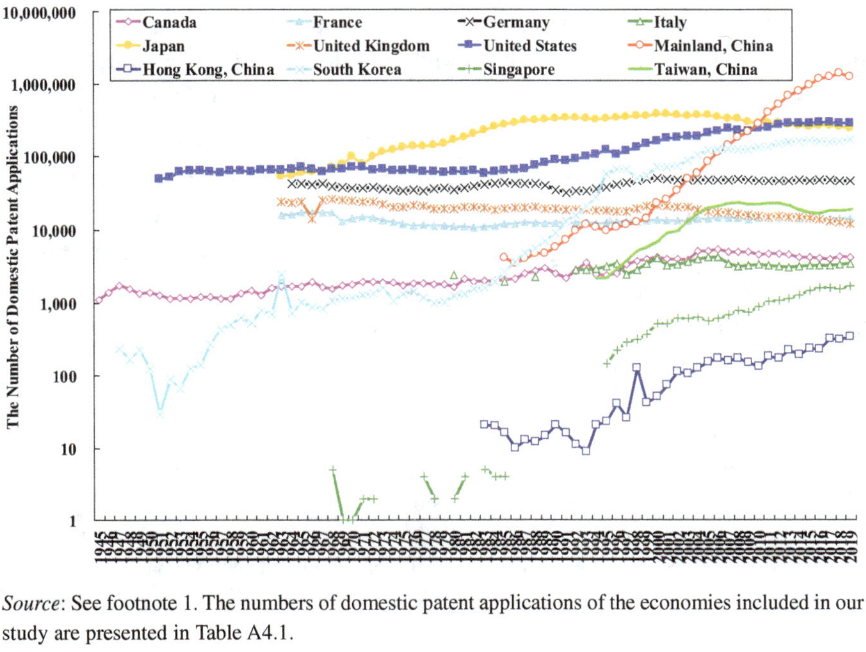

Source: See footnote 1. The numbers of domestic patent applications of the economies included in our study are presented in Table A4.1.

submitted domestically each year by domestic applicants in each of the economies under study is presented.[2]

Figure 4.1 shows that the United States (US) was the world leader in terms of the number of domestic patent applications submitted from 1951, the earliest year for which US data are available, to 1966. Between 1967 and 2009, Japan had the highest number of domestic patent applications in the world, until Mainland China caught up with it in 2011 (403,515 versus 287,580). The United States caught back up with Japan in 2013 (287,831 versus 271,731). Somewhat surprisingly, the number of domestic patent applications in Mainland China soared from only 4,064 in 1985 to 1,231,093 in 2019, overtaking those of both the United States and Japan, to become the highest in the world since 2011. Germany was in third place in the world[3] until overtaken by South Korea in 1995; it was also surpassed by Mainland China in 2003. The EANIEs have also seen a rapid rise in their number of domestic patent applications, with South Korea becoming the fourth highest in the world. The most remarkable feature of Figure 4.1 is the fact that for the developed G-7 economies, there have been little or no growth in the numbers of domestic patent applications in the past decade, with the exception of the US. This is despite fairly significant rates of growth in the quantities of their real R&D capital stocks (see Figure 3.2). In contrast, in Mainland China and the four EANIEs, the numbers of domestic patent applications have been growing quite rapidly.

However, for the smaller EANIEs such as Hong Kong and Singapore, where the domestic markets are relatively limited in size, the absolute numbers of domestic patent applications have remained low, with Singapore surpassing Hong Kong in the early 1990s. In fact, the numbers of the domestic patent applications of Hong Kong and Singapore are lower than the numbers of patent applications submitted by their residents to foreign jurisdictions such as the US. There are several reasons for this

[2] For Germany, Italy and the UK, WIPO provides two alternative sets of numbers for their domestic patent applications: "equivalent applications" and "applications counted by filing office". We used the latter, which avoids possible double counting.

[3] Unlike R&D expenditure data, patent application and grant data are available for a unified Germany back to 1964. However, both the USPTO and the WIPO publish data for a unified Germany only. Separate patent data for West Germany are not available after the reunification of Germany in 1990.

phenomenon. First, since patent application and its continued maintenance if granted, are costly, especially in jurisdictions outside the country or region of the discoverer/inventor, they are filed only if they show significant commercial potential, and only in countries or regions with potentially large and hence profitable markets. The United States is a potentially profitable market for almost all economies in the world because of its large size and a US patent is much more valuable commercially than a domestic patent for a discoverer/inventor in a small economy. Second, for the small economies, their own domestic markets may not be commercially important enough compared to the large foreign markets such as the United States to even warrant filing a patent application. This is especially the case if the discoverer/inventor is employed by the local subsidiary of a foreign, including US, corporation conducting its business globally. Thus, looking only at domestic patent applications and grants may not be sufficient — a comparison of the number of patent applications filed in other jurisdictions such as the US across economies may be a better indicator of their relative success in innovation.[4]

In order to adjust for the effect of the size of an economy, in Figure 4.2, the number of patent applications submitted domestically by domestic applicants divided by the total domestic population each year in each of the economies under study is presented. South Korea is currently by far the world leader in domestic patent applications per capita, with 3.35 applications per 1,000. Japan had had the highest number of domestic applications per capita from 1963, the first year for which Japanese data are available, and reached its peak in 2000. Then it began to decline and was surpassed by South Korea in 2007. Germany was in second place until it was overtaken by South Korea in 1993. It was further overtaken by both the US in 2001 and Taiwan, China in 2004. The US, which has always had a respectable number of domestic applications per capita, saw its domestic applications per capita more than tripled from 0.25/1,000 persons in 1983 to 0.87/1,000 persons in 2019. The number of domestic patent applications per 1,000 persons in Mainland China has also been rising rapidly since

[4]An examination of the US patent applications and grants is presented in Chapter 5. A comparison of the number of patent applications filed in European states may also be interesting as Europe as a whole is also a large market. This is done in Chapter 6.

Figure 4.2: The number of domestic patent applications per thousand persons, G-7 countries, Mainland China, and four EANIEs

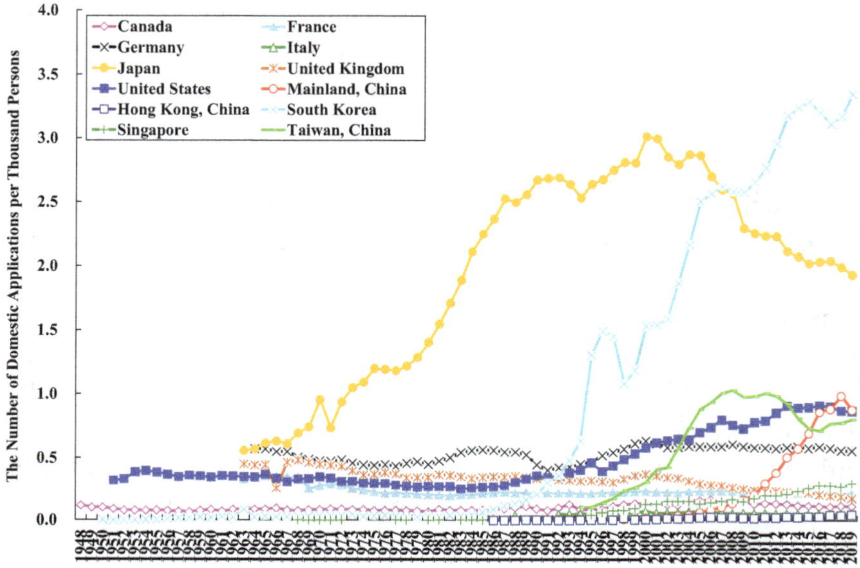

Source: The numbers of domestic patent applications of the economies are taken from Table A4.1. The population data are taken from International Financial Statistics (Canada, France, Germany, Italy, Japan, South Korea, Singapore and UK), World Development Indicators (US), and the local statistical agencies (Mainland China, Hong Kong, China and Taiwan, China).

1999 and reached 0.88/1,000 persons to rank third among economies in our sample in 2019, behind South Korea and Japan, but ahead of the US.[5]

4.2 The Quantities of Domestic Patent Grants of Selected Economies

An alternative, and perhaps more reliable, indicator of the degree of success in innovation is the number of patents granted, as opposed to the number of patent applications. In Figure 4.3, the number of patents granted domestically to domestic applicants by the relevant domestic

[5] There are, of course, other economies not represented in Figure 4.2, for example, Israel had a domestic patent application per capita of 0.16/1,000 persons, but an US patent application per capita of 0.98/1,000 persons in 2019.

Figure 4.3: The number of domestic patents granted to domestic applicants, G-7 countries, Mainland China, and four EANIEs

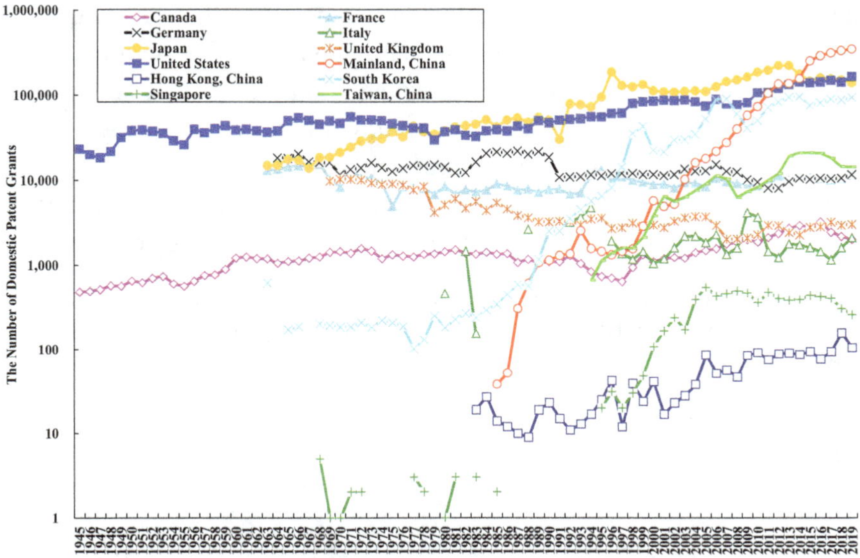

Source: See footnote 1. The numbers of domestic patent grants of the economies included in our study are presented in Table A4.2.

patent authority each year in each of the economies under study is presented. Mainland China started out with only 38 domestic patents granted in 1985, but increased rapidly to overtake Japan, the long-time champion since 1992, in 2015. Mainland China awarded a total of 354,111 domestic patents to domestic applicants in 2019. The US overtook Japan and came in second place in 2019, with 167,115 patents granted to domestic applicants. South Korea was in fourth place, behind Japan. France, Germany, and the UK, which used to rank right after Japan and the US, have fallen behind in terms of the number of domestic patents granted. More generally, the numbers of domestic patents granted in the European G-7 countries to domestic applicants all show a downward trend. Mainland China's rise in the number of domestic patent grants to domestic applicants has been extraordinarily rapid and it signifies China's determination to become an innovative country. Moreover, with so many domestic patents granted to domestic residents in China, it can be expected that there will be widespread domestic demand for the strengthening of the enforcement of intellectual property rights within China itself.

It is interesting to compare the domestic success rates of domestic patent applications across economies. The success rate may be defined as the number of domestic patents granted to domestic applicants divided by the number of domestic applications submitted by domestic applicants, lagged 1 year.[6] The 3-year moving-average domestic patent application success rates of the economies under study are presented in Figure 4.4, with the omission of those economies in which the number of patent applications to the USPTO exceeds the number of domestic applications on a regular basis.[7] These success rates vary significantly across

Figure 4.4: Three-year moving-average domestic patent application success rates, France, Germany, Japan, UK, US, Mainland China and South Korea

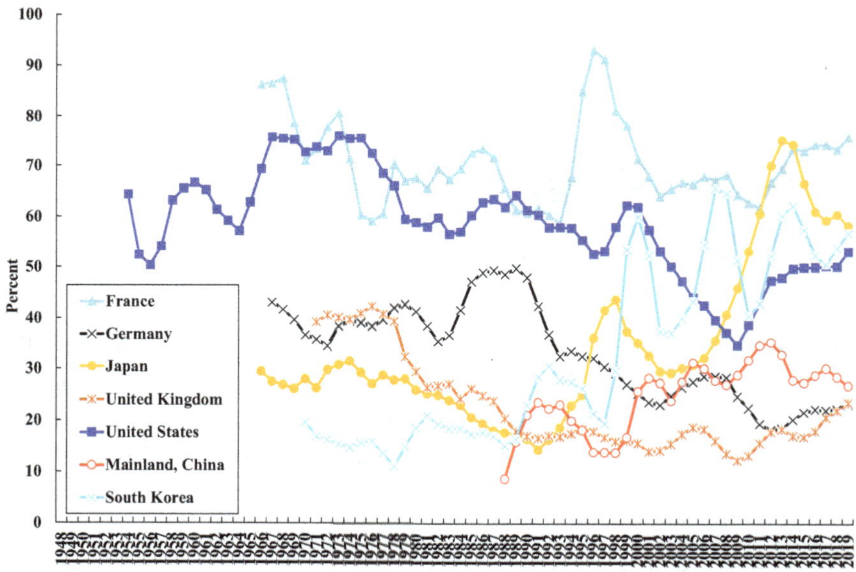

Source: Table A4.3.

[6] One can also choose a 2-year lag for the number of domestic applications. It all depends on the time required for processing of patent applications by the relevant domestic patent authorities.

[7] The economies omitted include Canada, Hong Kong, China, Italy, Singapore, and Taiwan, China all of which have had US patent application rates over 100% for long periods of time. The success rate may occasionally exceed 100%, as, for example in the case of the UK, because of variations in the time elapsed between the submission of a patent application and the award of a patent grant. However, in recent years, the number of USPTO patent applications of the UK has exceeded its domestic patent applications. This is why it has been left out from the econometric analyses in Chapters 10 and 11.

economies and also show significant fluctuations over time. In 2019, France had the highest domestic patent success rate among our sample of economies (75.6%), followed by Japan (58.1%), South Korea (56.7%), and the US (53.0%). The Chinese domestic patent success rate was 26.7%. Germany had the lowest rate at 23.2%, with the United Kingdom (UK) marginally ahead at 23.4%. Overall, a downward trend may be observed in the domestic patent success rates of non-Asian developed economies, and an upward trend for the East Asian economies of Mainland China, Japan and South Korea. We note that these domestic success rates may also reflect the varying procedures and standards used in the different jurisdictions. In addition, while they are clearly affected by the number of domestic applications, they may also in turn affect the future number of domestic applications.

4.3 The Effect of R&D Capital Stocks

The quantity of the real R&D capital stock of an economy can be expected to have a direct and positive causal relationship to the total number of domestic patent applications submitted by and patent grants to its domestic residents. In Figure 4.5, the annual total number of domestic patent applications submitted by the domestic residents of a country or region is plotted against the quantity of its real R&D capital stock at the beginning of each year. Figure 4.5 shows clearly that the higher the quantity of the real R&D capital stock of an economy is, the higher is the number of domestic patent applications submitted by its residents. The estimated simple linear regression line of the number of patent applications on the quantity of real R&D capital stock is statistically highly significant. The estimated "elasticity" of 1.034 is slightly greater than unity, that is, it implies that a 1% increase in the real R&D capital stock may be predicted to increase the number of domestic patent applications by domestic residents by 1.03%. However, it is worth noting that on an individual economy basis, the positive correlation is not so obvious for the European G-7 countries (see, for example, the data points for France, West Germany, Italy, and the UK) and for the US in its early phase. It is further worth noting that Japan, and the two East Asian NIEs, South Korea and Taiwan,

Figure 4.5: The number of domestic patent applications and the quantity of real R&D capital stock, G-7 countries, Mainland China, and four EANIEs

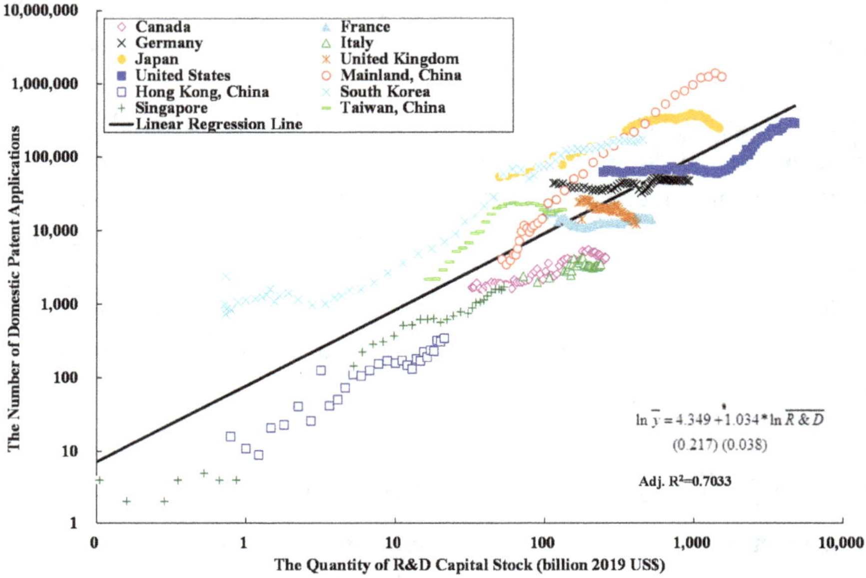

Note: The numbers in parentheses are the estimated robust standard errors of the coefficients.
Source: Data on the number of domestic patent applications are from Table A4.1 and data on the quantity of real R&D capital stock are from Table A3.2.

China, may be regarded as the "over-achievers", in the sense that at any given quantity of real R&D capital stock, their domestic residents submitted a higher number of domestic applications than that predicted by the linear regression line. However, all three show a tendency of levelling off. In contrast, Hong Kong, China and Singapore may be regarded as the "under-achievers", although this may well be due in part to the fact that they themselves have very small domestic markets and hence their discoverers and inventors may not find it worthwhile to apply for domestic patents. Finally, Mainland China was an "under-achiever" prior to 2000, but transformed into an "over-achiever" after 2000. In 2019, the number of domestic applications submitted by domestic residents in Mainland China was more than eight times what would have been if Mainland China had stayed on the estimated common linear regression line.

In Figure 4.6, the annual total number of domestic patents granted to the domestic residents of a country or region is plotted against the quantity of its real R&D capital stock at the beginning of each year. Figure 4.6 also clearly shows the positive relationship between the number of domestic patent grants of an economy and the quantity of its real R&D capital stock. The estimated simple linear regression line of the natural logarithm of the number of patent grants on the natural logarithm of the quantity of real R&D capital stock is also statistically highly significant, similar to the relationship between patent applications and R&D capital stock. The estimated "elasticity" of 1.076 implies that, on average, a 1% increase in the real R&D capital stock may be predicted to increase the number of domestic patent grants by more than 1%, 1.076% to be exact, that is, there are some increasing returns to scale to the generation of domestic patent grants from real R&D capital.

Figure 4.6: The number of domestic patent grants and the quantity of real R&D capital stock, G-7 countries, Mainland China, and four EANIEs

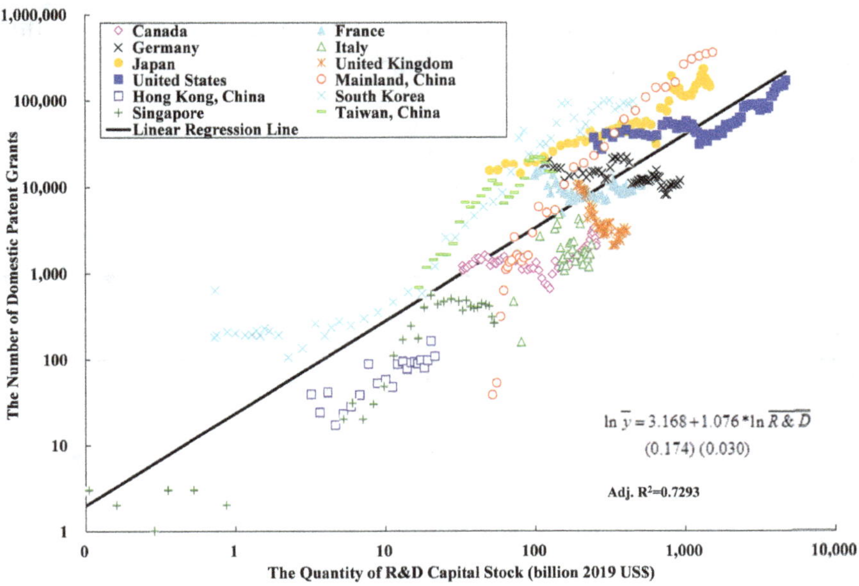

Note: The numbers in parentheses are the estimated robust standard errors of the coefficients.
Source: Data on the number of domestic patent grants are from Table A4.2 and data on the quantity of real R&D capital stock are from Table A3.2.

It is further worth noting that Mainland China (since 2000), Japan, and the two EANIEs, South Korea and Taiwan, China may also be regarded as the "over-achievers", in the sense that at any given quantity of real R&D capital stock, they were able to achieve a higher number of domestic patent grants than that predicted by the linear regression line. In contrast, Hong Kong, China and Singapore may also be regarded as the "under-achievers". In 2019, the number of domestic patent grants awarded in Mainland China was more than 5.6 times what would have been granted if Mainland China had stayed on the estimated common linear regression line. However, the non-Asian developed economies all appear to be "under-achievers" in the past decade or two.

A word of caution is necessary in the interpretation of the domestic patent grant data above as different economies may well have their own different standards in their patent grants, and moreover, these standards may also have changed systematically over time. For this reason, we cannot take the identified "over-achievement" and "under-achievement" of the different economies in innovation too literally. What is unmistakable is the general overall positive relationship between the numbers of domestic patent applications and patent grants on the one hand and the quantity of the real R&D capital stock on the other.

Appendix

Table A4.1: The number of domestic patent applications submitted by domestic residents, G-7 countries, Mainland China, and four EANIEs

Economy	Canada	France	United Germany	Italy	Japan	UK	US
1945	1,119						
1946	1,392						
1947	1,779						
1948	1,558						
1949	1,381						
1950	1,417						
1951	1,282						49,671
1952	1,156						52,405

(*Continued*)

Table A4.1: (*Continued*)

Economy	Canada	France	United Germany	Italy	Japan	UK	US
1953	1,173						62,006
1954	1,160						64,914
1955	1,236						64,121
1956	1,215						62,134
1957	1,167						60,278
1958	1,154						63,234
1959	1,348						63,302
1960	1,506						63,090
1961	1,310						66,335
1962	1,613						66,525
1963	1,703	15,825			53,876	24,300	66,715
1964	1,715	16,654	43,255		55,556	23,963	67,013
1965	1,734	17,509	43,504		60,796	24,274	**72,317**
1966	1,954	17,467	42,274		62,962	14,206	66,855
1967	1,655	17,347	42,581		61,721	25,786	61,651
1968	1,591	17,561	39,446		71,114	26,711	67,180
1969	1,785	12,974	38,538		77,132	25,904	68,243
1970	1,814	14,106	37,653		100,513	25,227	72,343
1971	1,986	14,962	37,444		78,425	24,771	71,089
1972	1,970	14,807	38,198		101,328	24,337	65,943
1973	1,942	13,458	36,421		115,221	22,472	66,935
1974	1,936	12,706	35,047		121,509	20,545	64,093
1975	1,782	12,110	34,757		135,118	20,842	64,445
1976	1,854	11,471	35,237		135,762	21,797	65,050
1977	1,883	11,811	34,413		135,991	21,114	62,863
1978	1,838	11,445	36,000		141,517	19,384	61,441
1979	1,796	11,303	36,991		150,623	19,468	60,535
1980	1,648	11,000	35,282	2,396	165,730	19,612	62,098
1981	2,164	10,945	37,261		184,244	20,808	62,404
1982	2,000	10,681	39,252		204,826	20,530	63,316

Table A4.1: (*Continued*)

Economy	Canada	France	United Germany	Italy	Japan	UK	US
1983	2,017	11,147	42,173		227,708	19,893	59,390
1984	2,026	11,333	43,455		256,195	19,093	61,841
1985	2,092	12,050	43,992	2,000	274,348	19,672	63,874
1986	2,161	12,155	43,629		290,132	20,040	65,487
1987	2,527	12,695	42,777		310,908	19,945	68,315
1988	2,772	12,437	42,894	2,289	308,775	20,536	75,192
1989	3,031	12,592	41,244		317,353	19,732	82,370
1990	2,549	12,378	35,282		332,952	19,310	90,643
1991	2,182	12,597	32,256		335,564	19,230	87,955
1992	2,807	12,539	33,919	2,847	337,498	18,848	92,425
1993	3,623	12,638	34,752	2,818	331,774	18,727	99,955
1994	2,480	12,519	36,715	2,961	319,261	18,384	107,233
1995	2,431	12,419	38,103	3,222	333,770	18,630	123,958
1996	2,583	12,916	42,322	3,505	339,045	18,184	106,892
1997	3,344	13,252	44,438	2,485	349,211	17,938	120,445
1998	3,809	13,251	46,523	2,845	357,379	19,530	135,483
1999	4,061	13,592	50,029	3,493	357,531	21,333	149,825
2000	4,187	13,870	51,736	4,166	384,201	22,050	164,795
2001	3,963	13,499	49,989	3,329	382,815	21,423	177,511
2002	3,959	13,519	47,598	3,336	365,204	20,624	184,245
2003	3,929	13,511	47,818	3,676	358,184	20,426	188,941
2004	5,231	14,230	48,448	3,998	368,416	19,178	189,536
2005	5,183	14,327	48,367	4,200	367,960	17,833	207,867
2006	5,522	14,529	48,012	4,197	347,060	17,484	221,784
2007	4,998	14,722	47,853	3,481	333,498	17,375	241,347
2008	5,061	14,658	49,240	3,230	330,110	16,523	231,588
2009	5,067	14,100	47,859	3,315	295,315	15,985	224,912
2010	4,550	14,748	47,047	3,339	290,081	15,490	241,977
2011	4,754	14,655	46,986	3,308	287,580	15,343	247,750
2012	4,709	14,540	46,620	3,174	287,013	15,370	268,782

(*Continued*)

Table A4.1: (*Continued*)

Economy	Canada	France	United Germany	Italy	Japan	UK	US
2013	4,567	14,690	47,353	3,125	271,731	14,972	287,831
2014	4,198	14,500	48,154	3,235	265,959	15,196	285,096
2015	4,277	14,306	47,384	3,281	258,839	14,867	288,335
2016	4,078	14,206	48,480	3,328	260,244	13,876	295,327
2017	4,053	14,415	47,785	3,251	260,292	13,301	293,904
2018	4,349	14,303	46,617	3,356	253,630	12,865	285,095
2019	4,238	14,103	46,632	3,471	245,372	12,061	285,113

Economy	Mainland, China	Hong Kong, China	South Korea	Singapore	Taiwan, China
1945					
1946					
1947			236		
1948			169		
1949			233		
1950			126		
1951			30		
1952			91		
1953			68		
1954			127		
1955			144		
1956			275		
1957			443		
1958			510		
1959			634		
1960			545		
1961			800		
1962			714		
1963			2,455		
1964			744		
1965			1,018		
1966			883		

Table A4.1: (*Continued*)

Economy	Mainland, China	Hong Kong, China	South Korea	Singapore	Taiwan, China
1967			855		
1968			1,086	5	
1969			1,157	1	
1970			1,202	1	
1971			1,283	2	
1972			1,377	2	
1973			1,622		
1974			1,093		
1975			1,326		
1976			1,436		
1977			1,177	4	
1978			989	2	
1979			1,034		
1980			1,241	2	
1981			1,319	4	
1982			1,556		
1983		21	1,599	5	
1984		20	1,997	4	
1985	4,064	16	2,702	4	
1986	3,494	10	3,640		
1987	3,975	13	4,871		
1988	4,751	12	5,696		
1989	4,685	15	7,020		
1990	5,705	21	9,082		
1991	7,192	16	13,253		
1992	9,663	11	15,951		
1993	11,687	9	21,449		
1994	10,722	21	28,554		2,197
1995	9,551	23	59,228	145	2,216
1996	10,857	41	68,405	224	2,938
1997	11,722	26	67,359	288	3,761

(*Continued*)

Table A4.1: (*Continued*)

Economy	Mainland, China	Hong Kong, China	South Korea	Singapore	Taiwan, China
1998	12,660	128	50,596	311	5,213
1999	14,403	42	55,970	374	5,804
2000	23,369	51	72,831	516	6,830
2001	26,200	74	73,714	523	9,170
2002	34,811	112	76,570	624	9,638
2003	50,326	107	90,313	626	13,049
2004	58,475	127	105,250	641	16,747
2005	84,052	156	122,188	569	20,093
2006	111,346	172	125,476	626	21,365
2007	141,210	160	128,701	696	23,132
2008	182,312	173	127,114	793	23,744
2009	218,111	149	127,316	750	22,594
2010	281,451	133	131,805	895	22,790
2011	403,515	181	138,034	1,056	23,432
2012	522,584	171	148,136	1,081	22,949
2013	693,170	226	159,978	1,143	21,633
2014	789,698	192	164,073	1,303	18,988
2015	957,291	239	167,275	1,469	17,262
2016	1,193,382	233	163,424	1,601	16,866
2017	1,233,592	324	159,084	1,609	18,199
2018	1,380,668	314	162,561	1,575	18,365
2019	1,231,093	346	171,603	1,727	18,984

Table A4.2: The number of domestic patent grants awarded to domestic residents, G-7 countries, Mainland China, and four EANIEs

Economy	Canada	France	United Germany	Italy	Japan	UK	US
1945	486						23,600
1946	495						20,203
1947	520						18,574

Table A4.2: (*Continued*)

Economy	Canada	France	United Germany	Italy	Japan	UK	US
1948	580						22,023
1949	570						32,119
1950	655						38,721
1951	627						39,548
1952	708						38,068
1953	742						36,206
1954	606						29,436
1955	570						26,457
1956	652						40,287
1957	761						36,599
1958	772						40,959
1959	899						44,196
1960	1,219						39,458
1961	1,258						40,139
1962	1,207						38,628
1963	1,194	13,230			14,937		**37,174**
1964	1,060	13,673	18,427		15,103		38,410
1965	1,116	14,570	18,373		17,797		50,331
1966	1,131	14,881	20,592		17,373		54,634
1967	1,222	15,246	16,646		13,877		51,274
1968	1,263	15,627	16,296		18,576		45,781
1969	1,433	10,288	16,312		18,787	9,807	50,394
1970	1,461	8,359	11,694		21,404	10,343	47,073
1971	1,395	13,696	13,425		24,795	10,376	55,975
1972	1,587	10,767	14,049		29,101	10,116	51,519
1973	1,486	10,817	16,167		30,937	9,357	51,501
1974	1,200	9,282	14,128		30,873	8,971	50,646
1975	1,336	4,962	12,740		36,992	9,120	46,710
1976	1,293	8,420	13,972		32,465	8,855	44,280
1977	1,260	8,361	14,992		43,047	7,722	41,488

(*Continued*)

Table A4.2: (*Continued*)

Economy	Canada	France	United Germany	Italy	Japan	UK	US
1978	1,352	8,083	14,886		37,648	8,464	41,250
1979	1,369	6,846	15,213		34,863	4,182	30,074
1980	1,450	8,438	14,281	466	38,032	5,158	37,350
1981	1,526	6,855	12,250		42,080	6,076	39,218
1982	1,386	7,764	12,404	1,475	43,794	4,686	33,890
1983	1,359	7,323	16,501	157	45,578	5,655	32,868
1984	1,427	7,651	20,940		51,690	4,442	38,373
1985	1,355	9,092	21,736		42,323	5,441	39,556
1986	1,377	8,574	20,813		51,276	4,610	38,126
1987	1,082	7,716	22,210		54,087	3,875	43,519
1988	1,184	7,875	20,368	2,646	47,912	3,633	40,498
1989	1,069	7,230	21,839		54,743	3,273	50,184
1990	1,109	7,816	18,813		50,370	3,265	47,391
1991	1,109	7,941	10,851		30,453	3,307	51,177
1992	1,305	6,891	11,021	3,251	78,994	3,331	52,253
1993	1,056	7,160	11,098	3,687	77,311	3,019	53,231
1994	852	11,551	11,736	4,785	72,757	3,517	56,066
1995	743	13,298	11,436		94,804	3,646	55,739
1996	709	10,105	12,071	1,944	187,681	2,737	61,104
1997	648	11,119	12,153	1,383	129,937	2,792	61,708
1998	949	10,045	12,162	1,178	125,704	3,168	80,289
1999	1,347	9,601	11,775	1,468	133,960	2,910	83,906
2000	1,117	8,937	11,772	1,057	112,269	3,003	85,068
2001	1,210	9,081	11,483	1,197	109,375	2,807	87,600
2002	1,253	8,189	11,841	1,613	108,515	3,339	86,971
2003	1,226	9,472	13,707	2,213	110,835	3,662	87,893
2004	1,425	9,371	12,925	2,217	112,527	3,780	84,270
2005	1,511	8,481	13,084	1,868	111,088	3,751	74,637
2006	1,588	10,697	15,457	2,317	126,804	2,978	89,823
2007	1,809	9,748	12,977	1,353	145,040	2,058	79,526

Table A4.2: (*Continued*)

Economy	Canada	France	United Germany	Italy	Japan	UK	US
2008	1,886	9,236	12,639	1,624	151,765	2,070	77,502
2009	2,029	9,228	10,284	4,201	164,459	2,118	82,382
2010	1,906	8,779	9,630	3,721	187,237	2,323	107,791
2011	2,150	8,815	8,208	1,462	197,594	2,992	108,622
2012	2,404	11,417	8,164	1,247	224,917	2,974	121,026
2013	2,756	10,235	9,792	1,806	225,571	2,464	133,593
2014	2,984	10,570	10,634	1,767	177,750	2,315	144,621
2015	2,858	11,043	10,411	1,630	146,749	2,838	140,969
2016	3,295	10,623	10,792	1,463	160,643	2,897	143,723
2017	2,500	10,216	10,564	1,168	156,844	3,267	150,949
2018	2,221	10,574	10,789	1,632	152,440	3,005	144,413
2019	2,035	11,673	11,770	2,130	140,865	3,081	167,115

Economy	Mainland, China	Hong Kong, China	South Korea	Singapore	Taiwan, China
1945					
1946					
1947					
1948					
1949					
1950					
1951					
1952					
1953					
1954					
1955					
1956					
1957					
1958					
1959					
1960					

(*Continued*)

Table A4.2: (*Continued*)

Economy	Mainland, China	Hong Kong, China	South Korea	Singapore	Taiwan, China
1961					
1962					
1963			625		
1964					
1965			177		
1966			191		
1967					
1968			207	5	
1969			200	1	
1970			190	1	
1971			192	2	
1972			213	2	
1973			188		
1974			227		
1975			212		
1976			191		
1977			104	3	
1978			133	2	
1979			258		
1980			186	1	
1981			232	3	
1982			274		
1983		19	245	3	
1984		27	297		
1985	38	14	349	2	
1986	52	12	458		
1987	311	10	596		
1988	616	9	575		
1989	1,083	19	1,181		

Table A4.2: (*Continued*)

Economy	Mainland, China	Hong Kong, China	South Korea	Singapore	Taiwan, China
1990	1,149	23	2,554		
1991	1,309	15	2,553		
1992	1,378	11	3,570		
1993	2,586	13	4,545		
1994	1,596	17	5,774		668
1995	1,471	25	6,575	20	1,138
1996	1,333	42	8,321	31	1,393
1997	1,472	12	14,497	20	1,611
1998	1,574	39	35,900	30	1,598
1999	2,906	24	43,314	48	2,139
2000	5,790	41	22,943	110	3,834
2001	4,955	17	21,833	170	6,477
2002	5,287	23	30,175	243	5,683
2003	10,334	28	30,525	175	6,399
2004	16,262	38	35,284	400	7,641
2005	18,247	87	53,419	555	9,124
2006	22,236	52	89,303	438	11,431
2007	28,181	57	91,645	469	10,445
2008	40,628	47	61,115	501	6,321
2009	58,514	86	42,129	473	7,392
2010	73,820	93	51,404	369	8,367
2011	105,824	76	72,258	484	10,035
2012	137,153	90	84,061	410	12,140
2013	138,337	92	95,667	393	19,532
2014	157,795	88	97,294	402	21,261
2015	256,400	96	76,319	446	21,401
2016	294,817	78	82,400	432	21,178
2017	320,242	96	90,847	414	18,569
2018	339,615	161	89,227	312	14,651
2019	354,111	107	94,852	264	14,481

Table A4.3: The domestic patent application success rate (3-year moving average), G-7 countries, Mainland China, and four EANIEs

Economy	Canada	France	United Germany	Italy	Japan	UK	US
1948	38.1						
1949	35.5						
1950	38.9						
1951	42.8						
1952	49.0						
1953	54.6						
1954	57.0						64.4
1955	55.0						52.4
1956	51.2						50.4
1957	54.8						54.2
1958	60.5						63.2
1959	68.9						65.6
1960	78.2						66.7
1961	84.0						65.3
1962	88.7						61.4
1963	83.2						59.2
1964	76.1						57.2
1965	67.1						62.9
1966	64.2	86.3			29.5		69.4
1967	64.3	86.6	43.1		27.6		75.8
1968	68.0	87.5	41.7		26.9		75.5
1969	76.3	78.7	39.7		26.2		75.3
1970	82.7	71.0	36.7		28.1		72.8
1971	82.9	73.4	35.8		26.3	39.3	73.8
1972	79.6	77.8	34.5		29.8	40.6	72.9
1973	77.4	80.7	38.5		30.8	40.1	76.0
1974	72.4	71.3	39.5		31.5	39.7	75.4
1975	68.7	60.4	39.2		29.3	40.9	75.5
1976	67.8	59.2	38.4		27.1	42.3	72.4

Table A4.3: (*Continued*)

Economy	Canada	France	United Germany	Italy	Japan	UK	US
1977	69.8	60.5	39.7		28.7	40.8	68.5
1978	70.8	70.3	42.0		27.8	39.3	66.0
1979	71.4	67.0	42.7		28.0	32.4	59.4
1980	75.7	67.6	41.4		25.9	29.4	58.8
1981	82.6	65.6	38.5		25.1	26.4	57.9
1982	79.1	69.3	35.5		24.8	26.7	59.7
1983	74.9	67.3	23.1	36.7		23.8	27.0
1984	67.6	69.4	25.6	41.7		22.9	24.1
1985	68.5	72.5	27.0	47.2		20.5	26.1
1986	67.8	73.3	32.8	49.0		19.3	24.8
1987	60.9	71.6	36.0	49.4		18.0	23.8
1988	54.2	65.6	37.4	48.6		17.6	20.3
1989	45.2	61.2	37.8	49.8		17.3	17.8
1990	40.7	60.7	36.7	48.0		16.3	16.9
1991	39.6	61.5	36.3	42.4		14.2	16.5
1992	46.6	60.3	35.2	36.8		16.2	17.0
1993	47.0	58.7	34.1	32.5		18.5	16.8
1994	40.3	67.7	33.6	33.6		22.8	17.4
1995	30.4	84.9	32.5	32.5		24.8	18.2
1996	27.5	93.0	32.2	32.2		36.0	17.8
1997	28.1	91.2	30.5	30.5		41.4	16.6
1998	27.5	81.1	29.3	29.3	49.1	43.5	15.9
1999	29.6	78.1	27.1	27.1	46.2	37.3	16.0
2000	30.4	71.3	25.4	25.4	43.1	35.0	15.5
2001	30.6	67.9	23.7	23.7	36.9	32.5	13.9
2002	29.3	64.0	23.1	23.1	35.8	29.4	14.1
2003	30.5	65.4	24.9	24.9	47.8	29.1	15.4
2004	33.0	66.7	26.5	26.5	58.4	30.0	17.3
2005	32.0	66.3	27.6	27.6	57.8	30.6	18.6
2006	31.9	67.9	28.7	28.7	54.1	32.0	18.3

(*Continued*)

Table A4.3: (*Continued*)

Economy	Canada	France	United Germany	Italy	Japan	UK	US
2007	30.8	67.1	28.7	28.7	44.7	35.5	16.0
2008	33.7	68.2	28.5	28.5	44.7	40.6	13.5
2009	36.9	64.3	24.8	24.8	69.6	45.7	12.2
2010	38.5	62.7	22.5	22.5	96.3	52.9	13.1
2011	41.7	61.7	19.5	19.5	95.3	60.4	15.6
2012	45.1	66.6	18.3	18.3	64.6	69.9	17.7
2013	52.1	69.4	18.6	18.6	46.1	75.0	18.2
2014	58.1	73.4	20.3	20.3	50.4	74.1	17.0
2015	64.0	72.8	21.7	21.7	54.6	66.4	16.7
2016	70.2	74.1	22.3	22.3	50.5	60.9	17.9
2017	68.8	74.1	22.1	22.1	43.3	59.2	20.6
2018	64.4	73.2	22.4	22.4	43.3	60.3	21.9
2019	58.1	75.6	23.2	23.2	49.6	58.1	23.4

Economy	Mainland, China	Hong Kong, China	South Korea	Singapore	Taiwan, China
1948					
1949					
1950					
1951					
1952					
1953					
1954					
1955					
1956					
1957					
1958					
1959					
1960					
1961					
1962					

Table A4.3: (*Continued*)

Economy	Mainland, China	Hong Kong, China	South Korea	Singapore	Taiwan, China
1963					
1964					
1965					
1966					
1967					
1968					
1969					
1970			19.7		
1971			16.9		
1972			16.3		
1973			15.4		
1974			14.7		
1975			15.7		
1976			15.9		
1977			13.7		
1978			11.0		
1979			14.9		
1980			18.5		
1981			20.9		
1982			19.2		
1983			18.4		
1984			18.4		
1985			17.3		
1986		91.2	17.7		
1987		81.7	16.9		
1988	8.6	81.4	15.0		
1989	15.7	109.2	16.3		
1990	20.9	127.0	23.0		
1991	23.4	127.7	28.4		
1992	22.2	97.8	30.5		

(*Continued*)

Table A4.3: (*Continued*)

Economy	Mainland, China	Hong Kong, China	South Korea	Singapore	Taiwan, China
1993	23.0	86.1	27.8		
1994	19.9	125.3	27.5		
1995	18.0	142.0	26.1		
1996	13.8	163.5	21.3		
1997	13.7	110.3	19.4		56.5
1998	13.6	120.6	29.5	13.6	53.4
1999	16.6	66.0	53.4	11.6	46.1
2000	25.5	88.8	60.0	18.4	49.9
2001	28.1	49.9	52.2	25.9	67.3
2002	27.2	54.0	37.3	36.3	74.3
2003	23.7	29.8	36.9	35.8	74.4
2004	27.4	30.5	40.0	46.1	62.3
2005	31.1	43.0	43.2	59.5	59.8
2006	30.0	45.8	54.3	75.8	56.6
2007	27.7	45.0	65.6	79.5	53.4
2008	26.8	31.9	64.5	74.6	44.4
2009	28.7	37.4	51.2	68.8	35.8
2010	31.6	47.2	40.3	60.3	31.8
2011	34.5	56.4	42.8	54.3	37.4
2012	35.1	56.4	52.0	47.4	44.3
2013	32.7	53.6	60.1	43.1	60.3
2014	27.7	47.5	62.1	36.8	78.4
2015	27.2	47.6	57.3	35.3	98.7
2016	28.7	40.5	52.2	32.9	111.2
2017	30.0	41.3	50.5	29.8	115.2
2018	28.4	41.2	53.6	24.9	104.4
2019	26.7	41.7	56.7	20.7	89.8

Chapter 5

United States Patent Applications and Grants

In this chapter, we assemble time-series data on another type of indicator of Research and Development (R&D) success — the annual numbers of United States (US) patent applications and grants, that is, the numbers of US patent applications from and grants to the residents of a country or region in our sample, including the US itself. We also explore the relationships between the numbers of the US patent applications from and grants to each economy on the one hand and the quantity of the real R&D capital stock of this economy on the other. We choose to look at the US patent applications and grants for all economies in our study so that their numbers of patent applications and grants are more comparable both across economies and times from the points of view of both quality and quantity. In addition, as the largest market by value in the world for more than seven decades, the US has always attracted the most foreign patent applications. The Chinese market has also been growing rapidly and already rivals the US market in size. China will be attracting more and more patent applications from foreign discoverers and inventors in the future, as no one can afford to ignore the potential of the Chinese market. Moreover, the protection of intellectual property in China has also been greatly strengthened since 2014, when specialised intellectual property courts were established.

In Figure 5.1, the total numbers of patent applications submitted to the United States Patent and Trademark Office (USPTO) each year by all

Figure 5.1: The total number of patent applications submitted to the USPTO by all applicants and by US applicants (thousands)

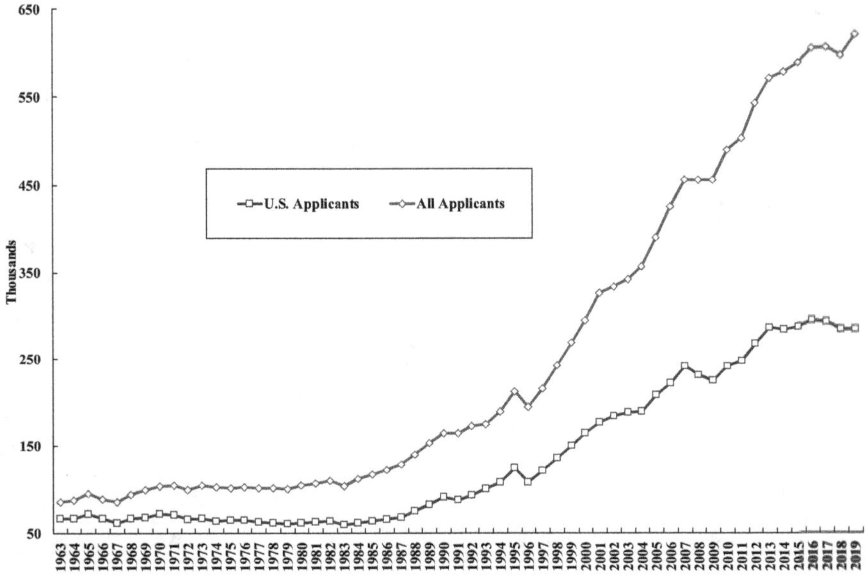

Source: USPTO.

applicants and by US applicants are presented. Three distinct phases may be identified. In the first phase, approximately between 1963 and 1986, the average annual total number of patent applications received by the USPTO was a relatively stable 101,202. In the second phase, 1986–1997, the average annual total number of patent applications received by the USPTO increased by almost 70% to 169,357. In the third and most recent phase, 1997–2019, the average annual total number of patent applications received by the USPTO increased by more than 1.6 times to 446,853. Similar trends are apparent with the annual total number of patent applications submitted to the USPTO by US applicants.

The share of total patent applications submitted to the USPTO by US residents declined steadily from 77.7% in 1963 to 45.9% in 2019. In 2019, the total number of US patent applications received was 621,453, with 285,113, or slightly less than half, coming from US applicants. However, over the decade from 2010 to 2019, the share of USPTO patent applications submitted by US residents remained fairly constant, averaging 48.7%.

Figure 5.2: The number of US patent applications, G-7 countries, Mainland China, and four EANIEs

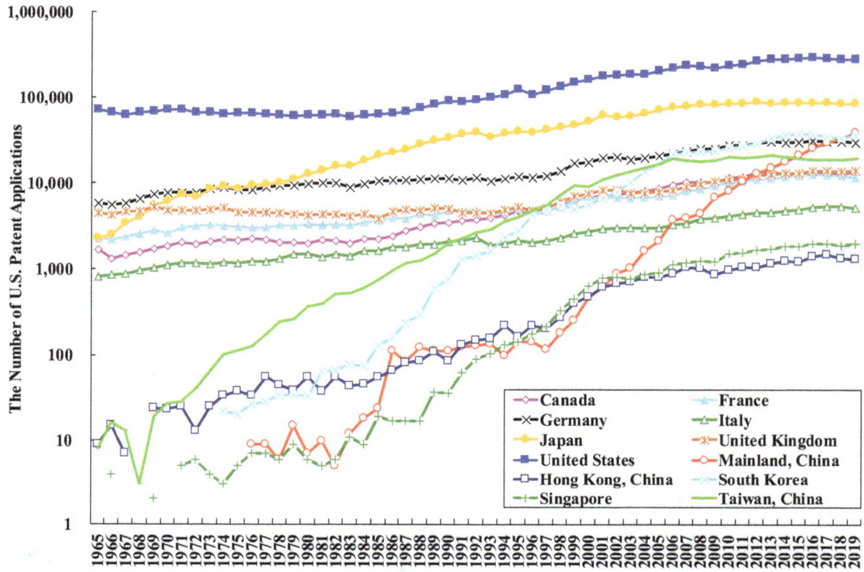

Source: The numbers of US patent applications are taken from Table A5.1.

In Figure 5.2, the number of patent applications submitted to the US each year by the residents of each of the economies under study, including those of the US itself, is presented. The US is clearly the world leader in terms of the number of patent applications filed in the US, followed by Japan. Germany was in third place from 1974 to 2011, when it was overtaken by South Korea. The growth of the number of patent applications from Mainland China has been phenomenal: in 1976, there were only nine applications, but the number grew to 39,055 applications in 2019, with Mainland China replacing South Korea in third place. The number of applications from the newly industrialised economy of Taiwan, China also grew rapidly from 1968, but began to level off in 2006. The numbers of applications from the developed economies of Canada, France, Italy and the United Kingdom (UK) have all fallen behind the East Asian economies with the exception of the two city economies of Hong Kong, China and Singapore. As noted in Chapter 4, for such small economies, the numbers of their US patent applications can far exceed the numbers of their respective domestic patent applications.

Figure 5.3: The number of US patent applications per 1,000 persons, G-7 countries, Mainland China, and four EANIEs

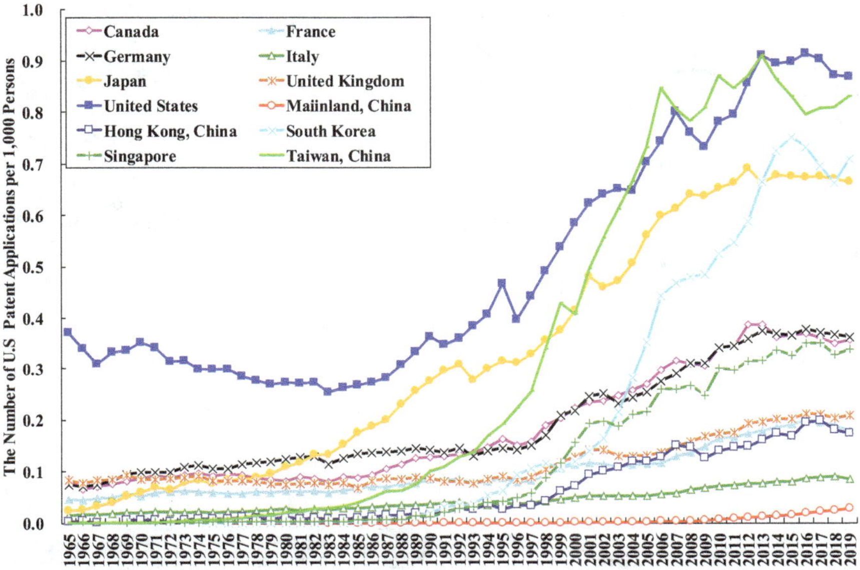

Source: The numbers of US patent applications of the economies are taken from Table A5.1. The population data are taken from *International Financial Statistics* (Canada, France, Germany, Italy, Japan, South Korea, Singapore and UK), *World Development Indicators* (US) and the local statistical agencies (Mainland China, Hong Kong, China and Taiwan, China).

Again, in order to adjust for the effect of the size of the economy, in Figure 5.3, the number of US patent applications submitted by the residents of each economy divided by its total domestic population each year is presented. The US was the world leader in the number of US patent applications per capita until it was overtaken by an East Asian newly industrialised economy, Taiwan, China, in 2004. The US recaptured the lead in 2013 (0.869 patents per 1,000 persons in 2019). South Korea (0.665/1,000), another East Asian newly industrialised economy, overtook Japan (0.662/1,000) in 2013 to become the third highest in our sample of economies and managed to retain its third place in 2019. Mainland China has remained in the last place even though its number of applications per capita has been rising, albeit slowly, mostly because it has a relatively low US patent application rate — its large population *per se* is not an important factor because the number of its domestic patent applications per capita was higher than that of the US in both 2018 and 2019.

Figure 5.4: US patent application rates, G-7 countries, Mainland China, and four EANIEs

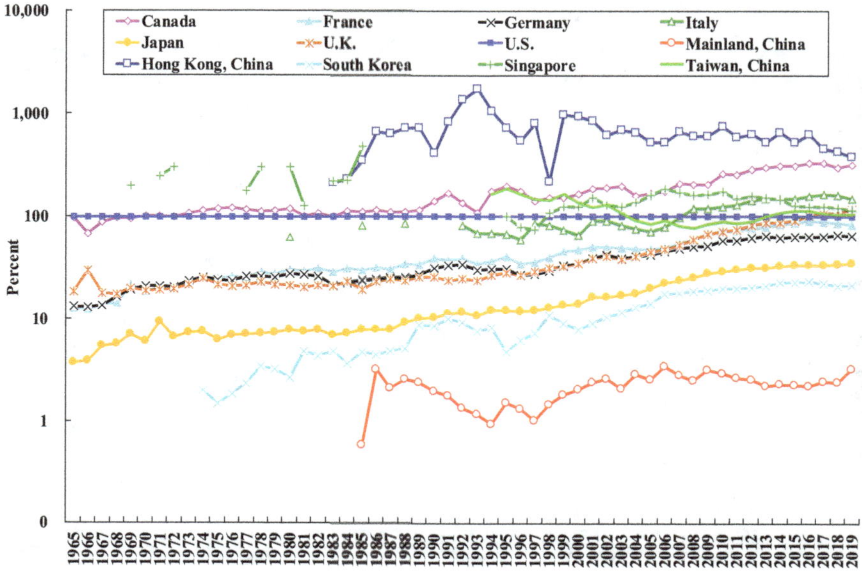

Source: Authors' Calculations. The numbers of US patent applications of the economies are taken from Table A5.1. The numbers of domestic patent applications of the economies are taken from Table A4.1 of Chapter 4.

An interesting indicator is the US patent application rate of each economy, defined as the ratio of the number of US patent applications to the number of domestic patent applications submitted by its domestic residents. Given that patent application and maintenance are costly, especially in a foreign jurisdiction, the US patent application rate may provide information on the self-perceived quality of the discoveries and inventions that underlie the patent applications. However, for economies in which the US patent application rate exceeds 100%, it is not going to be a good indicator of the self-perceived quality of the US patent applications from these economies. It is, instead, an indicator of the perceived relative unimportance of the domestic market compared to the US market.

The US patent application rates of selected economies are presented in Figure 5.4. It is clear that the US patent application rates differ significantly across economies. The US patent application rate of the US itself is of course 100%. The US patent application rates of the smaller economies such as Canada, Hong Kong, China, Singapore and Taiwan, China all exceed 100%, sometimes very substantially. The US patent application rates of Italy (since 2008) and the UK (since 2016) have also exceeded 100%.[1] In 2019, France had the highest US patent application rate (82.9%) among the group of economies with application rates below 100%, followed by Germany (65.0%) and Japan (34.4%). The Chinese application rate was a low 3.2%. We attribute this exceptionally low rate to the costs of application and maintenance, the language barrier, and possibly to the huge size of the Chinese domestic market itself.[2] In time, we expect the US patent application rate of Mainland China to rise significantly.

In the interests of better legibility, we have also reproduced Figure 5.4 without the logarithmic scale as Figure 5.5 and omitting the data of Hong Kong, China and Singapore as well as the off-chart data of Canada. Figure 5.5 (as well as Figure 5.1) shows that the US patent application rates of the other economies have on the whole been rising since the late 1990s, some more rapidly than others, with the exception of Mainland China, which has had by far the lowest US patent application rate of between 2% and 3% for the past two decades.

The quantity of the real R&D capital stock of an economy can be expected to have a direct and positive causal relationship to its total number of US patent applications and grants. In Figure 5.6, the annual total number of US patent applications submitted by the domestic residents of an economy is plotted against the quantity of its real R&D capital stock at the beginning of that year. Figure 5.6 shows clearly that the higher the quantity of the real R&D capital stock of an economy is, the higher is the number of US patent applications submitted by its domestic residents, similar to its number of domestic patent applications (see Figure 4.5). The estimated simple linear regression of the number of patent applications on the quantity of real R&D capital stock is statistically highly significant. The regression line indicates an estimated elasticity of 0.998, or almost

[1]The data on domestic applications of Italy, collected from the World Intellectual Property Organization (WIPO), appear to have some problems. They have been adjusted. The adjusted data have been used to calculate the US application rates for Italy.

[2]The Chinese domestic market is large enough for the Chinese discoverers and inventors.

Figure 5.5: US patent application rates, G-7 countries, Mainland China, and two EANIEs

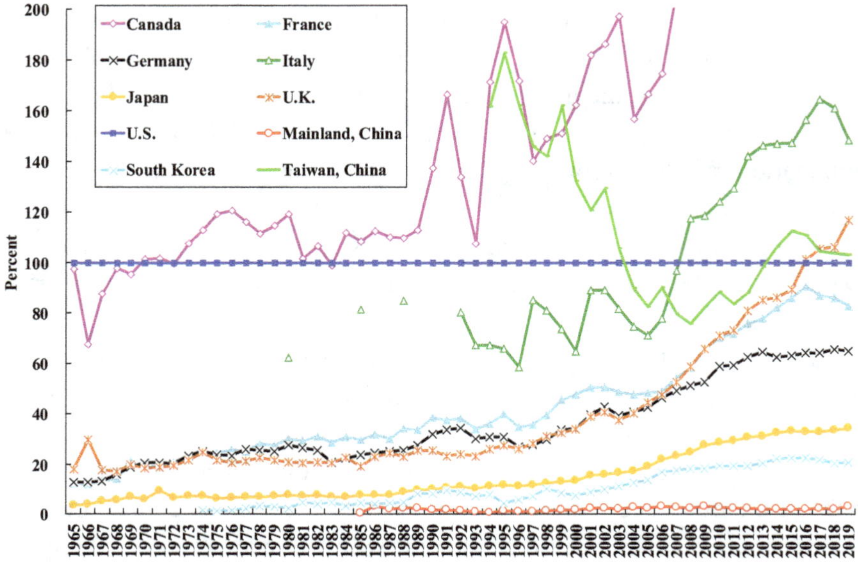

Note: The data for Hong Kong, China and Singapore, as well as the data for Canada since 2007, have been omitted because their inclusion will cause part of the rest of the chart to be illegible.
Source: Authors' Calculations. The numbers of US patent applications of the economies are taken from Table A5.1. The numbers of domestic patent applications of the economies are taken from Table A4.1 of Chapter 4.

exactly unity, that is, a 1% increase in the quantity of the real R&D capital stock increases the number of patent applications by 1%. The EANIEs all appear to be "over-achievers" whereas the data points for the G-7 countries seem to lie quite close to the linear regression line. In contrast, Mainland China has been an "under-achiever", but has also been able to reduce steadily its degree of "under-achievement".

In Figure 5.7, the total numbers of patents granted by the USPTO each year to all applicants and to US applicants are presented. Similar to the case for the total number of patent applications received, three distinct but different phases may be distinguished. In the first phase, between 1963 and 1986, the average annual total number of patents granted by the USPTO was a stable 64,963. In the second phase, 1986–2009, which was longer than the second phase for the patent applications, the average

Figure 5.6: The number of US patent applications and the quantity of real R&D capital stock, G-7 countries, Mainland China, and four EANIEs

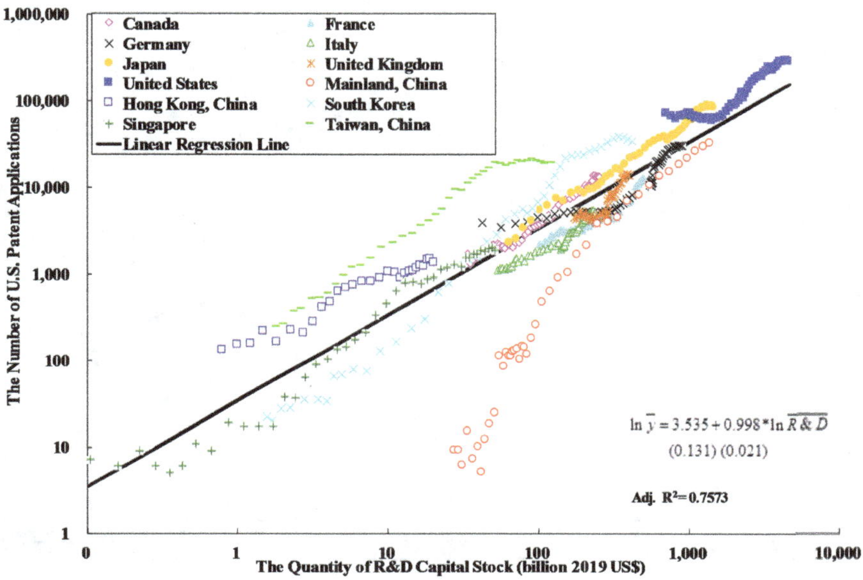

Note: The numbers in parentheses are the estimated robust standard errors of the coefficients of the linear regression line.
Source: Data on the number of US patent applications are from Table A5.1 and data on the quantity of real R&D capital stock are from Table A3.2.

annual total number of patents granted by the USPTO almost doubled to 127,492. The increases in patent grants seemed to lag behind the increases in patent applications. In the third and most recent phase, 2009–2019, the average annual total number of patents granted by the USPTO more than doubled again to 275,055. The same trend is evident with the annual total number of patents granted by the USPTO to US applicants.

However, the share of total USPTO patents granted to US residents started at a high of 81.4% in 1963 and declined steadily to 47.2% in 2019. In 2019, the total number of US patents granted was 354,430, with 167,115, or slightly less than half, going to US applicants. Over the decade from 2010 to 2019, the share of USPTO patent grants awarded to US residents remained fairly constant, averaging 47.8%.

Figure 5.7: The number of USPTO patents granted to all applicants and to US applicants (thousands)

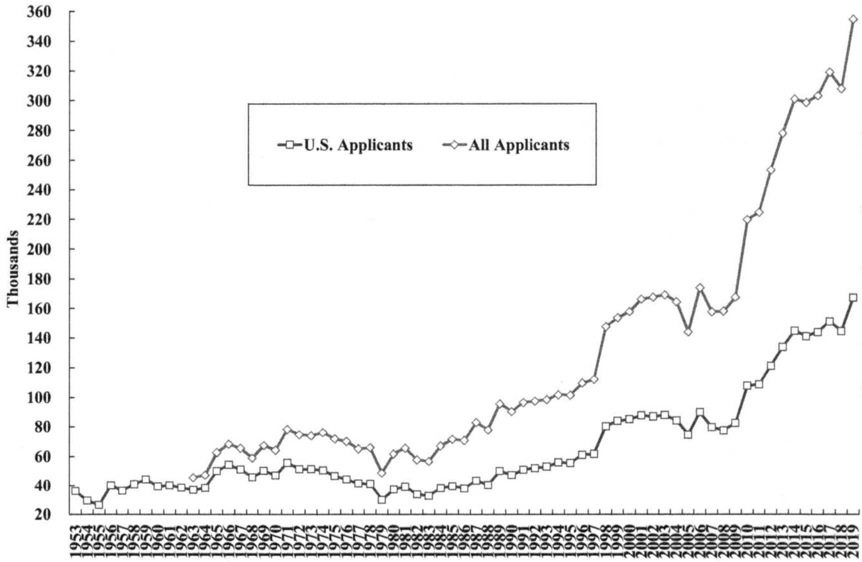

Source: USPTO.

In Figure 5.8, the number of patents granted in the United States by the USPTO each year to applicants from different economies, including the US itself, is presented. The US is the undisputed champion over the past 50 years, with more than 167,115 patent grants in 2019, followed by Japan, with 53,542 patent grants, and then South Korea (21,684) and Mainland, China (19,209). Germany started as number two in 1963 and was surpassed successively by Japan (1975), South Korea (2011) and Mainland China (2019) to settle into fifth place. Since these are patents granted in the US by the USPTO, the US may possibly have a "home court" advantage; however, for all the other economies, the comparison across them should be reasonably fair. The number of US patents granted to Chinese applicants each year has been increasing rapidly from single-digit levels in the early 1980s to almost 20,000 in 2019. The number of US patents granted to applicants from Taiwan, China was 11,489 in 2019, ahead of the UK, Canada, France and Italy.

Figure 5.8: The number of USPTO patent grants, G-7 countries, Mainland China, and four EANIEs

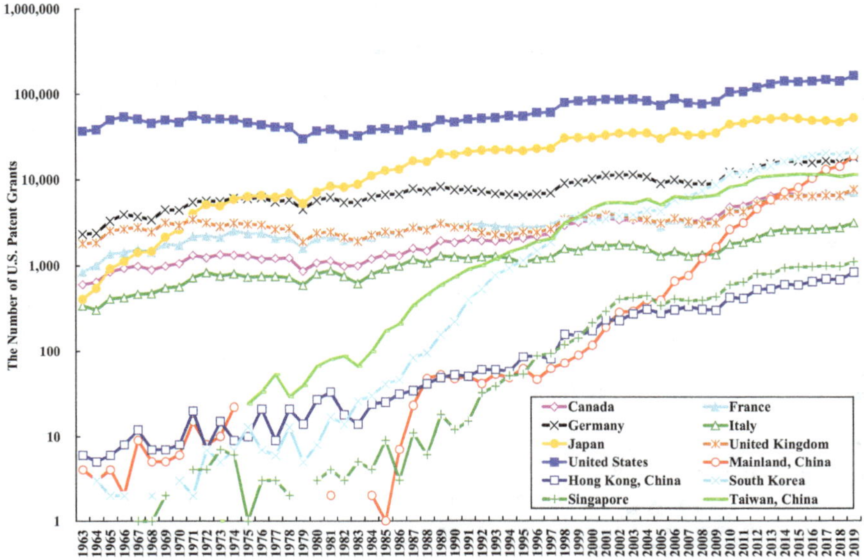

Source: The numbers of US patent grants of the economies are taken from Table A5.2.

In Figure 5.9, the number of patents granted in the United States by the USPTO each year to the applicants from different economies, including the US itself, divided by the population of the respective economies, is presented. On a per-capita basis, the US was the world champion until 2007, when it was overtaken by Taiwan, China and Japan. In 2019, the latest year for which published data on US patents are available, the US was the leader again, with 509 US patents granted per million persons, followed by Taiwan, China (487), South Korea (423), Japan (422), and Germany (220). Mainland China, because of its large population, was in last place among the economies under study, with slightly less than 14 US patents granted per million persons in 2019.

While using the number of patents actually granted by a specific country or region such as the United States as an indicator of innovation has the advantage of maintaining the same objective quality standard in the comparison of the output of R&D activities across the different countries and regions, it is also subject to possible changes in the procedures

Figure 5.9: The number of US patents granted per million persons, G-7 countries, Mainland China, and four EANIEs

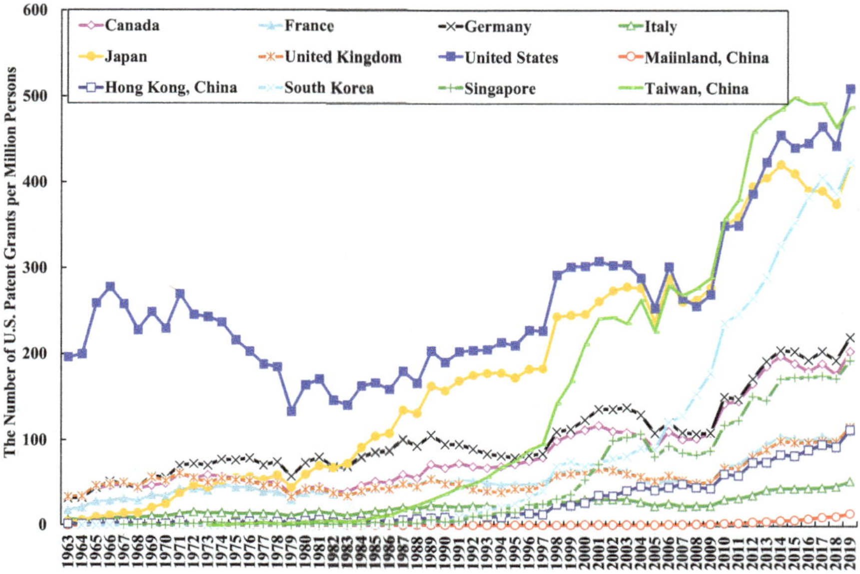

Source: The numbers of US patent grants of the different economies are taken from Table A5.2. The population data are taken from *International Financial Statistics* (Canada, France, Germany, Italy, Japan, South Korea, Singapore and UK), *World Development Indicators* (US) and the local statistical agencies (Mainland China, Hong Kong, China and Taiwan, China).

and standards of the granting country or region over time. Thus, neither the number of US patent applications nor the number of US patent grants by themselves can be a perfect measure of the (relative) R&D output of the different economies. It is interesting to examine the data on the success rates of the US patent applications of each economy over time. Since the number of patents granted must lag behind the number of applications, the success rate may be computed by dividing the number of patents granted in the current year by the number of patent applications in the previous year.

In Figure 5.10, the 3-year moving-average success rates of patent applications filed in the United States each year by the residents of different economies, including the US itself, over time, are presented. In 2019, Taiwan, China had the highest success rate, at 59.8%, and the UK had the lowest success rate, at 50.4%, with the US itself at an intermediate

Figure 5.10: Three-year moving-average US patent application success rates, G-7 countries, Mainland China, and four EANIEs

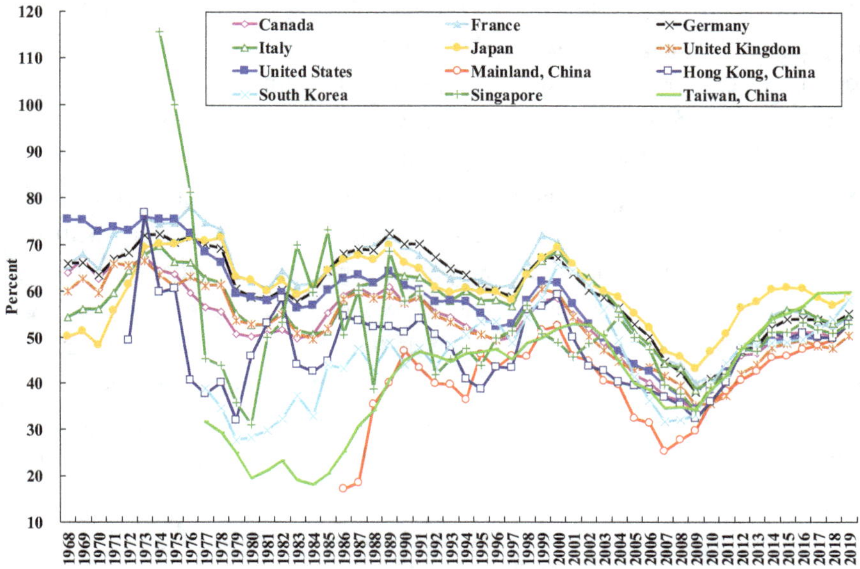

Source: Three-year moving-average US patent application success rates are taken from Table A5.3.

53.0%.[3] These success rates of almost all countries and regions in our sample, including the US itself, show strongly synchronous fluctuations over time, with the possible exceptions of some outliers in the years prior to 1990. There is, however, little evidence of any bias in favour of the United States, or for that matter, any other economy, in the 3-year moving-average success-rate data. Moreover, the success rates for all economies are actually contained in a relatively narrow band, which does move up and down over time. This indicates possible changes in the procedures and/or standards in the approval process by the USPTO in specific years. These changes will have to be taken into account in the econometric analysis to be conducted in Part Four of this study.

There are two possible measures of the degree of stringency of the standards applied by the USPTO. The first measure is its own total success rate of patent applications, defined as the total number of patents granted

[3]This may be taken as evidence that there is no obvious home bias in the US patent grants.

to all economies, including the US itself, divided by the total number of patent applications received from all economies in the previous year. The second measure is its total success rate of patent applications submitted by non-US applicants, defined as the total number of patents granted to all economies except the US, divided by the total number of patent applications received from all economies except the US in the previous year. In Figure 5.11, these two alternative US patent grant rates and their 3-year moving averages are presented. While the US total patent grant rates show significant year-to-year variations over time, they track closely with the individual-economy-specific US patent application success rates in Figure 5.10. Figure 5.11 shows that the two alternate US total patent grant rates, regardless of whether they include the US patent grant applications by US residents, have been practically the same every year since 1977. This is even truer of the 3-year moving averages. If anything, they show that foreign patent applicants have a slightly higher success rate than US

Figure 5.11: US total and foreign patent grant rates

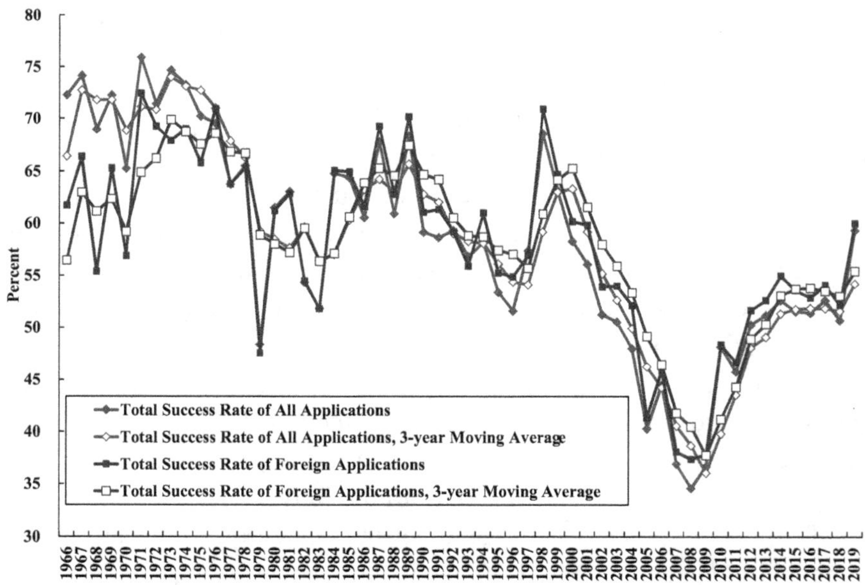

Source: Authors' calculations. Data on the number of US patent applications and grants are from Tables A5.1 and A5.2, respectively. The 3-year moving-average US patent application success rates are taken from Table A5.3.

applicants. This confirms that there is really no "home court" advantage for US domestic patent applicants.

Moreover, despite the fluctuations over time, there is also a distinct and unmistakable overall downward drift in the patent application success rates. The total USPTO patent application success rate declined from a peak of almost 76% in 1971 to just 60% in 2019, with significant fluctuations in between. What this means is that for any economy, even if the quantity and quality of its US patent applications are constant over time, the number of US patents granted may still fluctuate because of the changing US operating procedures and/or standards over time. These variations in the total patent grant rates of the USPTO will be taken into account in the econometric analysis in Part Four.

5.1 The Relationship between Domestic and U.S. Patent Grants

It is also interesting to examine the relationship between the US patent application success rate and the domestic patent application success rate of each economy. This can provide some indirect evidence on the quality of the domestic patents granted compared to the US patents granted and their evolution over time. In Figure 5.12, the US patent application success rate is plotted against the domestic patent application success rate of each economy each year, where we have omitted the data of economies with a US patent application rate that is over 100% on a regular basis. There appears to be a generally positive correlation between the US patent success rate and the domestic patent success rate for the selected economies — the higher the domestic success rate is, the higher the US success rate will be. The simple linear regression of the US success rate on the domestic success rate yields a statistically significant coefficient of 0.21. On average, an increase of 1% point in the domestic success rate of an economy increases its US success rate by 0.21% point, indicating a positive correlation. However, the overall goodness of fit is low (Adjusted $R^2 = 0.1166$), as is evident from the wide dispersion of the data points.

However, it is interesting to note that all the data points of Germany and the UK lie above the 45-degree line, which means that their US success rates are always higher than their domestic success rates. This

Figure 5.12: Scatter diagram between US and domestic patent application success rates, France, Germany, Japan, United Kingdom, Mainland China and South Korea

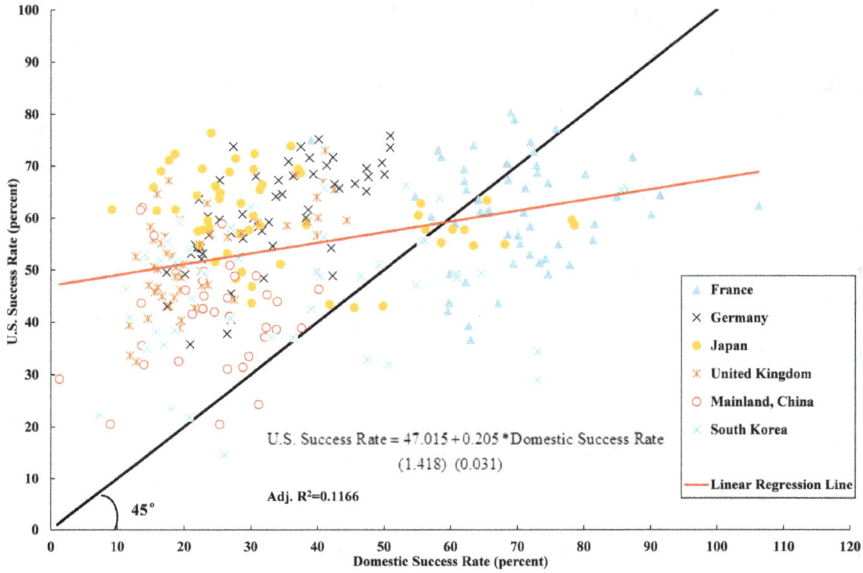

Source: Tables A5.3 and A4.3 of Chapter 4.

suggests that their application rates for respectively the domestic and US patents must be very different. The same is true of the Chinese data points except for the years 2005 and 2007. Japan was like Germany and the UK until 2008, after which its domestic success rate has been always higher than its US success rate except in 2015 and 2019. South Korea's experience was largely similar to that of Japan, with its US success rate exceeding its domestic success rate from 1975 to 2004 (except for 1979 and 1999) and vice versa for most years after 2005. France has had the opposite experience of Germany and the UK: in the 54 years between 1966 and 2019 — its domestic success rate was greater than its US success rate for 39 years; in particular, between 2000 and 2019, its domestic success rate was always greater than its US success rate.

In Figure 5.13, we plot the domestic and US success rates of each of the economies featured in Figure 5.12 as a time series. The domestic success rates were plotted as broken lines and the US success rates were plotted as continuous lines but with the same colours and markers. For

Figure 5.13: U.S. and domestic patent application success rates, France, Germany, Japan, United Kingdom, Mainland China and South Korea

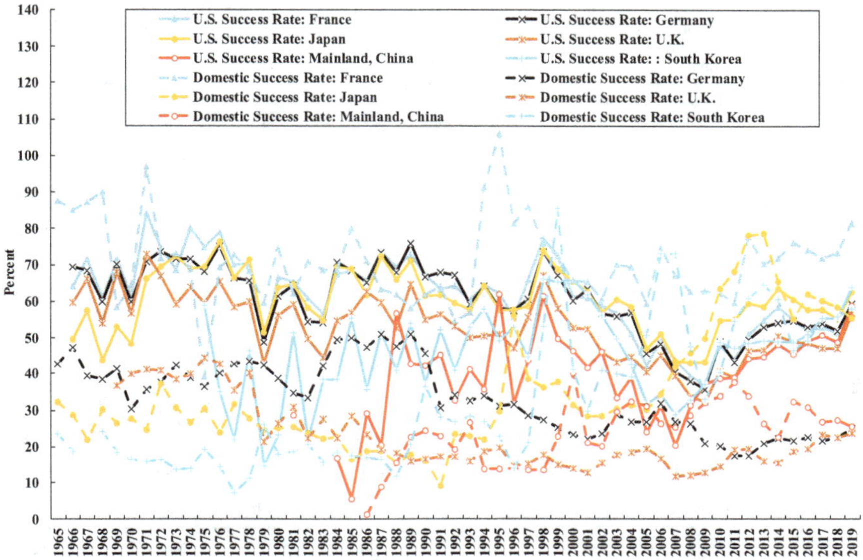

Source: Tables A5.3 and A4.3 of Chapter 4.

France, the domestic success rates have been higher than the US success rates. For Germany, the UK, and Mainland China, the US success rates have been consistently higher than the domestic success rates. For Japan, the US success rates were higher than the domestic success rates from 1966 to 2007, then became lower from 2008 onwards except for 2015 and 2019. The experience of South Korea was broadly similar to that of Japan.

In Figure 5.14,[4,5] the annual number of patents granted to the residents of an economy by the USPTO is plotted against the quantity of its real R&D capital stock at the beginning of that year. Figure 5.14 also shows clearly that in general the higher the quantity of the real R&D capital stock of an economy is, the higher the number of US patents granted to its

[4]Data for real R&D capital stocks are not available for a unified Germany before 1990. Data for US patents granted are not available separately for West Germany. Thus, only data for a united Germany are included in Figure 5.14.

[5]The data in Figure 5.14 are identical with those in Figure 1.1.

Figure 5.14: The number of USPTO patent grants and the quantity of real R&D capital stock, G-7 countries, Mainland China, and four EANIEs

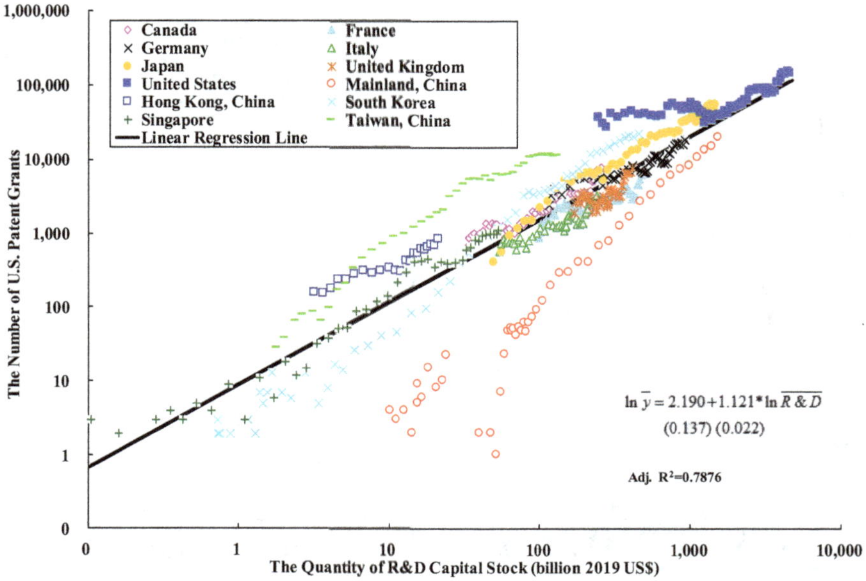

Source: Tables A5.2 and A3.2 of Chapter 3.

residents. The estimated simple linear regression is also statistically highly significant. It suggests that the elasticity of USPTO patent grants with respect to the quantity of real R&D capital stock may be estimated as 1.121. This implies the existence of fairly significant economies of scale in real R&D capital — a 1% increase in the quantity of real R&D capital increases the number of US patent grants by approximately 1.12%. Moreover, on an individual economy basis, the positive correlation is apparent even for the G-7 countries.[6] The EANIEs (South Korea and Singapore since 1991), including even Hong Kong, China, have all turned out to be "over-achievers", that is, at the same quantity of real R&D capital stock, they were awarded more US patent grants than the number predicted by the linear regression line. However, Mainland China has stood

[6]This is consistent with the view that the standards used by the USPTO are more stable than those of the patent authorities of the individual economies. This also confirms that the US patent grants data are more comparable across economies.

out as a significant "under-achiever", in the sense that at the same quantity of real R&D capital stock, it was only able to achieve a much lower number of US patents granted than the number predicted by the linear regression line. However, the degree of "under-achievement" has been steadily declining over time.

The perceived "over-" and "under-achievement" in the generation of domestic and USPTO patent grants may actually reflect significant systematic differences in not only the efficiency in the generation of domestic and US patent grants across economies but also in the standards used by the patent granting authorities of the different economies. Thus, Mainland China appears to have higher than average efficiency in the generation of domestic patents but lower than average efficiency in the generation of US patents. We believe that the relative efficiencies in the generation of US patent grants are probably more reliable because all economies face the same uniform standards of the USPTO as opposed to the possibly differing standards maintained by the respective domestic patent granting authorities.

The positive relationship between the number of patent grants and the quantity of real R&D capital stock appears stronger for US patent grants than for domestic patent grants (see Figure 4.6 of Chapter 4). The estimated elasticity is 1.12 compared to 1.08.[7] This may be due to the more uniform standards on patent grants on the part of the USPTO and also possibly to self-selection on the part of the non-US applicants who might choose to submit applications only for discoveries or inventions perceived to be of higher quality and therefore more likely to be approved. Taken as a whole, the overall positive relationship between patent grants, whether domestic or US, and the quantity of the real R&D capital stock, is unmistakable. The higher the quantity of real R&D capital stock is, the higher is the number of patent grants. In the empirical analysis in Part Four of this study, a more systematic econometric approach will be used to estimate this positive causal relationship between the numbers of patent applications and grants on the one hand and the quantity of real R&D capital stocks on the other.

[7]The adjusted R^2 for the simple linear regression of ln (number of domestic grants) on ln (quantity of R&D capital stock) as shown in Figure 4.6 of Chapter 4 is 0.7293, compared to the 0.7876 in Figure 5.14.

Appendix

Table A5.1: The number of US patent applications submitted by residents of selected economies, G-7 countries, Mainland China, and four EANIEs

Economy	Canada	France	United Germany	Italy	Japan	UK	US
1965	1,695	2,238	5,728	811	2,263	4,479	72,317
1966	1,323	2,174	5,504	849	2,479	4,238	66,855
1967	1,456	2,385	5,734	866	3,354	4,597	61,651
1968	1,558	2,522	6,455	960	4,051	4,660	67,180
1969	1,707	2,821	7,405	1,031	5,430	5,216	68,243
1970	1,843	2,625	7,798	1,105	6,093	4,746	72,343
1971	2,025	2,987	7,772	1,160	7,418	4,734	71,089
1972	1,966	3,122	7,800	1,162	6,831	4,811	65,943
1973	2,095	3,197	8,603	1,128	8,565	4,914	66,935
1974	2,191	3,157	8,897	1,192	9,163	5,109	64,093
1975	2,127	3,048	8,271	1,164	8,566	4,568	64,445
1976	2,237	3,005	8,369	1,230	9,365	4,529	65,050
1977	2,192	3,007	8,942	1,224	9,674	4,533	62,863
1978	2,050	3,257	9,303	1,328	10,189	4,468	61,441
1979	2,061	3,127	9,395	1,480	11,185	4,270	60,535
1980	1,969	3,331	9,765	1,501	12,951	4,178	62,098
1981	2,202	3,237	10,020	1,384	14,009	4,294	62,404
1982	2,138	3,336	10,109	1,500	16,068	4,351	63,316
1983	1,995	3,213	8,959	1,411	15,998	4,138	59,390
1984	2,273	3,507	9,829	1,636	18,473	4,370	61,841
1985	2,270	3,605	10,532	1,628	21,431	3,825	63,874
1986	2,438	3,884	10,725	1,799	22,895	4,641	65,487
1987	2,791	3,837	10,830	1,822	24,516	4,898	68,315
1988	3,046	4,301	11,018	1,943	28,357	4,788	75,192
1989	3,425	4,268	11,437	1,964	31,791	5,066	82,370
1990	3,511	4,771	11,292	2,093	34,113	4,959	90,643
1991	3,641	4,723	10,874	2,123	36,846	4,557	87,955
1992	3,761	4,828	11,652	2,288	38,633	4,587	92,425
1993	3,910	4,320	10,500	1,906	34,816	4,414	99,955

(Continued)

Table A5.1: (*Continued*)

Economy	Canada	France	United Germany	Italy	Japan	UK	US
1994	4,255	4,528	11,324	1,998	37,768	4,856	107,233
1995	4,745	5,001	11,853	2,128	39,872	5,202	123,958
1996	4,443	4,486	11,550	2,062	39,510	4,791	106,892
1997	4,694	4,759	12,333	2,119	41,767	5,147	120,445
1998	5,689	5,249	13,885	2,313	45,260	6,110	135,483
1999	6,149	6,216	16,978	2,577	47,821	6,948	149,825
2000	6,809	6,623	17,715	2,704	52,891	7,523	164,795
2001	7,221	6,852	19,900	2,967	61,238	8,362	177,511
2002	7,375	6,825	20,418	2,980	58,739	8,391	184,245
2003	7,750	6,603	18,890	3,011	60,350	7,700	188,941
2004	8,202	6,813	19,824	2,997	64,812	7,792	189,536
2005	8,638	6,972	20,664	2,993	71,994	7,962	207,867
2006	9,652	7,176	22,369	3,274	76,839	8,342	221,784
2007	10,421	8,046	23,608	3,376	78,794	9,164	241,347
2008	10,307	8,561	25,202	3,805	82,396	9,771	231,588
2009	10,309	9,331	25,163	3,940	81,982	10,568	224,912
2010	11,685	10,357	27,702	4,156	84,017	11,038	241,977
2011	11,975	10,563	27,935	4,282	85,184	11,279	247,750
2012	13,560	11,047	29,195	4,516	88,686	12,457	268,782
2013	13,675	11,462	30,551	4,580	84,967	12,807	287,831
2014	12,963	11,947	30,193	4,764	86,691	13,157	285,096
2015	13,201	12,327	30,016	4,839	86,359	13,296	288,335
2016	13,493	12,863	31,201	5,209	86,021	14,074	295,327
2017	13,301	12,584	30,783	5,355	86,113	14,057	293,904
2018	13,045	12,290	30,691	5,406	85,322	13,681	285,095
2019	13,432	11,690	30,290	5,154	84,435	14,124	285,113

Economy	Mainland, China	Hong Kong, China	South Korea	Singapore	Taiwan, China
1965		9			8
1966		15		4	16
1967		7			13
1968					3

Table A5.1: (*Continued*)

Economy	Mainland, China	Hong Kong, China	South Korea	Singapore	Taiwan, China
1969		24		2	19
1970		23			27
1971		25		5	28
1972		13		6	40
1973		25		4	66
1974		33	22	3	102
1975		38	20	5	113
1976	9	33	27	7	127
1977	9	56	28	7	174
1978	6	45	34	6	243
1979	15	39	34	9	262
1980	7	56	33	6	367
1981	10	38	64	5	394
1982	5	55	68	6	509
1983	12	44	78	11	530
1984	18	46	74	9	601
1985	24	56	129	19	760
1986	112	66	162	17	959
1987	83	82	235	17	1,182
1988	122	86	295	17	1,246
1989	112	108	607	37	1,507
1990	111	86	775	36	2,035
1991	126	132	1,321	63	2,252
1992	129	150	1,471	89	2,667
1993	135	155	1,624	104	2,874
1994	100	219	2,354	134	3,560
1995	144	163	2,820	144	4,054
1996	142	222	4,248	176	4,766
1997	117	207	4,920	213	5,492
1998	181	274	5,452	336	7,412
1999	257	403	5,033	460	9,411
2000	469	473	5,705	632	9,046

(*Continued*)

Table A5.1: (*Continued*)

Economy	Mainland, China	Hong Kong, China	South Korea	Singapore	Taiwan, China
2001	626	626	6,719	786	11,086
2002	888	681	7,937	807	12,488
2003	1,034	729	10,411	771	13,786
2004	1,655	815	13,646	879	15,057
2005	2,127	816	17,217	919	16,617
2006	3,768	889	21,685	1,143	19,301
2007	3,903	1,053	22,976	1,188	18,486
2008	4,455	1,027	23,584	1,266	18,001
2009	6,879	885	23,950	1,225	18,661
2010	8,162	995	26,040	1,540	20,151
2011	10,545	1,053	27,289	1,564	19,633
2012	13,273	1,070	29,481	1,688	20,270
2013	15,093	1,166	33,499	1,722	21,262
2014	18,040	1,253	36,744	1,869	20,201
2015	21,386	1,230	38,205	1,833	19,471
2016	26,026	1,435	37,341	1,988	18,718
2017	29,674	1,473	35,565	2,004	19,019
2018	32,615	1,349	33,961	1,888	19,103
2019	39,055	1,311	36,424	1,973	19,599

Table A5.2: The number of US patent grants awarded to residents of selected economies, G-7 countries, Mainland China, and four EANIEs

Economy	Canada	France	United Germany	Italy	Japan	UK	US
1963	606	853	2,338	345	407	1,813	37,174
1964	648	1,013	2,418	308	544	1,852	38,410
1965	853	1,372	3,338	414	919	2,558	50,331
1966	938	1,435	3,981	429	1,122	2,675	54,634
1967	992	1,558	3,766	471	1,424	2,800	51,274
1968	898	1,446	3,442	477	1,464	2,481	45,781
1969	993	1,809	4,524	556	2,152	3,181	50,394

Table A5.2: (*Continued*)

Economy	Canada	France	United Germany	Italy	Japan	UK	US
1970	1,068	1,731	4,439	571	2,625	2,954	47,073
1971	1,328	2,215	5,525	726	4,029	3,465	55,975
1972	1,242	2,230	5,728	838	5,151	3,168	51,519
1973	1,347	2,144	5,588	759	4,941	2,855	51,501
1974	1,326	2,569	6,156	807	5,894	3,146	50,646
1975	1,298	2,367	6,058	737	6,354	3,041	46,710
1976	1,193	2,408	6,212	754	6,542	2,991	44,280
1977	1,220	2,108	5,563	756	6,217	2,652	41,488
1978	1,227	2,119	5,874	725	6,912	2,722	41,250
1979	867	1,604	4,545	595	5,252	1,907	30,074
1980	1,083	2,087	5,782	806	7,124	2,405	37,350
1981	1,138	2,181	6,304	883	8,389	2,470	39,218
1982	993	1,975	5,469	753	8,149	2,137	33,890
1983	1,002	1,895	5,478	625	8,793	1,928	32,868
1984	1,202	2,163	6,323	794	11,110	2,268	38,373
1985	1,342	2,400	6,718	919	12,746	2,493	39,556
1986	1,314	2,369	6,856	995	13,209	2,403	38,126
1987	1,594	2,874	7,884	1,183	16,557	2,769	43,519
1988	1,489	2,661	7,352	1,076	16,158	2,582	40,498
1989	1,960	3,140	8,352	1,297	20,169	3,095	50,184
1990	1,859	2,866	7,614	1,259	19,525	2,791	47,391
1991	2,037	3,030	7,680	1,209	21,025	2,802	51,177
1992	1,964	3,029	7,309	1,271	21,925	2,425	52,253
1993	1,944	2,909	6,893	1,285	22,293	2,300	53,231
1994	2,008	2,779	6,731	1,215	22,384	2,231	56,066
1995	2,104	2,821	6,600	1,078	21,764	2,479	55,739
1996	2,232	2,788	6,818	1,200	23,053	2,450	61,104
1997	2,379	2,958	7,008	1,239	23,179	2,672	61,708
1998	2,973	3,674	9,095	1,584	30,840	3,460	80,289
1999	3,226	3,820	9,337	1,492	31,104	3,565	83,906
2000	3,419	3,819	10,235	1,714	31,295	3,659	85,068

(*Continued*)

Table A5.2: (*Continued*)

Economy	Canada	France	United Germany	Italy	Japan	UK	US
2001	3,606	4,041	11,260	1,709	33,223	3,955	87,600
2002	3,431	4,035	11,280	1,751	34,858	3,829	86,971
2003	3,427	3,868	11,444	1,722	35,515	3,619	87,893
2004	3,374	3,380	10,779	1,584	35,348	3,441	84,270
2005	2,894	2,866	9,011	1,296	30,341	3,141	74,637
2006	3,572	3,431	10,005	1,480	36,807	3,579	89,823
2007	3,318	3,130	9,051	1,302	33,354	3,291	79,526
2008	3,393	3,163	8,914	1,357	33,682	3,085	77,502
2009	3,655	3,140	9,000	1,346	35,501	3,173	82,382
2010	4,852	4,450	12,363	1,798	44,813	4,299	107,791
2011	5,014	4,532	11,919	1,885	46,139	4,292	108,622
2012	5,775	5,386	13,835	2,120	50,677	5,211	121,026
2013	6,547	6,083	15,498	2,499	51,919	5,806	133,593
2014	7,043	6,691	16,550	2,628	53,849	6,487	144,621
2015	6,802	6,565	16,549	2,645	52,409	6,417	140,969
2016	6,544	6,426	15,928	2,668	49,800	6,458	143,724
2017	6,934	6,816	16,846	2,718	49,677	6,635	150,949
2018	6,518	6,469	16,033	2,802	47,566	6,616	144,413
2019	7,595	7,233	18,293	3,175	53,542	7,791	167,115

Economy	Mainland, China	Hong Kong, China	South Korea	Singapore	Taiwan, China
1963	4	6			
1964	3	5	3		
1965	4	6	2		
1966	2	8	2		
1967	9	12		1	
1968	5	7	2	1	
1969	5	7		2	
1970	6	8	3		
1971	15	20	2	4	
1972	8	7	7	4	
1973	10	15	5	7	1

Table A5.2: (*Continued*)

Economy	Mainland, China	Hong Kong, China	South Korea	Singapore	Taiwan, China
1974	22	9	7	6	
1975		10	13	1	24
1976		21	7	3	33
1977		9	6	3	53
1978		21	13	2	29
1979		14	5		39
1980		27	8	3	66
1981	2	33	17	4	80
1982		18	14	3	88
1983		14	26	5	66
1984	2	24	30	4	99
1985	1	25	41	9	174
1986	7	31	46	3	210
1987	23	34	84	11	344
1988	47	41	96	6	457
1989	52	48	159	18	591
1990	47	52	225	12	732
1991	50	50	405	15	906
1992	41	60	538	32	1,001
1993	53	60	779	38	1,189
1994	48	57	943	51	1,443
1995	62	86	1,161	53	1,620
1996	46	88	1,493	88	1,897
1997	62	81	1,891	94	2,057
1998	72	160	3,259	120	3,100
1999	90	155	3,562	144	3,693
2000	119	176	3,314	218	4,670
2001	195	237	3,538	296	5,371
2002	289	233	3,786	410	5,431
2003	297	276	3,944	427	5,298
2004	403	312	4,428	449	5,938
2005	402	283	4,352	346	5,118
2006	661	308	5,908	412	6,361

(*Continued*)

Table A5.2: (*Continued*)

Economy	Mainland, China	Hong Kong, China	South Korea	Singapore	Taiwan, China
2007	772	338	6,295	393	6,128
2008	1,225	311	7,548	399	6,339
2009	1,655	305	8,762	436	6,642
2010	2,657	429	11,671	603	8,239
2011	3,174	419	12,262	647	8,781
2012	4,637	532	13,233	810	10,646
2013	5,928	540	14,548	797	11,071
2014	7,236	606	16,469	946	11,332
2015	8,166	601	17,924	966	11,690
2016	10,462	657	19,494	979	11,541
2017	13,243	706	20,717	998	11,580
2018	14,488	693	19,780	989	10,933
2019	19,209	846	21,684	1,119	11,489

Table A5.3: The US patent application success rate (3-year moving average), G-7 countries, Mainland China, and four EANIEs

Economy	Canada	France	United Germany	Italy	Japan	UK	US
1968		65.5	66.0	54.5	50.2	59.9	75.5
1969	66.8	68.0	66.2	56.2	51.4	62.8	75.3
1970	62.7	64.6	63.4	56.1	48.4	59.6	72.8
1971	66.1	72.5	67.0	59.7	55.9	66.0	73.8
1972	65.3	73.5	68.2	64.4	61.3	65.5	72.9
1973	67.3	75.9	72.1	67.8	69.3	66.4	76.0
1974	64.4	74.6	72.3	69.7	70.2	63.4	75.4
1975	63.7	74.7	70.4	66.2	70.2	61.0	75.5
1976	59.5	78.1	71.6	66.0	71.5	63.0	72.4
1977	56.6	74.7	69.9	62.7	70.7	61.2	68.5
1978	55.5	73.2	69.1	61.8	71.4	61.4	66.0
1979	50.9	63.3	60.3	55.2	63.1	53.8	59.4

Table A5.3: (*Continued*)

Economy	Canada	France	United Germany	Italy	Japan	UK	US
1980	50.3	62.2	58.7	52.8	62.2	53.0	58.8
1981	50.9	60.5	58.3	52.7	60.0	52.7	57.9
1982	51.8	64.4	60.2	55.9	62.2	55.1	59.7
1983	49.9	61.1	57.8	51.6	59.2	51.1	56.5
1984	50.7	61.7	59.8	50.8	60.8	49.6	56.9
1985	55.4	64.2	64.4	51.4	64.4	52.1	60.2
1986	59.1	67.2	68.0	57.9	66.7	58.2	62.8
1987	60.8	69.4	69.0	61.0	67.7	59.8	63.4
1988	58.9	69.7	68.8	62.0	66.6	58.4	61.8
1989	61.0	72.1	72.4	63.9	69.8	59.0	64.2
1990	57.3	69.8	70.1	63.3	66.2	57.5	61.2
1991	58.9	67.9	70.1	62.9	64.7	58.7	60.2
1992	55.4	64.9	67.3	60.6	60.9	54.9	57.8
1993	54.5	62.6	64.8	57.9	59.6	53.3	57.8
1994	52.3	62.9	63.5	59.9	60.5	51.3	57.7
1995	50.8	62.3	60.5	58.0	59.9	50.6	55.2
1996	49.3	60.8	60.0	58.0	59.9	49.6	52.5
1997	50.0	61.3	58.8	56.8	58.0	51.3	53.0
1998	54.6	66.3	64.0	63.7	63.4	56.7	57.9
1999	57.9	72.0	67.2	66.4	67.1	60.4	62.1
2000	58.5	70.5	67.1	68.6	69.3	59.4	61.8
2001	55.1	65.1	63.7	64.7	65.7	54.5	57.3
2002	52.0	60.4	60.2	62.9	61.7	50.3	53.0
2003	49.0	58.9	58.8	60.0	60.1	47.2	50.0
2004	45.8	55.6	56.6	56.5	58.7	44.5	47.1
2005	41.8	50.0	52.9	51.2	55.3	42.7	43.9
2006	40.1	47.5	50.3	48.4	52.2	43.3	42.4
2007	37.0	45.0	44.8	44.2	47.1	41.6	39.5
2008	36.1	44.0	42.2	43.1	45.8	39.4	37.1
2009	34.1	39.9	38.0	38.4	43.1	35.2	34.5
2010	38.4	41.2	40.9	40.4	46.8	35.6	38.5

(*Continued*)

Table A5.3: (*Continued*)

Economy	Canada	France	United Germany	Italy	Japan	UK	US
2011	41.8	42.7	42.6	42.1	50.9	37.3	42.8
2012	46.1	47.5	47.2	46.8	56.4	41.9	47.2
2013	46.5	49.9	48.5	50.1	57.6	43.9	47.8
2014	49.3	54.8	52.3	54.1	60.5	47.8	49.6
2015	50.8	56.1	54.0	56.1	60.8	48.7	49.8
2016	51.2	55.2	54.0	56.0	60.5	49.3	49.8
2017	51.1	53.4	54.0	54.3	58.6	48.2	50.1
2018	50.0	52.2	53.0	53.2	56.9	47.6	50.0
2019	52.9	54.4	55.2	54.4	58.6	50.4	53.0

Economy	Mainland, China	Hong Kong, China	South Korea	Singapore	Taiwan, China
1968					
1969					
1970					
1971					
1972		49.4			
1973		76.8			
1974		59.8		115.6	
1975		60.6		100.0	
1976		40.5		81.1	
1977		37.6	38.8	45.4	31.5
1978		40.0	34.6	43.8	29.2
1979		32.0	27.8	35.7	24.8
1980		45.9	28.2	31.0	19.3
1981		53.1	29.9	50.0	21.0
1982		58.5	32.3	53.3	23.1
1983		43.9	37.2	70.0	19.0
1984		42.5	32.9	59.9	18.0
1985		44.8	44.0	73.2	20.2
1986	17.1	54.8	43.2	50.7	25.1
1987	18.4	53.7	47.6	60.2	30.8
1988	35.4	52.3	42.8	38.6	34.1

Table A5.3: (*Continued*)

Economy	Mainland, China	Hong Kong, China	South Korea	Singapore	Taiwan, China
1989	39.9	52.4	48.9	68.6	40.7
1990	47.1	51.3	43.9	57.9	44.9
1991	43.2	54.0	47.7	60.0	46.8
1992	39.8	50.6	43.4	41.6	45.8
1993	39.6	47.9	48.6	45.1	44.5
1994	36.4	40.7	50.6	47.5	46.4
1995	46.2	38.7	53.4	43.8	46.8
1996	43.2	43.3	53.4	49.9	47.5
1997	45.9	43.2	48.9	51.4	45.2
1998	45.7	55.9	54.6	57.0	48.8
1999	51.6	56.8	58.7	50.9	49.8
2000	52.5	59.2	65.8	48.9	52.0
2001	45.9	50.1	64.4	45.7	52.9
2002	44.7	43.7	61.4	48.8	52.7
2003	40.4	42.6	56.0	50.6	50.3
2004	39.5	40.2	49.5	54.4	44.8
2005	32.2	39.4	41.4	50.2	39.8
2006	31.4	38.4	36.2	47.5	38.4
2007	25.3	36.8	31.7	39.5	34.7
2008	27.7	35.1	32.1	37.6	34.8
2009	29.7	32.4	33.0	34.1	34.3
2010	35.7	35.9	39.6	39.1	38.4
2011	38.2	40.1	44.3	41.9	41.5
2012	40.5	47.0	48.1	47.7	47.3
2013	42.5	47.7	48.3	47.0	50.8
2014	45.5	51.0	49.0	51.3	54.0
2015	46.0	50.1	49.1	51.3	55.3
2016	47.4	51.1	49.7	53.3	56.8
2017	48.4	50.2	51.8	51.8	59.7
2018	49.5	49.9	54.0	51.0	59.5
2019	52.9	53.0	58.3	52.9	59.8

Chapter 6

European Patent Grants

The United States (US) has been the largest consumers' market in the world since the end of World War II, but more recently, the Chinese consumers' market has caught up with it. In terms of the total value, the Chinese consumers' market is today the same size as the US market. But the European Union is also a very large consumers' market, with huge consumption potential because of the size of its population (447.7 million as of 1 January 2020) and the high value of its Gross Domestic Product (GDP) per capita (US$37,104 in 2019). It is therefore just as important, in principle, for discoverers and inventors everywhere to secure patents in the European states in order to protect their intellectual property rights in this vast market (and of course eventually also in China).

The European Patent Office (EPO) was established in 1973 and is headquartered in Munich, Germany. The EPO grants European patents for the 38 "Contracting States" to the European Patent Convention,[1] but is not itself legally part of the European Union. However, while the EPO provides a single patent application and grant process for all European patents, it does not grant a European Union patent or even a Europe-wide patent, but instead a bundle of European national patents.[2] The EPO is an organ of the

[1] In addition, there are two extension states (in Europe) and four validation states (outside of Europe). Detailed information can be found on the official website: https://www.epo.org/about-us/at-a-glance.html.

[2] The patents granted by the EPO have the same legal rights and are subject to the same conditions as national patents granted by the respective national patent offices. However, they must be validated at the national patent offices of the countries selected by the applicant for them to be effective.

European Patent Organisation, which was set up on the basis of the European Patent Convention and is sometimes also referred to as EPO.

In 2019, the total numbers of patent applications received and patent grants awarded by the EPO were respectively 181,407 and 137,784, compared to 621,453 applications and 354,430 grants for the United States Patent and Trademark Office (USPTO). The US is still the largest technology market in the world even though it has been surpassed by Mainland China in terms of the total numbers of patent applications received and patent grants awarded in 2019. The China National Intellectual Property Administration (CNIPA), China's patent office, received a total of 1,400,661 patent applications and awarded 452,804 patent grants in 2019.

In this chapter, we study the data on the numbers of patents granted by the EPO to the different economies in our sample from 2004 to 2019.[3] In Figure 6.1, the number of EPO patents granted to each economy in our

Figure 6.1: The number of EPO patent grants and the quantity of real R&D capital stock, G-7 countries, Mainland China, and four EANIEs

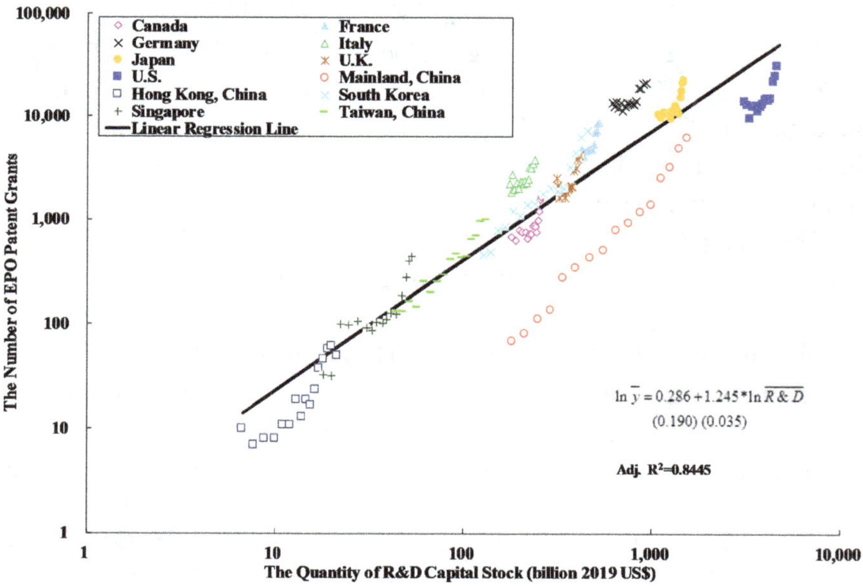

Source: Data on patent grants were collected from the EPO website; the quantities of real R&D capital stocks were estimated by the authors (see Chapter 3).

[3]Unfortunately, data on patents granted by the EPO in years earlier than 2004 are not readily available.

sample in each year is plotted against the quantity of its real R&D capital stock at the beginning of that year. There are fewer data points in Figure 6.1 compared to the case of patents granted by the USPTO, as presented in Figure 5.14 of Chapter 5. Nevertheless, a similar positive relationship between the number of EPO patent grants awarded to each economy and the quantity of its real R&D capital stock is visually clearly apparent.

However, the slopes of the individual economy-specific patent grants with respect to the quantities of the R&D capital stock all show clear signs of increases for the more recent years. We believe this is due to the rise in the EPO patent grant rate since 2016 (see the discussion below and Figure 6.4). Moreover, significant differences in the degree of R&D efficiency also appear to exist across economies, that is, for a given quantity of the real R&D capital stock, the number of EPO patent grants can vary widely. For example, Figure 6.1 shows that, holding the quantity of the real R&D capital stock constant, the number of EPO patent grants received by Mainland China is in general much lower than those received by the European countries and Japan. The same relative R&D inefficiency appears to be true for the US as well. However, this may be due to different propensities for different economies to apply for EPO patents.

The implied elasticity of the number of EPO patent grants with respect to the quantity of real R&D capital stock is 1.245, indicating highly significant economies of scale to real R&D capital — a 1% increase in the quantity of R&D capital leads to a 1.25% increase in the number of EPO patent grants. We believe this may, in part, be an artefact of the continuous increase in the EPO patent grant rate since 2016. What would have been the situation if the EPO patent grant rate had stayed at the 2015 level for the period 2016–2019? The EPO grant rate was 44.81 in 2015, and it increased annually from 2016 onwards to 59.96, 66.40, 76.61, and ending with 78.97 in 2019. The probability of a patent application being approved during these years was significantly increased. A simple way to estimate what the numbers of EPO grants would have been if there were no change in the patent grant behaviour of the EPO is to deflate the number of patent grants in proportion to the annual grant rates. Thus, for 2016, the number of patent grants of every economy is multiplied by 44.81/59.96. Similar adjustments are made for the years 2017–2019 based on the EPO grant rates. The resulting adjusted number of

Figure 6.2: The number of EPO patent grants and the quantity of real R&D capital stock, G-7 countries, Mainland China, and four EANIEs (using hypothetical data for 2016–2019)

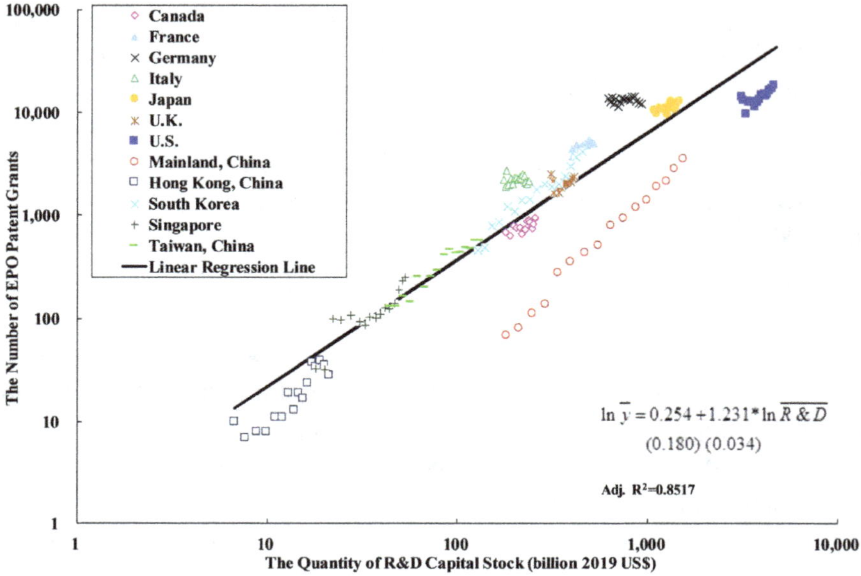

Source: Data on patent grants were collected from the EPO website, with the data for 2016–2019 deflated in accordance with the EPO patent grant rates; the quantities of real R&D capital stocks were estimated by the authors (see Chapter 3).

patent grants, together with the unadjusted data prior to 2015, are presented in Figure 6.2.

Figure 6.2 shows the same positive relationship between the number of EPO patent grants and the quantity of real R&D capital stock. However, the rising slopes in Figure 6.1 are no longer evident, coupled with a slight improvement in the goodness of fit. Moreover, the implied elasticity of the number of EPO patent grants with respect to the quantity of real R&D capital stock has been slightly reduced, from 1.245 to 1.231, but still indicating significant economies of scale.

We next compare the economy-specific annual numbers of EPO patent grants with those of the USPTO patent grants, in the form of a scatter diagram, in Figure 6.3. Each point in the scatter diagram records the number of USPTO patent grants (on the vertical axis) and the number of EPO patent

Figure 6.3: The number of USPTO patent grants versus the number of EPO patent grants, G-7 countries, Mainland China, and four EANIEs

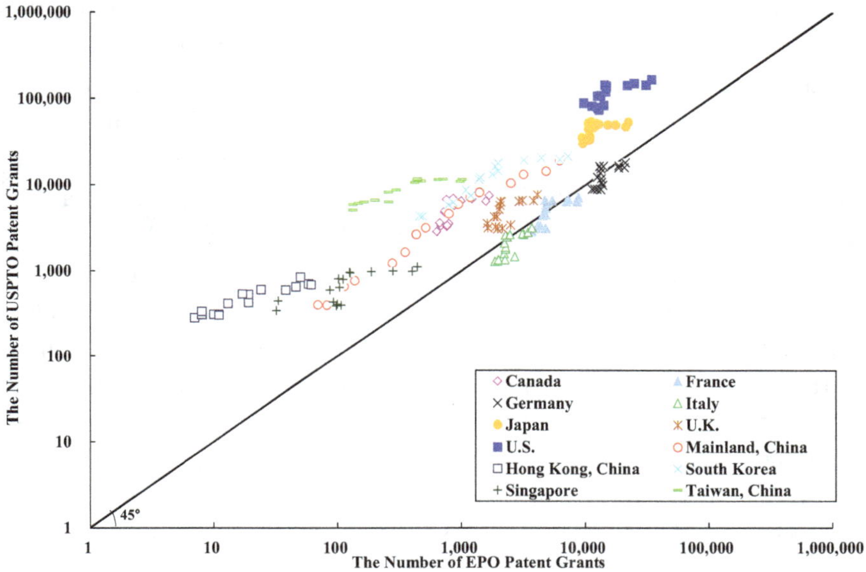

Source: EPO patent grants statistics were collected from the EPO website, and USPTO patent grants statistics were collected from the USPTO website.

grants (on the horizontal axis) for a specific economy in a given year. If the numbers of USPTO and EPO patent grants are the same, the point will lie exactly on the 45° line. If there are more USPTO than EPO patent grants, the point will lie above the 45° line, and otherwise below the line.

Figure 6.3 shows that the economy-specific numbers of USPTO and EPO patent grants are positively correlated across all economies, that is, a higher number of USPTO patents is typically associated with a higher number of EPO patents and vice versa. This shows that either number can in principle be used as a measure of the relative degree of innovation success across economies. However, for the continental European G-7 countries (France, Germany, and Italy), the number of USPTO patent grants is typically similar to the number of EPO patent grants, as indicated by the fact that their data points all lie on or close to the 45° line. With the exception of these three continental European G-7 countries, for all the other economies in our sample, including North American economies, the

United Kingdom (UK), and the East Asian economies, the number of USPTO patent grants consistently exceeds the number of EPO patent grants. This is indicated by the fact that all their data points lie above the 45° line. This may be due in part to a lower EPO patent application rate on the part of these latter economies. Given that patent application and maintenance can be costly, applications are only submitted in the potentially most important markets. For the continental European countries, the European home market is just as important as the US market, whereas for the other economies, the US market is still considered to be the most important market. For the latter group of economies, USPTO patent grants have a much higher priority than EPO patent grants. In addition, it is also possible that the continental European countries may have had a "home-court" advantage in their applications for EPO patents, meaning that they may enjoy higher EPO patent application success rates. For this, we would have to look at the economy-specific EPO patent grant rates.

In Table 6.1, we present the ranks of each of the economies in our sample by their numbers of EPO and USPTO patent grants respectively in

Table 6.1: Economies ranked by the number of EPO and USPTO patent grants in 2019

Rank		**USPTO Patent Grants**		**EPO Patent Grants**
1	US	167,115	US	34,614
2	Japan	53,542	Japan	22,423
3	South Korea	21,684	Germany	21,198
4	Mainland, China	19,209	France	8,800
5	Germany	18,293	South Korea	7,247
6	Taiwan, China	11,489	Mainland, China	6,229
7	UK	7,791	UK	4,119
8	Canada	7,595	Italy	3,713
9	France	7,233	Canada	1,683
10	Italy	3,175	Taiwan, China	1,014
11	Singapore	1,119	Singapore	440
12	Hong Kong, China	846	Hong Kong, China	50

Source: EPO patent grants statistics were collected from the EPO website, and USPTO patent grants statistics were collected from the USPTO website.

2019. We note that the US and Japan ranked first and second for both USPTO and EPO patent grants, confirming their statuses as the top two inventor and discoverer nations in the world. However, Germany, France and Italy, the three continental European G-7 countries, had more EPO than USPTO patent grants. As a result, Germany and France ranked higher in terms of EPO patents compared to USPTO patents, in which South Korea and Mainland China ranked third and fourth. The UK, Canada, Taiwan, China, Singapore, and Hong Kong, China all had far fewer EPO patents compared to USPTO patents. Table 6.1 shows that the rankings according to USPTO patent grants may be more reliable as an indicator of relative success in innovation across economies.

Of course, the numbers of patents granted by respectively the EPO and the USPTO also depend on the patent grant rates of the two patent offices, which may well be different. In Figure 6.4, we compare the annual aggregate patent grant rates (the total number of patent grants divided by the total number of patent applications received in the previous year) of the EPO and the USPTO. Figure 6.4 shows that the patent grant rates of the EPO were generally lower than those of the USPTO prior to 2015,

Figure 6.4: The EPO and the USPTO aggregate patent grant rates

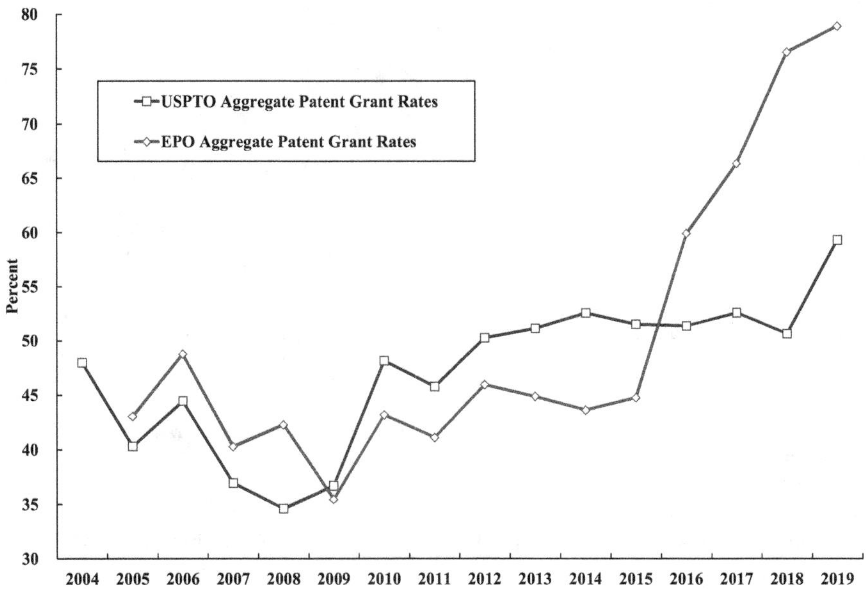

Source: Calculated by the authors.

suggesting that the EPO might have maintained somewhat higher standards than the USPTO then. However, beginning in 2016, the EPO patent grant rate started to rise, from 45% to almost 80% in 2019,[4] far surpassing the USPTO grant rate, although the latter also showed a significant increase between 2018 and 2019.

In Figures 6.5 and 6.6, we compare the annual economy-specific patent grant rates (the number of patent grants divided by the number of patent applications submitted in the previous year by an economy) of the EPO and the USPTO separately for the two periods 2004–2015 and 2016–2019, respectively. We separate the data by the two periods because of the significant changes in the EPO aggregate patent grant rates beginning in 2016. The data of Hong Kong, China have been omitted from

Figure 6.5: A comparison of the economy-specific EPO and USPTO patent grant rates, 2004–2015

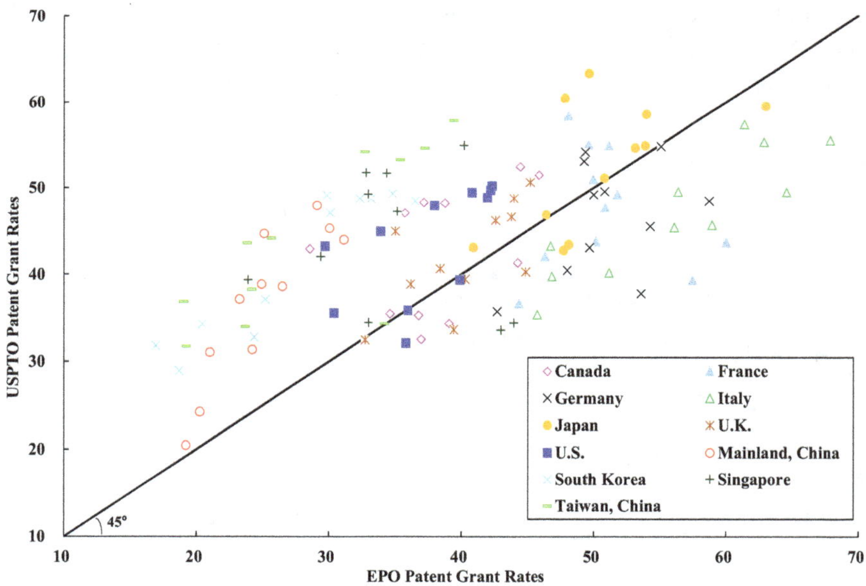

Source: Calculated by the authors from EPO and USPTO statistics. Patent grant rates as defined may exceed 100% as processing by the patent offices may take more than 1 year.

[4]The surge beginning in 2016 was partly attributed by the EPO to improvements in its work efficiency.

both charts because there were very few patent applications and grants and the grant rates are therefore not very meaningful. Figure 6.5 shows that there was a positive correlation between the USPTO and EPO grant rates. However, economy-specific patent grant rates of the EPO were in general lower than those of the USPTO (with the exception of the continental European G-7 countries), suggesting that the EPO maintained somewhat higher standards than the USPTO except perhaps for the continental European G-7 countries. In other words, the continental European countries appeared to have a "home-court" advantage in terms of their EPO patent applications.

Figure 6.6 shows that for the period 2016–2019, the EPO grant rates were almost always higher than the USPTO patent grant rates for not only the continental European G-7 countries but also all other economies. This is indicated by almost all of the data points lying below the 45° line. We believe this may be due to the higher aggregate patent grant rates of the EPO. It remains to be seen whether the high aggregate and economy-specific patent grant rates of the EPO will persist over time.

Figure 6.6: A comparison of the economy-specific EPO and USPTO patent grant rates, 2015–2019

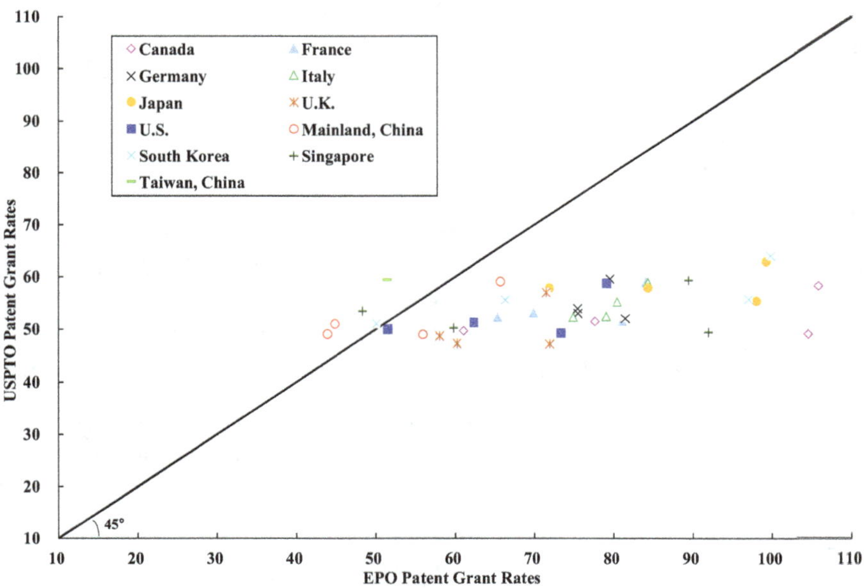

Finally, we compare directly the numbers of domestic,[5] EPO and USPTO patent grants received each year by Mainland China, Japan and the US from 2004 to 2019. This allows us to assess the comparability of the three different sources of patent grants as indicators of the relative innovation capacities across economies. The results are presented in Figure 6.7, which shows that as of 2019, Mainland China had the highest number of domestic patent grants, followed by Japan, with the US as a very close third. In terms of USPTO patent grants, in 2019, the US was still the world's leader, with 167,115 patents, followed by Japan, with 53,542 patents. Despite a very rapid rate of increase, Mainland China received only 19,209 USPTO patents. In terms of EPO patent grants, the US was also the world's leader, with 34,614 patent grants, followed by

Figure 6.7: The domestic, EPO and the USPTO patent grants, Mainland China, Japan and the US (2004–2019)

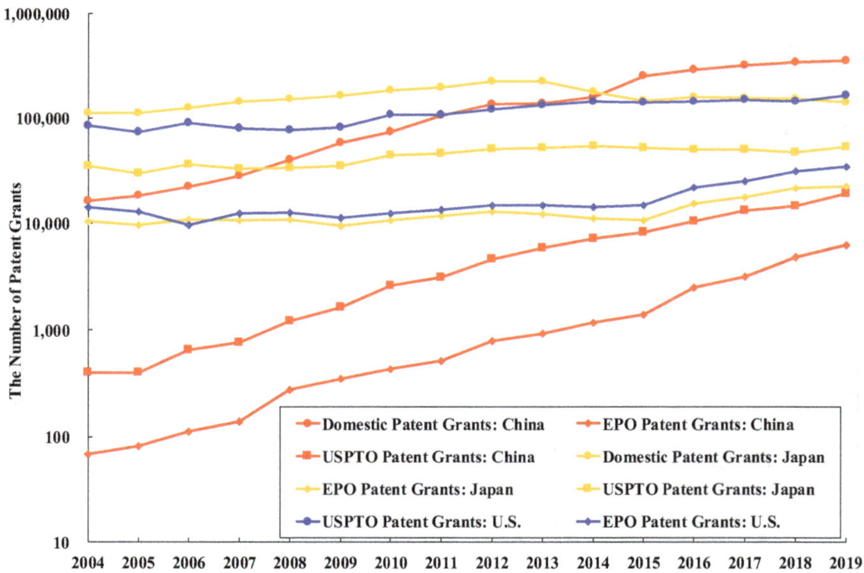

Source: The numbers of EPO and USPTO patent grants were collected from WIPO, EPO, and USPTO websites. The numbers of Chinese and Japanese patent grants were collected from Chinese Statistical Yearbooks and WIPO, respectively.

[5]For the US, domestic patent grant means USPTO patent grant.

Japan, with 22,423 patent grants. Mainland China received only 6,229 EPO patent grants. The overall picture is that there is still a large gap between the number of USPTO and EPO patent grants received by the US and Japan on the one hand and Mainland China on the other. However, the numbers of Chinese USPTO and EPO patents have been increasing at average annual rates of 27.3% and 32.5%, respectively. If these rates of growth continue, the number of Chinese USPTO and EPO patent grants may reach parity with the US in another decade.

The ratios of Chinese and Japanese USPTO patent grants to US USPTO patent grants in 2019 were 11.5% and 32%, respectively. The corresponding ratios for EPO patent grants were 18% and 65%, respectively. The numbers of EPO patent grants in 2019 seemed to understate the patent or technology gap between the US and Japan.[6] The changes in the EPO aggregate and economy-specific patent grant rates over time, as revealed in Figures 6.5–6.7, also raise questions of intertemporal comparability of EPO patent grants. We conclude that the number of patent grants awarded by the USPTO is a more reliable measure of the relative innovation success across economies than the number of patent grants awarded by EPO or the number of domestic patent grants.

[6]This is also apparent from Table 6.1.

Chapter 7

Chinese Patent Grants

The United States (US) has been the largest consumers' market in the world since World War II, but more recently, the Chinese consumers' market has also been catching up. By one measure, the total value of retail sales, the Chinese market is already the same size as the US market. In 2019, retail sales in China reached US$5.8 trillion[1] compared to US$5.5 trillion in the US.[2] However, these numbers depend on the underlying definitions and the exchange rate used and may not be strictly comparable. But it is clear that the two markets have become similar in size, and therefore discoverers and inventors everywhere should also want to apply for Chinese patents to protect their intellectual property rights in a not only vast but also rapidly growing market, in addition to US patents.

The China National Intellectual Property Administration (国家知识产权局) (CNIPA) is responsible for assessing patent applications and awarding patent grants in Mainland China, as well as for the comprehensive coordination of foreign-related affairs in the field of intellectual property. Based in Beijing, it was established in 1980 as the Patent Office of the People's Republic of China. It then changed its name to "State Intellectual Property Office (SIPO)", before assuming its current name. In this chapter, we study the data on patent applications received from and patent grants awarded to the different economies in our study, including Mainland China itself, by CNIPA and its predecessor organisations

[1] National Bureau of Statistics, People's Republic of China.

[2] Bureau of Economic Analysis, US Department of Commerce.

between 1985 and 2019. In considering CNIPA patent applications and grants, we have to bear in mind that this was a period of explosive growth for the CNIPA. The total number of patent applications received by CNIPA grew from 8,558 in 1985 to 1,400,661 in 2019.[3] Similarly, the number of patent grants awarded grew from 40 in 1985 to 452,804 in 2019. The one-year total success rate of CNIPA applications rose from 0.47% (less than 1 in 200) in 1985 to 32.33% (almost 1 in 3) in 2019, a huge leap.

The success rates of non-Mainland applicants were even higher. The number of patent applications received by CNIPA from non-Mainland applicants grew from 4,494 in 1985 to 169,865 in 2019. The number of patent grants awarded to them grew from 2 in 1985 to 98,693 in 2019. They imply success rates of 0.045% (less than 1 in 2,000) in 1985 and 58.10% (almost 3 out of 5) in 2019. However, for non-Mainland applicants, patenting on the Mainland was almost an afterthought until the late 1990s, when it began to appear that Mainland China would soon become a major market that cannot be ignored. Thus began a rush into China, with large annual increases in CNIPA patent applications from abroad. We should note that despite the high rates of growth, the economy-specific numbers of CNIPA patent applications (and grants) remain low relative to the economy-specific number of United States Patent and Trademark Office (USPTO) and the European Patent Office (EPO) patent applications (and grants), suggesting that there are still large pools of past discoveries and inventions yet to be patented in China. For this reason, the annual numbers of CNIPA patent applications and grants of these economies may not be dependent on the quantities of their current-period real Research and Development (R&D) capital stocks.

In Figure 7.1, we compare the total numbers of annual patent applications and patent grants of the three major patent offices — CNIPA, EPO and USPTO. CNIPA (and its predecessor organisations) used to have the lowest annual number of applications, but since 1999, its number of patent applications has been growing rapidly and surpassed the EPO in 2004 and

[3]The numbers in this paragraph and the next are taken from China Statistical Yearbook, various years.

Figure 7.1: The total numbers of patent applications and grants of CNIPA, EPO and USPTO

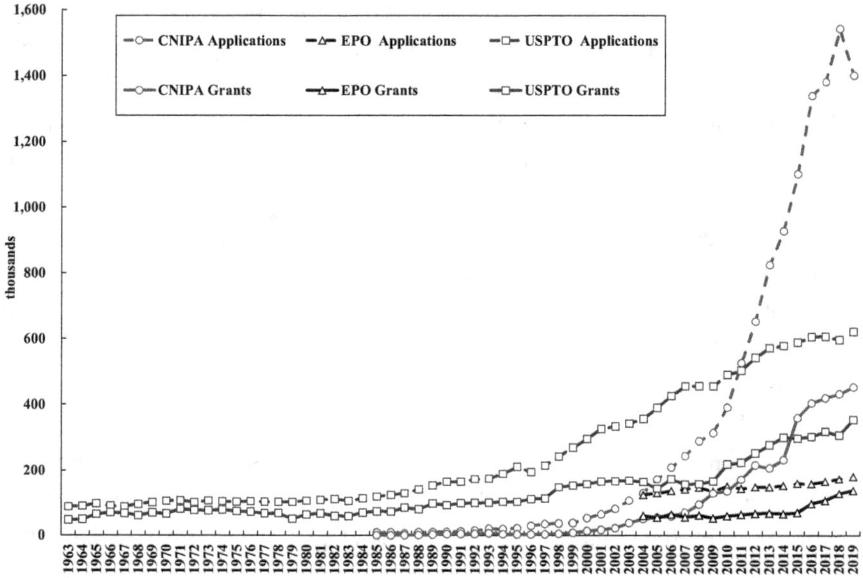

Source: The numbers of CNIPA, EPO, and USPTO patent applications and grants were collected from China Statistical Yearbook, various years, and EPO and USPTO websites, respectively.

USPTO in 2011. In 2019, CNIPA received 1.4 million patent applications worldwide, more than twice the number of patent applications received by the second-placed USPTO. It has also been awarding the highest annual number of patent grants worldwide since 2015, with 452,804, compared to the 354,430 of the USPTO, in 2019. EPO is in third place in both patent applications and patent grants.

Of course, the numbers of patents granted respectively by CNIPA, EPO, and USPTO also depend on their respective patent grant rates, which may well be quite different. In Figure 7.2, we compare the aggregate patent grant rates of CNIPA, EPO, and USPTO, defined as the total number of annual patent grants divided by the total number of patent applications received in the previous year. Figure 7.2 shows that the patent grant rate of the CNIPA has been among the lowest of the three major

Figure 7.2: The aggregate patent grant rates of CNIPA, EPO, and USPTO

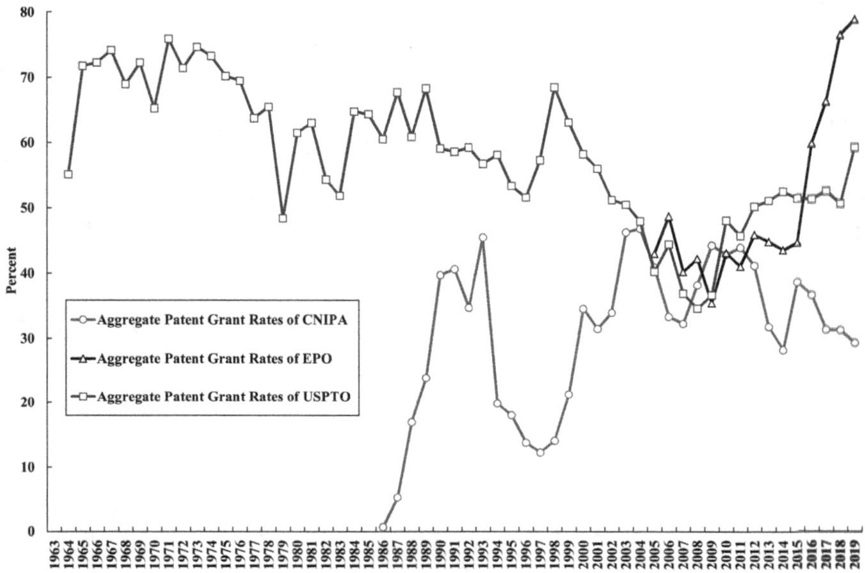

Source: The numbers of CNIPA, EPO and USPTO patent applications and grants were collected from China Statistical Yearbook, various years, and EPO and USPTO websites, respectively.

patent offices, and moreover has been on a declining trend, despite significant fluctuations, since 2004. The patent grant rate of the EPO has been the highest since 2016 and appears to continue to rise, reaching 79% in 2019. By comparison, the USPTO grant rate was 59% and rising, and the CNIPA grant rate was only 29%. The significantly lower patent grant rates of the CNIPA suggest that it may perhaps have maintained somewhat higher standards than the other two patent offices; however, the aggregate patent grant rates of the CNIPA also depend on the patent application rates of the potential applicants from China and the other economies.

In Figure 7.3, the number of patent applications submitted to CNIPA each year by the residents of each of the economies under study is presented.[4] These numbers have all been rising very rapidly over time. In the two

[4]The number of Chinese patent applications for Hong Kong, China and Taiwan, China are from the China Science and Technology Statistics database (http://www.sts.org.cn/data/). Others are from the World Intellectual Property Organization (WIPO) database.

Figure 7.3: The number of patent applications submitted to the CNIPA, G-7 countries, Mainland China, and four EANIEs

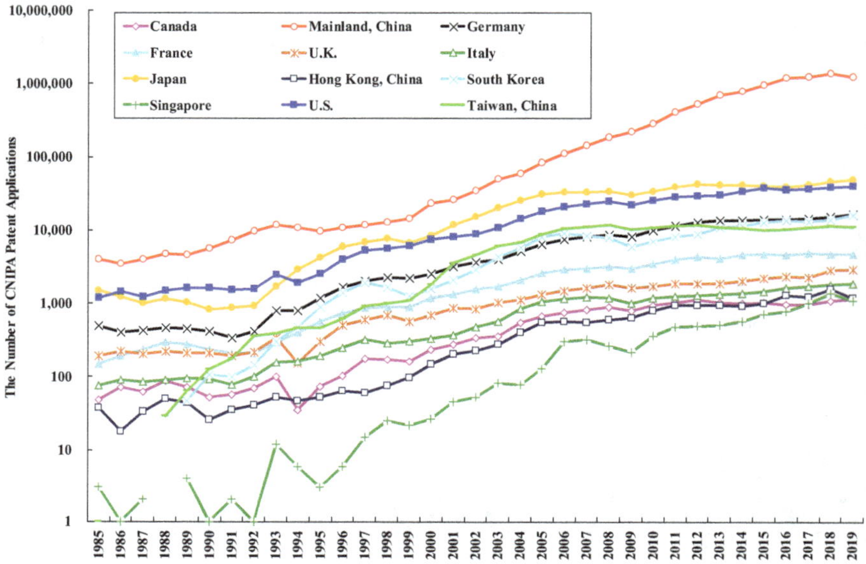

Source: China Statistical Yearbook, various years.

decades between 1999 and 2019, the number of CNIPA patent applications submitted by Mainland Chinese applicants grew at an average annual rate of 22.2%, higher than that of any other economy. Even the United Kingdom (UK), with the lowest average annual rate of growth of its CNIPA patent applications among the G-7 countries, was able to achieve 8.2%. This may be referred to as the World Trade Organization (WTO) effect. As China was poised to join the WTO and open its market, no economy would want to be left out. The most important source of patent applications for CNIPA turns out to be Mainland China itself. Japan comes in second, with the US a close third. Germany and South Korea are neck and neck in the fourth and fifth places. However, we note that these CNIPA patent applications from applicants outside Mainland China may also be based on discoveries or inventions made in some prior year but not yet patented on the Mainland. Thus, their annual numbers may not bear any relation to the current-year R&D activities and hence are not dependent on the quantities of the current-year real R&D capital stocks.

Figure 7.4: The number of patents granted by CNIPA, G-7 countries, Mainland China, and four EANIEs

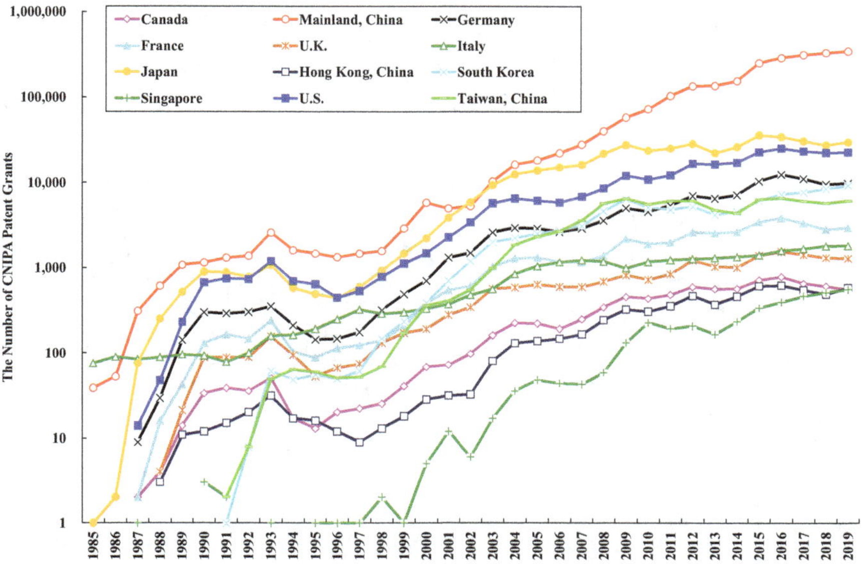

Source: China Statistical Yearbook, various years.

In Figure 7.4, the numbers of patent grants awarded by CNIPA each year, to applicants from different economies, including Mainland China itself, are presented. These numbers have also been rising over time. Mainland China itself has since 1987 been and still is the top recipient of CNIPA patents, followed by Japan and then the US, with Germany and South Korea in fourth and fifth places. The rank order is the same as for the number of CNIPA patent applications submitted by each of the economies. The increases in the numbers of economy-specific patent grants have been brought about by the following: (1) the increases in their respective CNIPA patent applications rates, which, as noted above, may have been caused, in part, by the filing of patent applications for discoveries and inventions made in prior years but not yet patented in China; (2) the increases in the economy-specific CNIPA grant rates; and (3) the increases in R&D activities in these economies, as reflected in the increases in the quantities of their real R&D capital stocks.

Figure 7.5: The economy-specific patent grant rates of CNIPA, G-7 countries, Mainland China, and four EANIEs

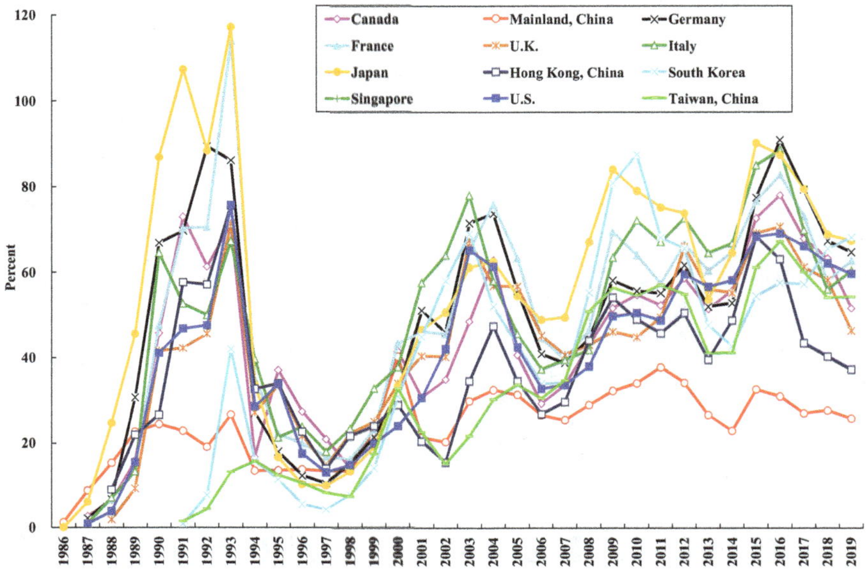

Source: China Statistical Yearbook, various years.

In Figure 7.5, we present the economy-specific patent grant rates of CNIPA, defined as the number of annual patent grants awarded to an economy, divided by the number of patent applications submitted by it in the previous year. Figure 7.5 shows significant intertemporal but synchronous fluctuations of the economy-specific CNIPA patent grant rates, not unlike those for the USPTO (see Figure 5.10). The synchronicity of the fluctuations shows that there is no obvious bias for or against the applicants of any particular economy. Overall, South Korea (68% in 2019) and Japan (67% in 2019) seem to have the highest patent grant rates, and Hong Kong, China (37% in 2019) the lowest (excluding Mainland China itself). The US has had respectable intermediate CNIPA patent grant rates (59% in 2019). However, Mainland China, with consistently the lowest patent grant rate since 2005 (26% in 2019), appears to have a "home-court" disadvantage.

In Figure 7.6, the number of CNIPA patents granted to each economy in our study in each year is plotted against the quantity of its real R&D

Figure 7.6: The number of patent grants awarded by CNIPA and the quantity of R&D capital stock, G-7 countries, Mainland China, and four EANIEs

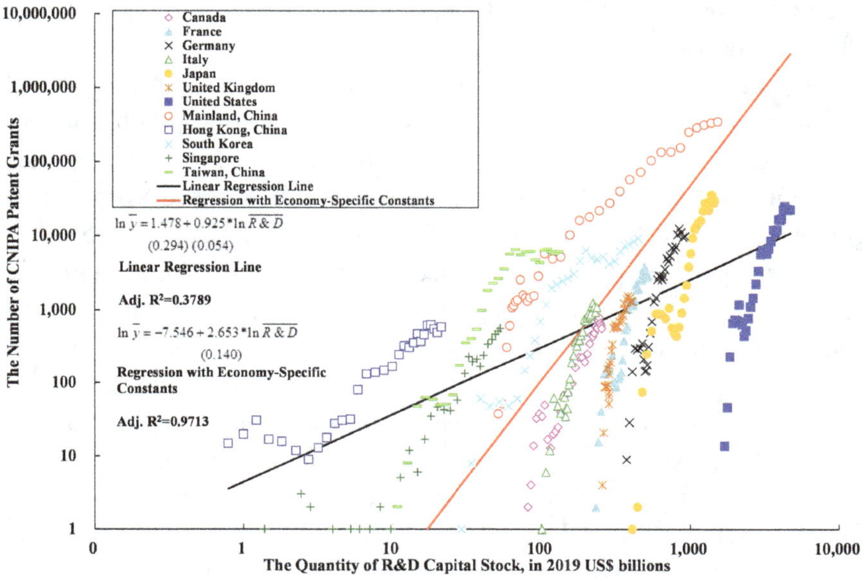

Source: Data on patent grants were collected from China Statistical Yearbook, various years; the quantities of real R&D capital stocks are estimates of the authors (see Chapter 3).

capital stock at the beginning of that year. Figure 7.6 shows a positive relationship between the number of CNIPA patent grants and the quantity of real R&D capital stock of each individual economy, similar to those shown in Figures 5.14 of Chapter 5 and Figure 6.1 of Chapter 6 for USPTO and EPO patent grants, respectively — the higher the quantity of the real R&D capital stock, the higher is the number of patent grants. The estimated implied elasticity of the number of patent grants with respect to the quantity of real R&D capital stock from the simple linear regression is 0.925, not too far from unity.

However, there also exist significant differences: in particular, the slopes of the economy-specific number of CNIPA patent grants-quantity of the real R&D capital stock lines all seem to be much steeper than the estimated common slope (0.925) of the linear regression line of the natural logarithm of the number of patents on the natural logarithm of the quantity of real R&D capital stock (the black line). Moreover, the goodness of fit, as measured by the adjusted R^2 (0.3789), of the simple linear regression is much lower than those for USPTO patent grants in Figure 5.14 of Chapter 5 (0.7876) and EPO patent grants in Figure 6.1 of Chapter 6 (0.8445).

A second simple linear regression, incorporating individual economy-specific constant terms, was run (the red line), with a much-improved goodness of fit (adjusted $R^2 = 0.9713$). The red line captures the common positive slope of the relationship between CNIPA patent grants and real R&D capital stocks of the different economies.[5] However, it also seems to imply the existence of an incredibly high degree of economies of scale in the quantity of real R&D capital, with an estimated elasticity of 2.65, that is, a 1% increase in the quantity of real R&D capital of an economy leads to a 2.65% increase in its number of CNIPA patents.[6] We believe this may have been caused by the spurious statistical correlation between a rapidly growing number of CNIPA patent grants and a much more slowly but steadily growing quantity of real R&D capital stock over the past two decades. As pointed out above, the annual number of CNIPA patent grants awarded to an economy is not necessarily determined by the quantity of its current real R&D capital stock. In fact, the number of CNIPA patent grants of a typical economy is regularly exceeded by the number of its USPTO patent grants (see Figure 7.9), which shows that it is not constrained by the lack of discoveries or inventions but by the number of CNIPA patent applications that it decides to submit.

Figure 7.6 also seems to indicate that for a given quantity of the real R&D capital stock, the number of CNIPA patent grants awarded to Mainland Chinese applicants is significantly higher than those of other economies, at least since 2003. There appears to be, at least superficially, a significantly higher degree of Chinese R&D efficiency in generating CNIPA patent grants. At first sight, one may attribute this observed

---

[5] As might be expected, the linear regression with economy-specific constants fits much better. The red line in Figure 7.6 is drawn with a constant term set equal to the weighted average of all the economy-specific constants with the shares of the number of observations of each economy in the total number of observations as weights.

[6] See also our econometric analyses in Chapters 10 and 11.

relative efficiency to a Chinese "home-court" advantage; but as Figure 7.5 shows, CNIPA's domestic patent grant rate is already lower than that of any other economy in our study. We believe the apparent R&D efficiency has been the result of a significantly higher domestic patent application rate, so that even with the lowest domestic patent grant rate, the total number of CNIPA patent grants is still the highest.

Moreover, we note that the red line in Figure 7.6 also divides the economies in our study into two distinct groups. To the right of the red line are all the data points of the G-7 countries; and to the left are all the data points of Mainland China and the four East Asian Newly Industrialised Economies (EANIEs), with the exception of one data point of South Korea for 1991. This suggests that perhaps the two groups of countries should be analysed separately.

In Figures 7.7 and 7.8, we present the data for the two groups of economies separately. Figure 7.7, which presents only the data for

Figure 7.7: The number of patent grants awarded by CNIPA and the quantity of R&D capital stock, Mainland China and four EANIEs

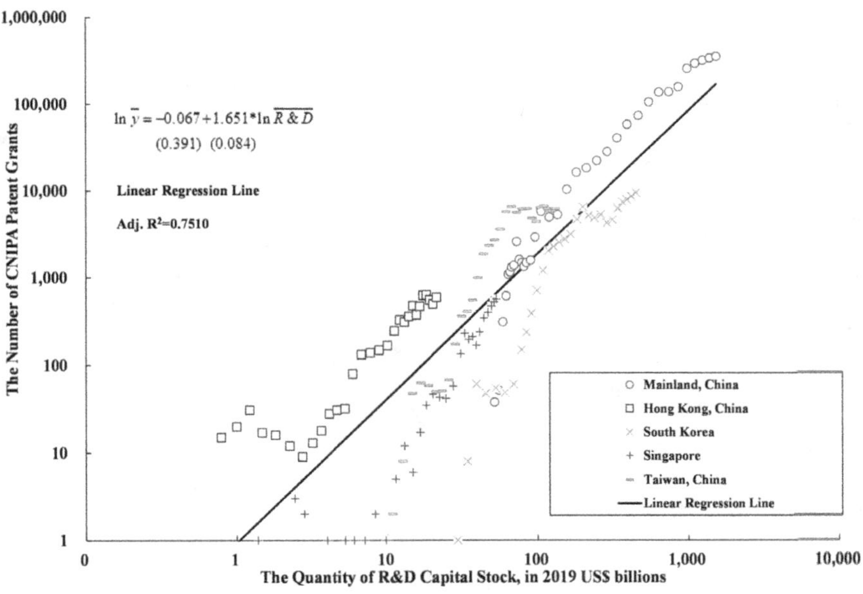

Source: Data on patent grants were collected from China Statistical Yearbook, various years; the quantities of real R&D capital stocks are estimates of the authors (see Chapter 3).

Mainland China and the four EANIEs, shows the same positive and monotonic effect of the quantity of real R&D capital of an economy on the annual number of CNIPA patent grants awarded to it. The fit of the simple linear regression is good, with an adjusted R^2 of 0.7510. The estimated elasticity of 1.651 still seems to be on the high side and may be similarly explained as for Figure 7.6.

In Figure 7.8, the data of only the G-7 countries are presented. The fit of the simple linear regression is reasonable, with an adjusted R^2 of 0.4957 and a statistically significant estimated elasticity of 1.584. This also indicates a high degree of economies of scale in the generation of CNIPA patent grants, similar to that observed for Mainland China and the four EANIEs (see Figure 7.7). It is also clear from the scatter diagram that significant differences exist across the different economies. The fit of the linear regression with economy-specific constant terms is much better, with an adjusted R^2 of 0.9880, but the estimated elasticity is an incredibly

Figure 7.8: The number of patent grants awarded by CNIPA and the quantity of R&D capital stock, G-7 countries

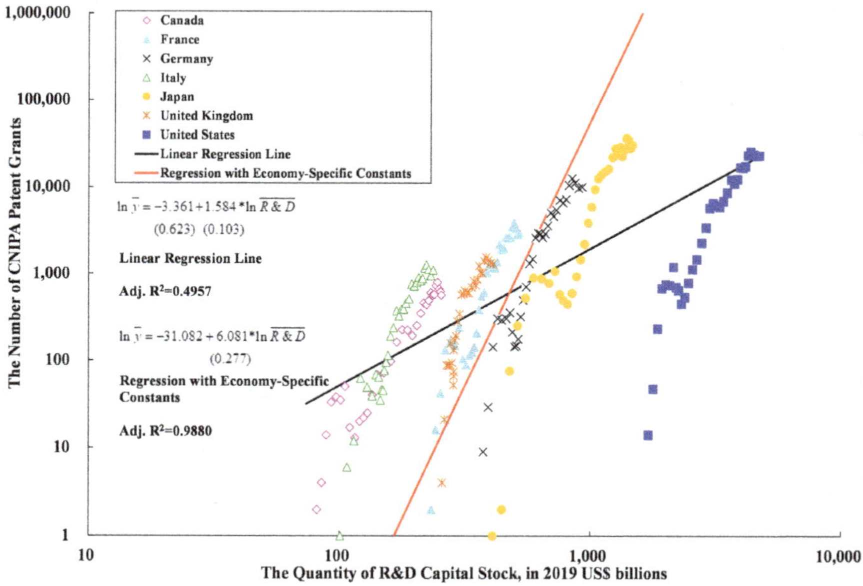

Source: Data on patent grants were collected from China Statistical Yearbook, various years; the quantities of real R&D capital stocks are estimates of the authors (see Chapter 3).

high 6.081.[7] We believe this may also be due to the spurious correlation between a rapidly rising number of economy-specific CNIPA patent grants since the mid-to-late 1990s, and a more slowly rising quantity of economy-specific real R&D capital stock. We remain sceptical that the actual elasticity of CNIPA patent grants with respect to the quantity of real R&D capital stock can be so high.

We would like to provide a plausible explanation of why the economy-specific CNIPA patent grant-real R&D capital stock lines in Figure 7.8 (and to a lesser extent in Figures 7.6 and 7.7) all seem to have very steep slopes (it is the steepness that accounts for the high estimated elasticity of patent grants with respect to real R&D capital stock in the regression with economy-specific constants). One way to understand it is through the trends of rapidly rising economy-specific patent grant rates (see Figure 7.5) and patent application rates. What this means is that even if the quantity of the real R&D capital stock remains constant over time, the numbers of economy-specific CNIPA patent applications and grants will continue to increase. Basically, the number of CNIPA patents granted to a G-7 country at any time is not determined or constrained by its then R&D capacity, but by the number of CNIPA patent applications it submitted, which is up to the discoverers and inventors of the G-7 country itself. The number of its CNIPA patent grants during this period of rapid growth is therefore not subject to any binding constraint from its R&D capacity, unlike its USPTO patent grants. Over time, an increasing number of CNIPA applications is submitted by each G-7 country and therefore an increasing number of CNIPA patent grants is awarded to each of them. At the same time, the quantity of real R&D capital stock of each G-7 country also continues to grow, but at a lower rate than the number of CNIPA patent grants. This results in the appearance of a steep slope for the economy-specific CNIPA patent grant-real R&D capital stock line. The fact is that the CNIPA has a relatively short history and unlike the USPTO, it is still far from its steady state. The USPTO picture, as shown in Figure 5.14, reflects the long-term steady-state relationship between patent grants and real R&D capital stock more accurately.

[7]The red line in Figure 7.8 is drawn with a constant term set equal to the weighted average of all the estimated economy-specific constants with the shares of the number of observations of each economy in the total number of observations as weights.

We next compare the number of CNIPA patent grants with the number of USPTO patent grants received by each of the economies. In Figure 7.9, a scatter diagram between economy-specific USPTO patent grants and CNIPA patent grants is presented. Figure 7.9 shows that the numbers of USPTO and CNIPA grants are positively correlated across all economies, that is, a higher number of USPTO patents is typically associated with a higher number of CNIPA patents and vice versa. The simple linear regression between the natural logarithms of the numbers of USPTO and CNIPA patent grants yields a statistically highly significant coefficient, even though the goodness of fit is low (adjusted $R^2 = 0.3083$).

However, for all economies in our study other than Mainland China, the number of USPTO patent grants always exceeded the number of CNIPA patent grants, sometimes significantly so. This may be easily seen, as the data points for all economies other than Mainland China lie above the 45° line (a data point that lies exactly on the 45° line has exactly the same number of USPTO and CNIPA patent grants). We believe this phenomenon is

Figure 7.9: The number of USPTO patent grants vs. the number of CNIPA patent grants, G-7 countries, Mainland China, and four EANIEs

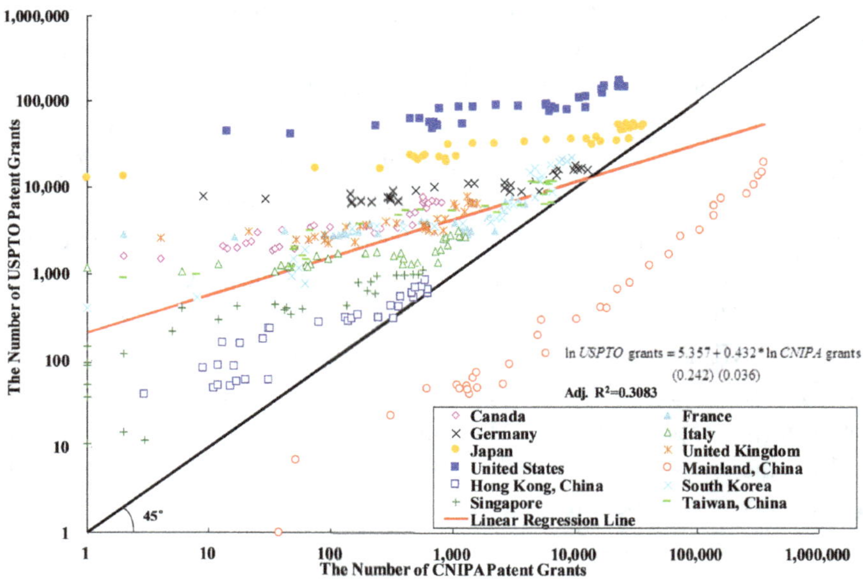

Source: CNIPA patent grant statistics were collected from China Statistical Yearbook, various years, and USPTO patent grant statistics were collected from the USPTO website.

not because the CNIPA has higher standards than the USPTO, but because the number of patent applications submitted by each of the economies to USPTO has been higher than the number submitted to CNIPA, which is consistent with the idea of the existence of a reserve pool of potentially CNIPA patentable discoveries and inventions. Finally, we note that Mainland China has had a systematically lower number of USPTO patent grants compared to other economies, other things being equal. We believe this is due, in part, to the low USPTO application rates of Mainland China.

In Table 7.1, we present the ranks of each of the economies in our study by their numbers of CNIPA, EPO, and USPTO patent grants respectively in 2019. Table 7.1 shows that the US was awarded the highest

Table 7.1: Economies ranked by the number of CNIPA, EPO, and USPTO patent grants in 2019

Rank		USPTO Patent Grants in 2019		EPO Patent Grants in 2019		CNIPA Patent Grants in 2019
1	U.S.	167,115	U.S.	34,614	Mainland, China	354,111
2	Japan	53,542	Japan	22,423	Japan	30,401
3	South Korea	21,684	Germany	21,198	U.S.	23,114
4	Mainland, China	19,209	France	8,800	Germany	9,989
5	Germany	18,293	South Korea	7,247	South Korea	9,437
6	Taiwan, China	11,489	Mainland, China	6,229	Taiwan, China	6,197
7	U.K.	7,791	U.K.	4,119	France	2,997
8	Canada	7,595	Italy	3,713	U.K.	1,310
9	France	7,233	Canada	1,683	Italy	1,102
10	Italy	3,175	Taiwan, China	1,014	Hong Kong, China	592
11	Singapore	1,119	Singapore	440	Canada	568
12	Hong Kong, China	846	Hong Kong, China	50	Singapore	566

Source: CNIPA patent grant statistics were collected from China Statistical Yearbook, various years; EPO patent grant statistics were collected from the EPO website; and USPTO patent grant statistics were collected from the USPTO website.

number of patent grants by both the USPTO and EPO, and the third highest number by CNIPA. Mainland, China was awarded the highest number of patent grants by CNIPA, fourth highest by USPTO and the sixth highest by EPO. Japan, as a sign of its technological strength, was in second place by the number of patent grants from all three major patent offices. South Korea was third-placed by USPTO patent grants and fifth-placed by EPO patent grants, in both cases ahead of Mainland China. Germany, the technology leader in Europe, was fifth-placed by USPTO patent grants, third-placed by EPO and fourth-placed by CNIPA.

Table 7.1 also provides evidence that all the economies in our study, except for Mainland China, could have had more CNIPA patent grants if they would submit more patent applications on the basis of their already existing discoveries and inventions. Every one of them had significantly more USPTO patent grants than CNIPA patent grants. It is also interesting to note that while the European economies and the US and Canada had more EPO than CNIPA patent grants, Japan, South Korea, Taiwan, China, Singapore, and Hong Kong, China all had more CNIPA than EPO patent grants.

Finally, we compare directly the numbers of CNIPA, EPO and USPTO patent grants received each year by Mainland China, Germany, Japan and the US from 2004 to 2019. This allows us to assess the comparability of the patent grants by the three major patent offices as indicators of their relative innovation success and standards. The results are presented in Figure 7.10.

Figure 7.10 shows clearly the rapid and continuing rise in the numbers of patent grants received by Mainland China from all three patent offices, CNIPA, EPO, and USPTO (the three red lines). However, the number of Chinese domestic patent grants far exceeds its numbers of foreign patent grants by an order of magnitude. The numbers of CNIPA patent grants received by Japan (the yellow line with circular markers), the US (the blue line with circular markers) and Germany (the black line with circular markers) have also been rising over time. Among the four economies, the US is first in the numbers of both EPO and USPTO patents and third in the number of CNIPA patents; China is first in the number of CNIPA patents, third in USPTO patents and fourth in EPO patents[8]; Japan comes in

[8] It should be pointed out that South Korea had more USPTO as well as EPO patents than Mainland China in 2019 (see Table 7.1).

Figure 7.10: The CNIPA, EPO and the USPTO patent grants, Mainland China, Germany, Japan and the United States

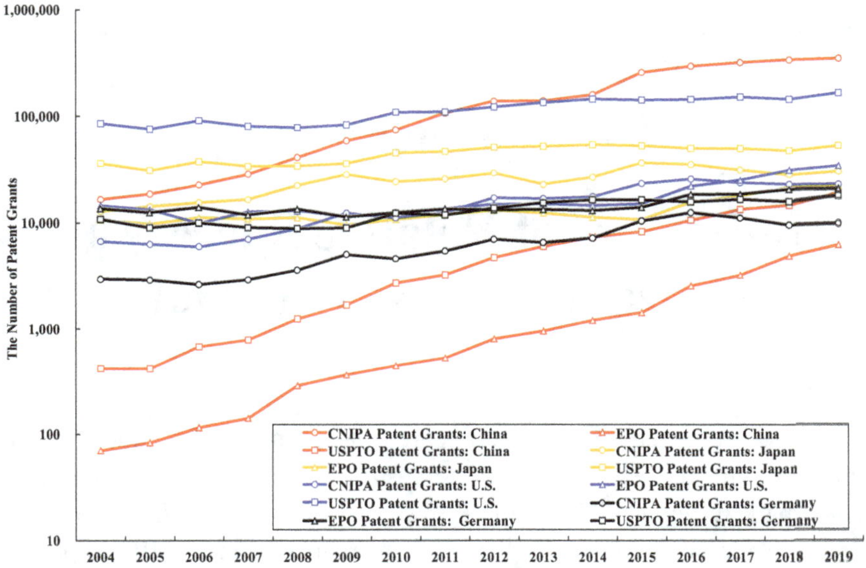

Source: The numbers of CNIPA, EPO and USPTO patent grants were collected from China Statistical Yearbooks, WIPO, EPO and USPTO websites.

second in the numbers of patent grants awarded by all three major patent offices; and Germany comes in third in the number of EPO patents and fourth in the numbers of both CNIPA and USPTO patents. We conclude that the number of patent grants by the USPTO still appears for the time being to be the best indicator of the relative innovation success across economies. In time, when more patent applications are received by CNIPA from outside of Mainland China, the number of CNIPA patent grants may also serve as a useful indicator of relative innovation success across economies.

Chapter 8

Indicators of Relative Success in Innovation across Economies

In previous chapters, we have compared the economies included in our study in terms of their numbers of domestic, the United States Patent and Trademark Office (USPTO), the European Patent Office (EPO) and the China National Intellectual Property Administration (CNIPA) patent applications and/or grants. In this chapter, we develop several indicators of relative success in innovation based on their numbers of patent applications and grants and use them to assess the relative performance of the economies in innovation.

In Table 8.1, we tabulate the numbers of domestic, USPTO, EPO and CNIPA patent grants received by the residents of the different economies in 2019. From the tabulation, we also derive the relative rankings of each economy in accordance with the number of patent grants under each category. In 2019, Mainland China had the largest number of domestic patent grants, followed by the United States (US) and Japan, with South Korea in fourth place. The US had the largest number of USPTO and EPO patent grants, but only the third largest number of CNIPA patent grants, after Japan. Japan demonstrated its formidable strength in innovation by becoming the second highest recipient of, respectively, the USPTO, EPO and CNIPA patent grants. Germany was the strongest European country in innovation, ranking first among European countries in all three categories of patent grants — USPTO, EPO and CNIPA. (It was third in EPO patent grants, fourth in CNIPA patent grants, and fifth in USPTO patent

Table 8.1: The numbers of domestic, USPTO, EPO and CNIPA patent grants received by the residents of the different economies and their relative ranks in 2019

	Domestic Patent Grants		USPTO Patent Grants		EPO Patent Grants		CNIPA Patent Grants			
	Number	Rank	Number	Rank	Number	Rank	Number	Rank	Weighted Rank	Weighted Rank Integerised
Canada	2,035	10	7,595	8	1,683	9	568	11	9.58	10
France	11,673	7	7,233	9	8,800	4	2,997	7	7.31	7
Germany	11,770	6	18,293	5	21,198	3	9,989	4	4.23	4
Italy	2,130	9	3,175	10	3,713	8	1,102	9	9.23	9
Japan	140,865	3	53,542	2	22,423	2	30,401	2	2.00	2
United Kingdom	3,081	8	7,791	7	4,119	7	1,310	8	7.48	8
United States	167,115	2	167,115	1	34,614	1	23,114	3	1.96	1
Mainland, China	354,111	1	19,209	4	6,229	6	354,111	1	2.85	3
Hong Kong, China	107	12	846	12	50	12	592	10	11.04	11
South Korea	94,852	4	21,684	3	7,247	5	9,437	5	4.25	5
Singapore	264	11	1,119	11	440	11	566	12	11.48	12
Taiwan, China	14,481	5	11,489	6	1,014	10	6,197	6	6.58	6

Sources: Data on the number of domestic and US patent grants are from Tables A4.2 and A5.2, respectively. Data on EPO patent grants were collected from the European Patent Office website. Data on CNIPA patent grants were collected from China Statistical Yearbook, various issues.

grants.) South Korea, also an up-and-coming powerhouse in innovation, came in third in USPTO patent grants, ahead of both Mainland China and Germany, and fifth in both EPO and CNIPA grants. Hong Kong, China and Singapore were in the last places.[1]

Looking simply at the aggregate total number of patent grants received by each economy from all three major patent offices — CNIPA, EPO and USPTO — in 2019, Mainland China would come in first, with 379,549 patent grants, followed by the US (224,843) and Japan (106,366). However, this result is, in part, the artefact of the overwhelmingly large total number of CNIPA patent grants (452,804), the bulk of which (354,111) were awarded to Chinese applicants, even though as a group they had the lowest CNIPA grant rate. Instead, we compute a weighted rank for the 12 economies, using their ranks in each of the categories of USPTO, EPO and CNIPA patent grants in Table 8.1. The weights are the total numbers of patent grants of USPTO (354,430), EPO (137,784) and CNIPA (452,804), respectively, in 2019, divided by the aggregate total number of patent grants of all three patent offices (945,018). The results, presented in the "Weighted Rank" column, indicate that the US would still be number one by a hair, followed by Japan, with Mainland China in third place. Germany was ranked fourth, followed by South Korea and Taiwan, China. Four of the top 10 patent-generating economies were in East Asia, four were in Europe, and two were in North America.[2] The weighted ranks have been converted into whole integer ranks in the last column of Table 8.1.

The rank correlation coefficient between the integerised weighted ranks and the USPTO ranks is a high 0.937, which means that the USPTO rank order is a good summary indicator of the relative success in innovation across economies. We have also previously established, in Chapter 5, that the procedures and standards employed by the USPTO do not appear to be biased in favour of either US applicants or any of the foreign applicants. Of course, counting only the number of USPTO patent grants does penalise economies with a low USPTO patent application rate, such as Mainland China. But we expect that both the Chinese USPTO patent

[1] Hong Kong, China however, was ahead of Canada in CNIPA patent grants in 2019 (592 vs. 568).

[2] Israel is one of the innovative economies that has not been included in this study.

application rate and the CNIPA patent application rates of the US and other economies will increase over time, since no enterprise in the world, whatever its geographical or national origin, can afford to ignore the huge markets of China and the US in the long run.

In Figure 8.1, we compare the numbers of USPTO patent grants received by each economy each year, using the number of patent grants received by US residents as a benchmark (100). Figure 8.1 shows that the US has been the leader in USPTO patent grants from the very beginning. Since the mid-1970s, Japan has been a persistent number two behind the US, followed more recently by South Korea, which overtook Germany in the mid-2010s. However, Mainland China also managed to overtake Germany in 2019 to become the economy with the fourth highest number of USPTO patent grants. The US lead in USPTO patent grants has been commanding, accounting for almost 50% of all USPTO patent grants. The second-placed Japan received no more than a third of the number of patent grants received by the US, and South Korea, Mainland China and

Figure 8.1: An index of USPTO patent grants (the number of patent grants received by US residents = 100)

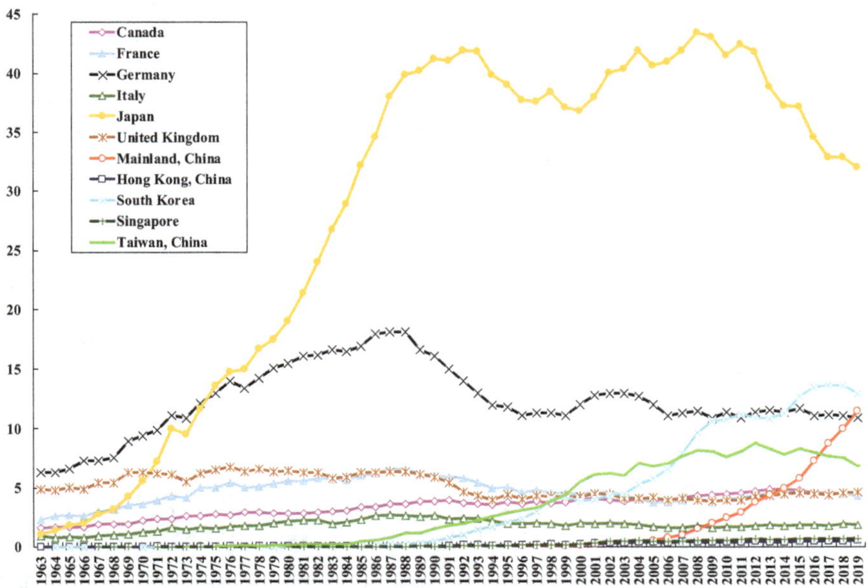

Source: Data on the number of US patent grants are from Table A5.2.

Germany each received approximately one-tenth of the number received by the US. With this as a performance indicator of innovation, the rank order is the US, Japan, South Korea, Mainland China and Germany.

A second possible indicator is the relative efficiency of the real R&D capital stock across economies. If the efficiency is the same between two economies, then the numbers of patent grants received per unit quantity of the real R&D capital stock should be identical. To the extent that they differ, they may reflect differences in R&D efficiency. In Figure 8.2, we compare the R&D efficiency in terms of the number of domestic patent grants per billion 2019 US dollars of R&D capital stock, across the economies included in our study. Mainland China has had the highest R&D efficiency in the generation of domestic patent grants since 2015, despite a very low domestic patent grant rate (see Figure 7.5), followed by South Korea and Taiwan, China. Japan was the leader in R&D efficiency in domestic patent grants between 1969 and 1996, but lost out to first South

Figure 8.2: The number of domestic patent grants per unit quantity of the real R&D capital stock in billion 2019 US dollars

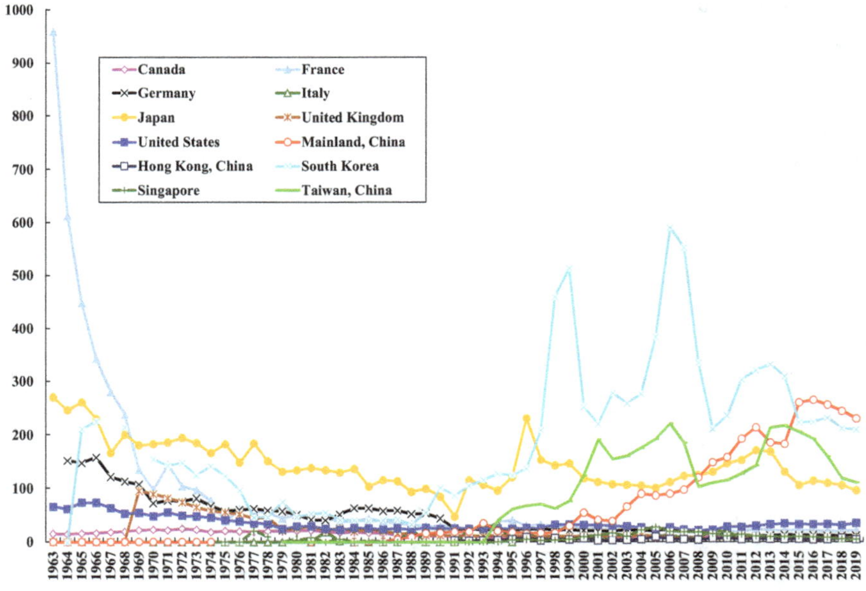

Sources: Data on the number of domestic patent applications are from Table A4.2 and data on the quantity of real R&D capital stock are from Table A3.2.

Korea, then Taiwan, China and then Mainland China, ending up in fourth place in 2019. The US had the highest efficiency among the G-7 countries except Japan. With this as a performance indicator of innovation, the rank order is Mainland China, South Korea, Taiwan, China, Japan and the US. We should add that the quantity of R&D capital stock in 2019 US dollars of an economy is sensitive to the value of the exchange rate of its currency relative to the US dollar in 2019. A low value of its exchange rate would result in a lower quantity of its real R&D capital stock, and hence a higher R&D efficiency in the generation of domestic patent grants, and vice versa.

In Figure 8.3, we compare the R&D efficiency in terms of the number of USPTO patent grants per billion 2019 US dollars of R&D capital stock, across the economies in our study. It turns out that Taiwan, China had the highest R&D efficiency, with the largest number of USPTO patent grants per unit quantity of its real R&D capital stock. South Korea was in second place, followed by Hong Kong, China, Japan and the US. The US has had

Figure 8.3: The number of USPTO patent grants per unit quantity of the real R&D capital stock in billion 2019 US dollars

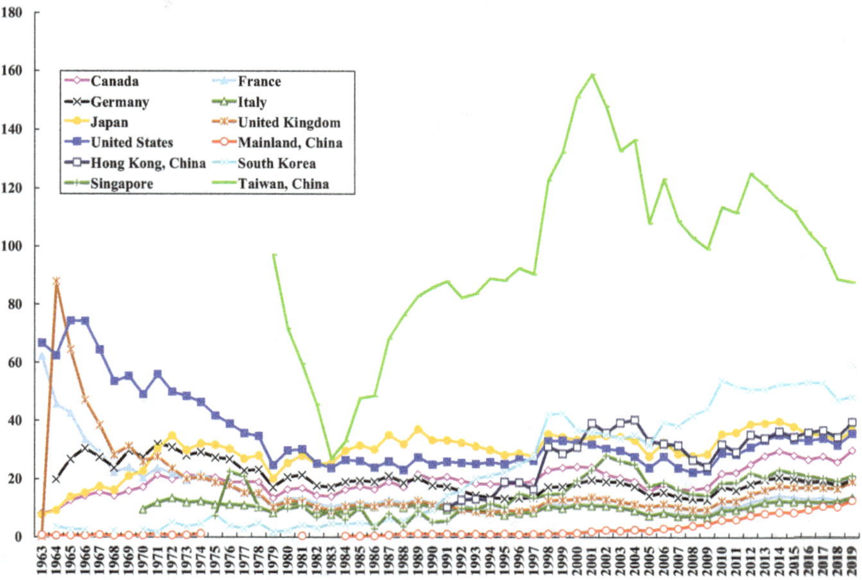

Sources: Data on the number of USPTO patent applications are from Table A5.2 and data on the quantity of real R&D capital stock are from Table A3.2.

the highest R&D efficiency in the generation of USPTO patent grants among all G7 countries except Japan since 1965. Mainland China has had the lowest R&D efficiency in the generation of USPTO patent grants, but this may also have to do with its low US patent application rate. In any case, Chinese R&D efficiency in the generation of USPTO patent grants has been rising steadily since 2000. With this as a performance indicator of innovation, the rank order is Taiwan, China, South Korea, Hong Kong, China, Japan and the US. Similar to the case for R&D efficiency in the generation of domestic patent grants, the relative efficiency in the generation of USPTO patent grants is also sensitive to the values of exchange rates in 2019. A low value of the exchange rate would result in a lower quantity of the real R&D capital stock in US dollars, and hence a higher R&D efficiency in the generation of USPTO patent grants, and vice versa.

A third possible indicator is based on a scatter diagram of the number of USPTO patents and the quantity of real R&D capital stock presented as Figure 5.14 and reproduced as follows. There is an overall linear

Figure 5.14: The number of USPTO patent grants and the quantity of real R&D capital stock, G7 countries, Mainland China and four EANIEs

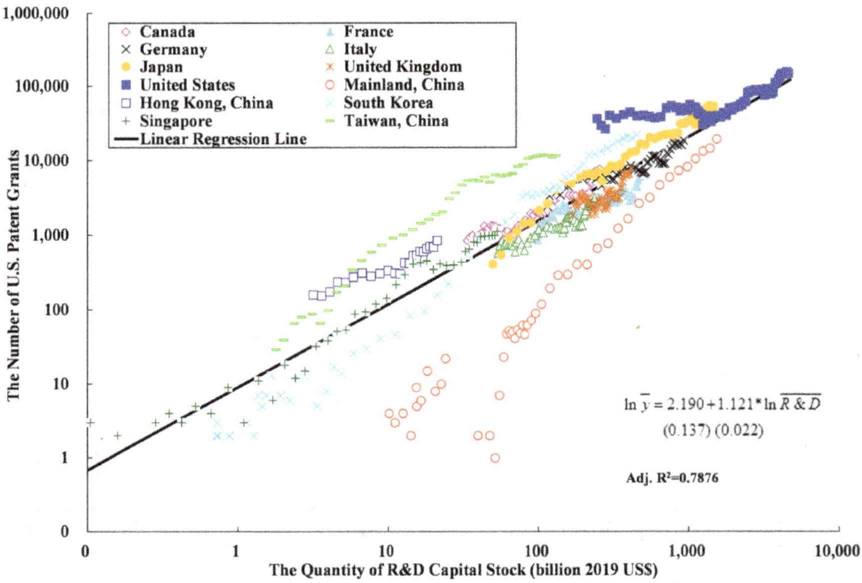

Sources: Table A5.2 of Chapter 5 and Table A3.2 of Chapter 3.

regression line estimated from the data, which can be used to predict the number of USPTO patents that an economy with a given quantity of real R&D capital stock would be expected to be able to generate under normal circumstances. The vertical distance of each economy's data point from the linear regression line (the residual of the regression) is then a measure of its degree of under- or over-achievement. If an economy operates below the overall linear regression line, it is an "under-achiever"; if it operates above the line, it is an "over-achiever". For every economy and in every year between 2000 and 2019, we compute the additional percentage (positive or negative) of USPTO patent grants that the economy would have been awarded, given its quantity of real R&D capital stock, if it had operated on the linear regression line.

The results of this exercise are presented in Figure 8.4. These results are both retrospective and prospective. Taiwan, China had the highest

Figure 8.4: The percentage of over- and under-achievement in USPTO patent grants, G-7 countries, Mainland China, and four EANIEs (2000–2019)

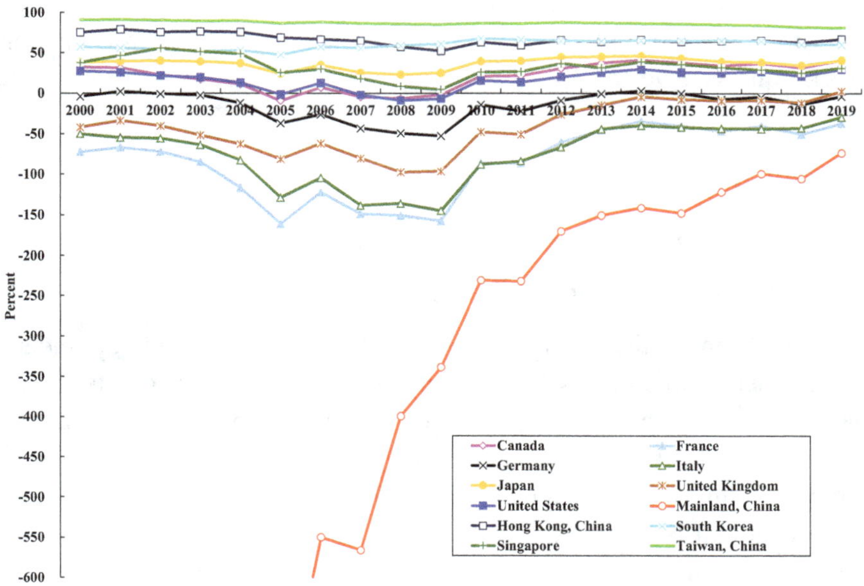

Note: The graph is truncated at –600% in order to maintain legibility of the rest of the graph. In 2000, the under-achievement of Mainland China in USPTO patent grants was –1,291%.
Source: Data are taken from Table A8.1.

degree of "over-achievement", followed by Hong Kong, China, South Korea, Canada, Japan and Singapore. The US has been an "over-achiever" since 2010. However, all the European economies in our study — France, Italy, the UK, and Germany — have been habitual "under-achievers". As has been Mainland China. However, the Chinese degree of "under-achievement" has greatly improved over time, increasing from –1,291% in 2000 to –73% in 2019. The "under-achievers" such as Mainland China, and France and Italy (both with "under-achievement" somewhere between 30% and 40%) have a great deal of room for further improvement. With this as a performance indicator of innovation, the rank order is Taiwan, China, Hong Kong, China, South Korea, Canada and Japan. We should add that the degree of over- and/or under-achievement can also be sensitive to the values of the exchange rates in 2019. In the first place, the overall linear regression line itself will be affected by the changes in the quantities of R&D capital stocks in 2019 US dollars. Moreover, if the exchange rate was under-valued, the quantity of R&D capital stock in 2019 US dollars would also be under-estimated, and this might result in an "apparent" over-achievement (the same number of patent grants with a lower quantity of real R&D capital stock), and vice versa.

Appendix

A8.1 *Estimation of the degree of over- and under-achievement in USPTO patent grants*

The first step in the estimation of the degree of over- and/or under-achievement is to predict what the number of USPTO patent grants would have been for each economy, based on its quantity of real R&D capital stock of that year, if the economy were operating on the overall linear regression line. Once the predicted number of USPTO patent grants is derived, it can be subtracted from the actual number of USPTO patent grants and then divided by the actual number of USPTO patent grants to arrive at a percentage over- or under-achievement. This is done for each economy for every year from 2000 to 2019. The results of these calculations are presented in Table A8.1.

Table A8.1: Estimated percentage over- and under-achievements in USPTO patent grants, G-7 countries, Mainland China and four EANIEs (2000–2019)

	Canada	France	Germany	Italy	Japan	United Kingdom	United States	Mainland, China	Hong Kong, China	South Korea	Singapore	Taiwan, China
2000	32.2	–72.0	–4.0	–50.2	38.0	–42.0	27.3	–1,290.6	75.3	57.7	37.7	91.0
2001	31.4	–66.8	2.1	–54.7	39.3	–33.7	25.9	–876.4	79.1	56.4	46.6	91.3
2002	22.5	–71.9	–1.0	–55.8	40.0	–40.6	21.9	–659.0	75.5	54.9	55.6	90.6
2003	17.5	–84.5	–2.6	–63.7	39.1	–51.8	19.8	–767.0	76.4	52.5	51.7	89.4
2004	11.4	–116.1	–12.0	–82.7	36.7	–62.7	13.3	–651.9	75.8	53.7	48.9	89.6
2005	–9.2	–160.6	–37.2	–128.6	23.9	–81.1	–1.2	–794.2	69.0	48.1	25.6	86.7
2006	7.0	–121.9	–26.4	–104.5	34.9	–62.1	13.0	–550.0	66.8	58.0	29.9	88.3
2007	–4.7	–148.2	–43.4	–138.6	25.4	–80.4	–2.0	–566.3	65.1	56.3	18.1	86.5
2008	–6.5	–150.4	–49.5	–136.0	23.2	–97.6	–8.8	–399.5	57.4	59.5	8.5	85.7
2009	–2.0	–157.3	–53.0	–145.0	24.8	–96.6	–6.7	–338.6	52.4	61.4	4.7	84.9
2010	20.9	–85.8	–14.4	–88.0	39.4	–47.9	15.7	–230.9	63.2	68.1	26.2	86.7
2011	21.8	–86.3	–22.2	–83.7	40.2	–50.8	13.8	–231.8	59.3	66.4	26.6	86.4
2012	30.6	–60.3	–9.0	–66.7	44.5	–26.4	20.3	–169.8	65.8	65.3	36.7	87.7
2013	37.6	–45.1	–0.7	–44.4	45.0	–14.9	25.9	–150.4	64.2	64.9	31.7	87.2
2014	41.1	–34.7	2.9	–40.0	45.8	–4.5	29.8	–141.3	66.2	65.8	38.9	86.5
2015	37.9	–40.4	–0.1	–42.1	43.0	–7.8	26.0	–147.8	63.9	65.4	35.8	86.0
2016	34.4	–46.4	–7.2	–43.7	39.0	–9.4	25.4	–121.8	65.1	65.6	31.9	84.9
2017	37.0	–40.4	–4.6	–44.1	38.1	–8.9	26.9	–99.3	65.6	65.2	29.2	84.0
2018	32.0	–50.5	–13.9	–42.9	34.4	–11.8	21.2	–105.3	62.9	60.6	25.3	81.9
2019	41.2	–36.9	–3.5	–29.4	40.8	2.6	29.7	–73.5	67.5	61.0	31.4	81.6

Source: Author's calculations

Chapter 9

Innovation at the Microeconomic Level

In Chapters 4–7, we have shown, visually through many charts and in simple linear regressions, that the quantity of real Research and Development (R&D) capital stock of an economy has a positive and statistically significant effect on its numbers of patent applications and grants. This is found to be true for not only the domestic patent applications and grants in each economy in our study but also the patent applications and/or grants of the United States Patent and Trademark Office (USPTO), the European Patent Office (EPO) and the China National Intellectual Property Administration (CNIPA). In general, the higher the total quantity of real R&D capital stock in an economy is, the more domestic and international patent applications will be submitted by and patent grants awarded to its residents.

In this chapter, we examine data from selected individual Chinese and US enterprises to see whether the same relation holds at the microeconomic level, that is, whether a higher number of patent grants is awarded to an individual enterprise with a higher quantity of real R&D capital stock. Cross-sectional US firm-level data have been analysed by Hausman, Hall and Griliches (1984) and Hall, Griliches and Hausman (1986) in their pioneering studies on the relationship between the number of patent applications and R&D expenditure. We use a different approach: we assemble time-series data on the R&D expenditures of specific, selected Chinese and US enterprises as well as the numbers of Chinese and US patents granted to these enterprises. From the data on R&D expenditures, we construct estimates of the time series of the quantities of real R&D capital stock for each enterprise in 2019 US dollars. Then we attempt to relate the annual numbers of Chinese and US patent grants to each enterprise to the quantities of its real R&D capital stock in the previous year.

The specific Chinese enterprises that we have selected are China Petroleum and Chemical Corporation (Sinopec), Huawei Technologies Co., Ltd. (Huawei), and ZTE Corporation (ZTE). They have been consistently among the annual top ten Chinese recipients of CNIPA patent grants. The specific US enterprises that we have selected are Apple Inc. (Apple), General Electric Company (GE), Hewlett-Packard Corporation (H-P),[1] International Business Machines Corporation (IBM), Microsoft Corporation (Microsoft), and Qualcomm, all well-known US high-technology companies.

9.1 The Quantities of Real R&D Capital Stock

First, we construct estimates of the time series of the quantities of real R&D capital stock for each enterprise from its time series of real R&D expenditures.[2] The quantity of real R&D capital stock is derived as the cumulative past R&D expenditures in 2019 US dollars less a 10% depreciation per year.[3] In Figure 9.1, the estimated quantities of real R&D capital stock of all the individual Chinese and US enterprises under study are presented. As of 2020, Microsoft had the highest quantity of real R&D capital stock, followed by Huawei Technology Co., Ltd., and Apple. IBM

---

[1]The data for Hewlett-Packard Corporation are available up to 2015, after which it was split up into more than one successor corporation.

[2]The R&D expenditures are converted into real R&D expenditures in national or regional currencies in 2019 prices using the GDP deflators of the respective economies. Annual GDP deflators are collected from International Financial Statistics (IFS) database and domestic official statistical sources. The real R&D expenditures in national or regional currencies are then converted to US dollars, using the 2019 year-end exchange rates.

[3]The initial real R&D capital stock for each enterprise is estimated by dividing the real R&D expenditure in the first year that R&D expenditure data are available by the sum of the rate of growth of real R&D expenditure in the first 5 years and the annual rate of depreciation, assumed to be 10%.

Figure 9.1: The quantity of real R&D capital stock, selected Chinese and US enterprises

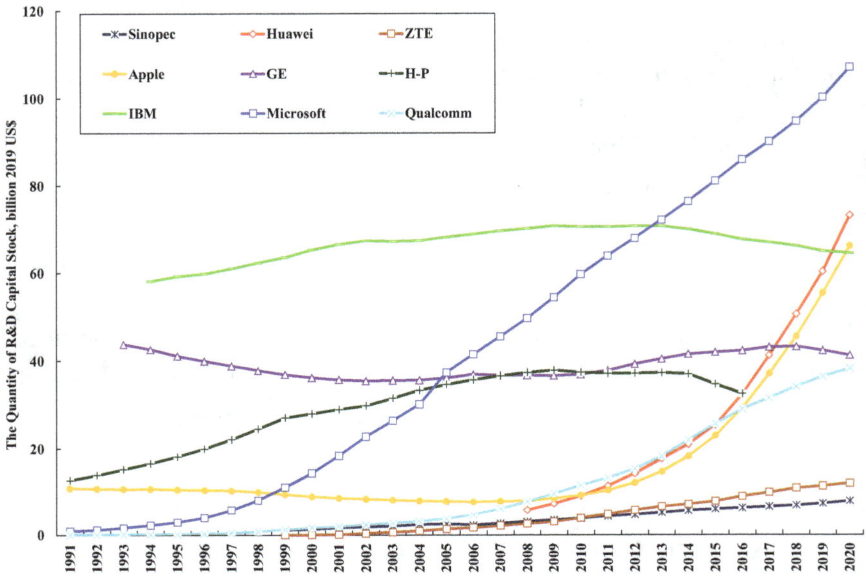

Source: Authors' calculations. R&D expenditures for Chinese enterprises are collected from their annual reports (various years), supplemented by their financial reports from the Osiris Database. R&D expenditures for US enterprises are collected from the US Securities and Exchange Commission and the Orbis Americas database.

Corporation was the global leader until it was surpassed by Microsoft in 2013, and then by both Huawei and Apple in 2020. General Electric used to be number two, but fell to fifth place in 2020. Qualcomm, whose real R&D capital stock had been rising fast, was in sixth place. ZTE and Sinopec still lagged behind the other enterprises significantly in terms of the quantity of real R&D capital stock.

9.2 The Number of Patent Grants

In Figure 9.2, the numbers of USPTO patent grants awarded to our selected enterprises are plotted against time. IBM Corporation had a commanding lead in the number of USPTO patent grants. In 2019, it was awarded 9,253 patents, compared to 3,080 for Microsoft. Huawei, in

Figure 9.2: The number of USPTO patent grants, selected Chinese and US enterprises

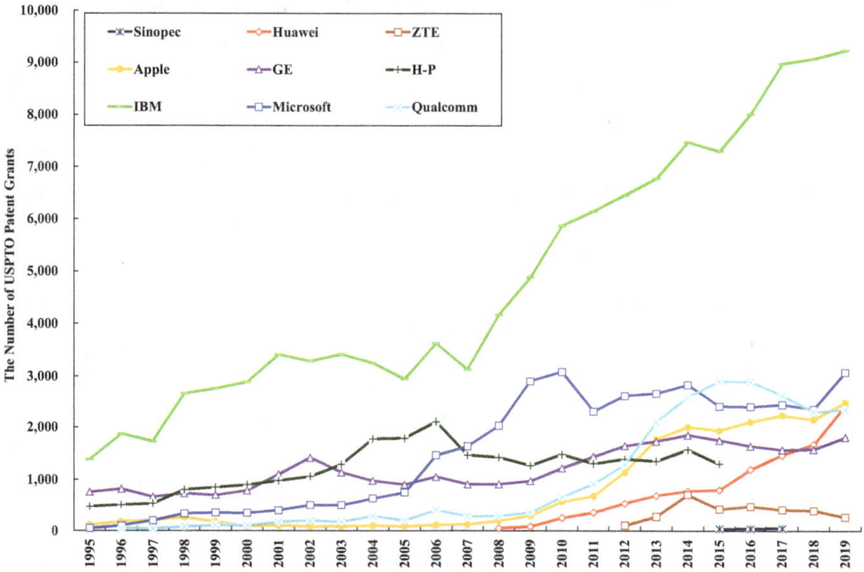

Note: Organisations with less than 40 patent grants awarded are not separately listed on the USPTO website.
Source: USPTO.

fourth place with 2,417 USPTO patent grants, was just behind Apple with its 2,483 patent grants. ZTE and Sinopec were at the bottom.[4]

However, we note that the number of USPTO patents awarded to Apple has been almost stationary over time, even though the quantity of its real R&D capital stock has been rising rapidly (see Figure 9.1). This is a little anomalous. We conjecture that the slowdown in the number of patent grants awarded to Apple is due to the slowdown in the number of patent applications submitted by Apple, and not necessarily due to a slowdown of the discoveries and inventions at Apple. There may possibly be two reasons for the slowdown in patent applications: disclosure

[4]The number of patent grants awarded to Sinopec is available for only 3 years. This does not necessarily mean that Sinopec received no USPTO patent grants in the other years, but the USPTO published patents grants to a given applicant separately only if the number of patent grants awarded in a given year is greater than or equal to 40.

avoidance or tax avoidance. Disclosure avoidance is a strategy sometimes used by a corporation to avoid alerting the competitors of its product development strategy and progress thereof. The corporation may forego patent applications altogether or may apply for patents at relatively obscure locations so as to avoid widespread dissemination of the disclosure. Tax avoidance is a strategy to vest the ownership of patents in a subsidiary in a low-tax jurisdiction, such as the Republic of Ireland, so as to reduce the profit or income tax payable on any potential royalties and license fees to be earned from the patents.

In Figure 9.3, the number of CNIPA patent grants awarded to our selected enterprises are plotted against time. It is clear that the numbers of CNIPA patent grants of all the selected enterprises, Chinese and US, have been rising rapidly over time, much more so than their respective numbers of USPTO patents. In 2020, Huawei had the highest number of CNIPA patent grants (6,413), followed by Sinopec (2,954) and ZTE (1,348). Qualcomm had the highest number of CNIPA patents among US enterprises (1,158 in 2020), followed by Microsoft and Apple. For reasons not

Figure 9.3: The number of CNIPA patent grants, selected Chinese and US enterprises

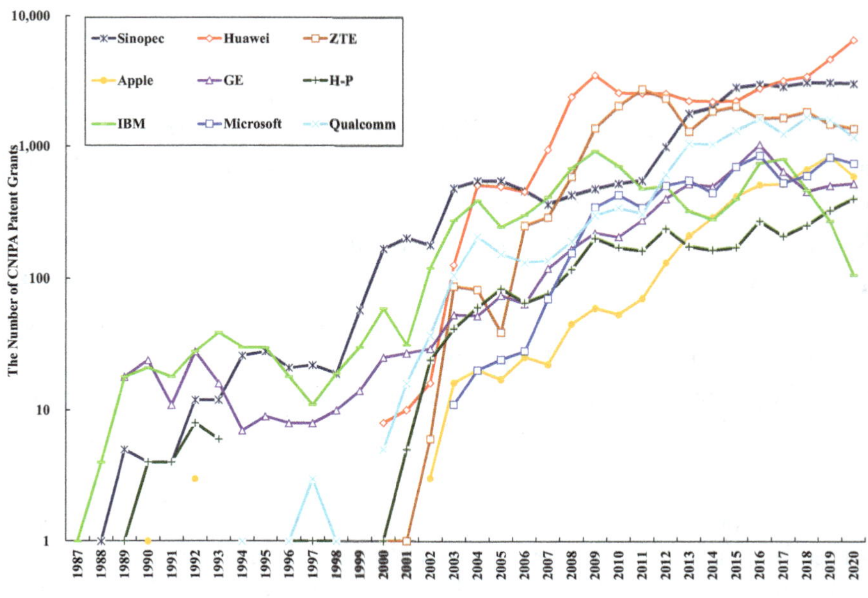

Source: Patsnap database (https://www.zhihuiya.com/).

apparent, the number of CNIPA patent grants of IBM has been declining over time since 2017.

We note an interesting but not unexpected phenomenon — for all of these enterprises, the numbers of their home patent grants have always been greater than the numbers of their foreign patent grants over our period of study. Thus, Sinopec, Huawei, and ZTE have had more CNIPA patent grants than USPTO patent grants awarded to them each year. Similarly, Apple, GE, H-P, IBM, Microsoft, and Qualcomm have had more USPTO patent grants than CNIPA patent grants awarded to them each year, with the exception of the years 2016–2019 for H-P.[5]

9.3 The Relationship between the Number of Patent Grants and the Quantity of Real R&D Capital Stock

In Figure 9.4, the annual number of USPTO patent grants awarded to each enterprise is plotted against the quantity of its R&D capital stock in 2019 US dollars of the previous year. We find the same positive relationship between the number of patent grants and the quantity of real R&D capital stock found at the macroeconomic level of an economy in the earlier chapters. The linear regressions, with and without enterprise-specific constants, both fit quite well and yield statistically significant coefficients.[6] The estimated elasticity of the number of USPTO patent grants with respect to the quantity of real R&D capital stock lies between 0.968 and 1.056, or approximately one, that is, a 1% increase in the real R&D capital stock increases the number of USPTO patent grants by approximately 1%. However, IBM seems to be an outlier, and perhaps also GE. The problem appears to be that the quantity of its real R&D capital stock is no longer growing but the number of its patent grants keeps rising, resulting in a

[5] See Tables A9.2 and A9.3. By 2016, Hewlett-Packard Corporation has already been split into several independent entities and Mainland China has become the manufacturing hub for them.

[6] As might be expected, the linear regression with enterprise-specific constants fits much better. The red line in Figure 9.4 is drawn with a constant term set equal to the weighted average of all the enterprise-specific constants with the shares of the number of observations of each enterprise in the total number of observations as weights.

Figure 9.4: The number of USPTO patent grants and the quantity of real R&D capital stock, selected Chinese and US enterprises

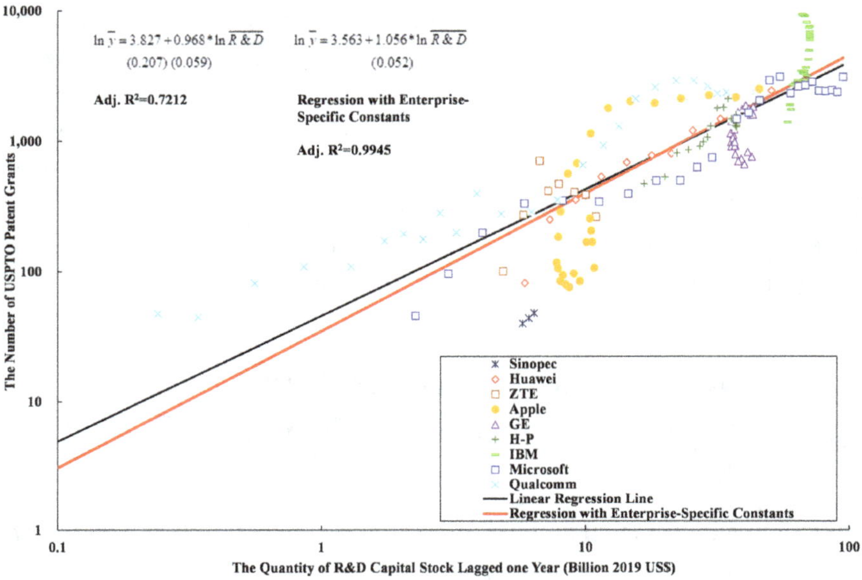

Source: Tables A9.1 and A9.2.

very steep enterprise-specific USPTO patent grant-real R&D capital stock line. One possible conjecture is that the rate of depreciation of 10% per annum may have been too high for these enterprises if a high proportion of their R&D expenditures were devoted to basic research, in which case a higher quantity of real R&D capital would have been implied.

In Figure 9.5, the annual number of CNIPA patent grants awarded to each enterprise is plotted against the quantity of its R&D capital stock in 2019 US dollars of the previous year. However, the scatter diagram itself, unlike Figure 9.4, does not show a clear correlation between the number of CNIPA patent grants and the quantity of real R&D capital stock. The fit of the simple linear regression is poor, with an adjusted R^2 of only 0.0507, even though the estimated coefficient of the natural logarithm of the quantity of real R&D capital stock is positive and statistically significant. Yet the implied elasticity of the number of patent grants with respect to the quantity of real R&D capital stock is an implausibly low 0.329. We believe this low estimate is the result of the very diverse behaviour of the Chinese and US enterprises. The linear regression with enterprise-specific

Figure 9.5: The number of CNIPA patent grants and the quantity of real R&D capital stock, selected Chinese and US enterprises

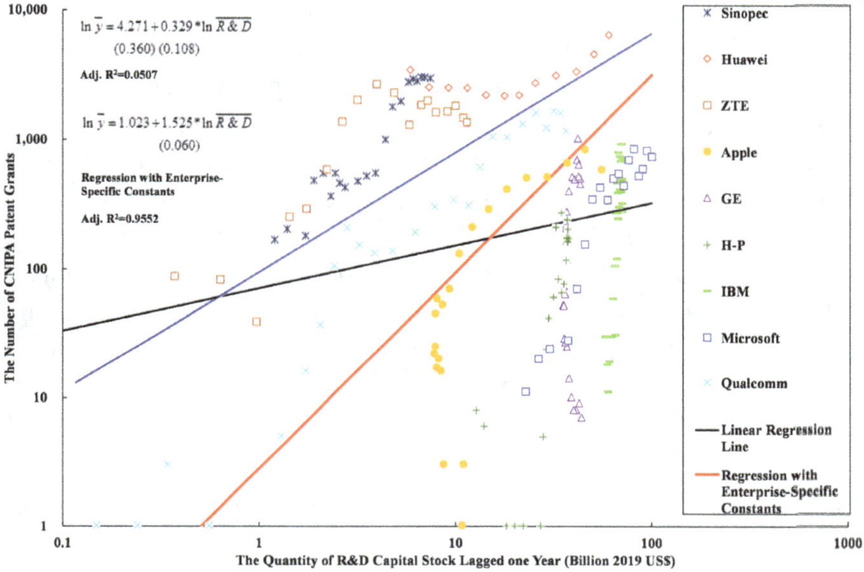

Source: Tables A9.1 and A9.3.

constants fits much better, with an adjusted R^2 of 0.9552, but yields an incredibly high elasticity of 1.525 (the red line).[7] Moreover, it is also apparent from the scatter diagram that a straight line (the blue line) can be drawn so that the data points for all of the Chinese enterprises (except for one observation for ZTE in 2005) lie on one side and those of all US enterprises lie on the other. This suggests that the experiences of the selected Chinese and US enterprises with the CNIPA must have been quite different. We believe this may be due to the differences in the CNIPA patent application rates between the Chinese and US enterprises.[8] At the economy-wide level, CNIPA grant rates for the US (59% in 2019) have

[7]The red line in Figure 9.5 is drawn with a constant term set equal to the weighted average of all the enterprise-specific constants with the shares of the number of observations of each enterprise in the total number of observations as weights.

[8]For US enterprises, it may be necessary to strike a balance between the avoidance of disclosure and the need for intellectual property right protection.

been consistently higher than those for Mainland China (26% in 2019).[9] Unfortunately, it has not been possible to find data on enterprise-specific CNIPA patent application rates. We note, however, that the appearance of the scatter of data points in Figures 9.4 and 9.5 for both IBM and GE are quite similar (the respective data points are on top of one another), even though they apply to different patent grants, USPTO and CNIPA, respectively. This suggests that perhaps the quantities of real R&D capital stocks of these two enterprises may have been under-estimated because of the possible over-depreciation of their basic research capital.

In Figures 9.6 and 9.7, we present the data for the selected Chinese and US enterprises separately. Figure 9.6 shows the same positive and monotonic effect of the quantity of real R&D capital stock of a Chinese enterprise on the annual number of CNIPA patent grants awarded to it. The fit of the simple linear regression is good, with an adjusted R^2 of

Figure 9.6: The number of CNIPA patent grants and the quantity of real R&D capital stock, selected Chinese enterprises

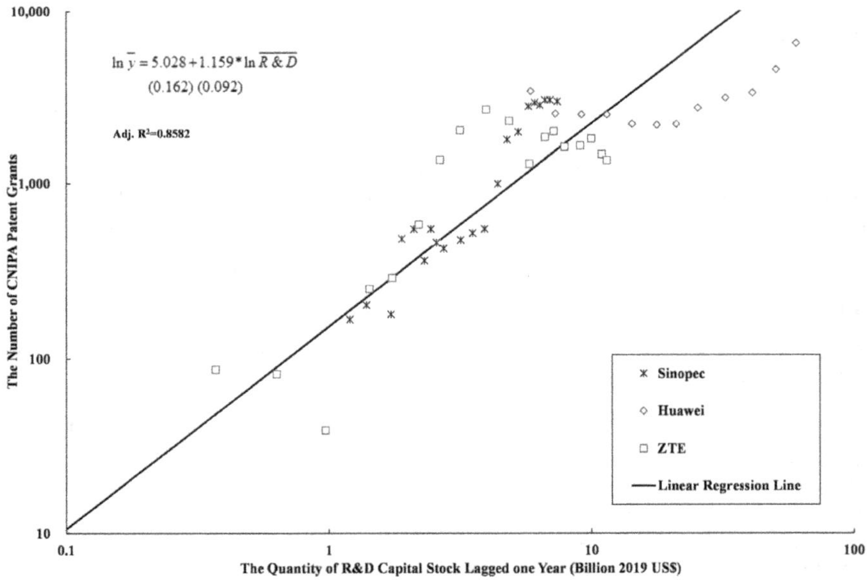

Source: Tables A9.1 and A9.3.

[9] See Chapter 7.

0.8582. The estimated elasticity of 1.159 suggests the existence of a reasonable degree of economies of scale in real R&D capital at the enterprise level.

In Figure 9.7, the data of only the US enterprises are presented. The fit of the simple linear regression is not that good, with an adjusted R^2 of only 0.2338, even though the estimated coefficient of 0.799 is statistically significant. The fit of the linear regression with enterprise-specific constants is much better, with an adjusted R^2 of 0.9313 (the red line).[10] However, the estimated coefficient of 1.765 also implies an incredibly high degree of economies of scale. We believe this may be due to the possible over-depreciation of real basic research capital in a couple of the US

Figure 9.7: The number of CNIPA patent grants and the quantity of real R&D capital stock, selected US enterprises

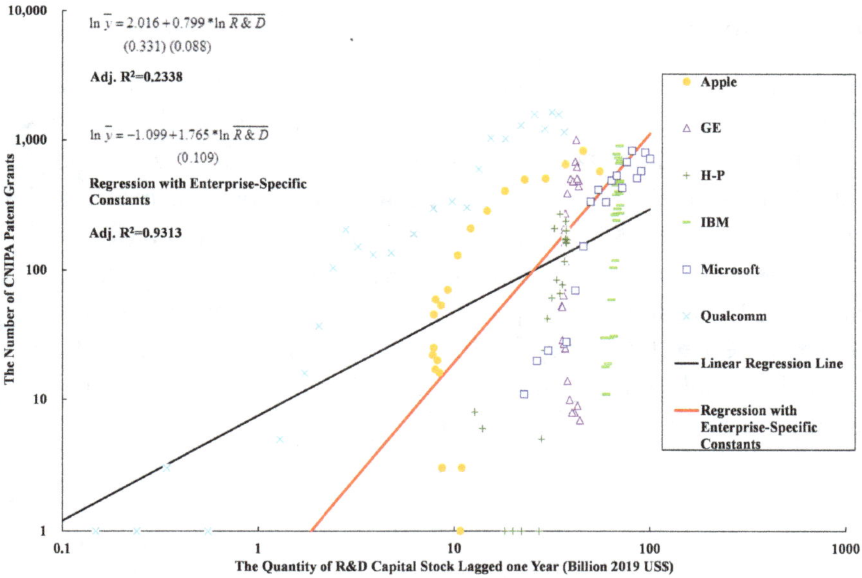

Source: Tables A9.1 and A9.3.

[10] Similar to the red lines in Figures 9.4 and 9.5, the red line in Figure 9.7 is drawn with a constant term set equal to the weighted average of all the enterprise-specific constants with the shares of the number of observations of each enterprise in the total number of observations as weights.

enterprises as well as the rapidly rising enterprise-specific patent application and patent grant rates over time. We note that the steep enterprise-specific CNIPA patent grant-real R&D capital lines in Figure 9.7 are not dissimilar to the corresponding economy-specific lines in Figure 7.8. For US enterprises, Mainland China is a large and rapidly growing new market and CNIPA patenting is a new game, leading to continuing large increases in patent applications (and patent grants), based in part on their reserve pools of not-yet-CNIPA-patented discoveries and inventions, which are not affected by the current levels of real R&D capital stock. As in Chapter 7, we do not believe that the actual elasticity of patent grants with respect to real R&D capital can be so high. The high estimate is probably an artefact of the rapid increases in the CNIPA patent application and patent grant rates of the selected US enterprises.

9.4 Summary

From our analysis of the data from an admittedly limited number of Chinese and US enterprises, the evidence suggests that there exists a positive and monotonic dependence of the number of patent grants on the quantity of the real R&D capital stock at the microeconomic level as at the macroeconomic level. In addition, there also appears to be some degree of economies of scale in the creation of patents from R&D activities at the enterprise level. However, there is also some evidence that real R&D capital may have a useful life beyond 10 years, depending on the share of basic research in total R&D expenditures, the verification of which will have to await further study.

Appendix

Table A9.1: The estimated quantities of real R&D capital stock, selected Chinese and US enterprises (billion 2019 US dollars)

	Chinese Enterprises			US Enterprises					
	China Petroleum and Chemical Corporation	**Huawei Technologies Co., LTD.**	**ZTE Corporation**	**Apple Inc.**	**General Electric Company**	**Hewlett-Packard Corporation**	**International Business Machines Corporation**	**Microsoft Corporation**	**Qualcomm**
1991				10.933		12.761		0.888	0.088
1992				10.835		13.982		1.201	0.118
1993				10.756	43.790	15.287		1.668	0.148
1994				10.764	42.597	16.629	58.147	2.268	0.178
1995				10.588	41.116	18.201	59.295	3.014	0.239
1996				10.489	39.962	19.980	59.885	4.057	0.341
1997				10.368	38.861	22.154	61.041	5.850	0.556
1998				10.063	37.829	24.584	62.296	8.170	0.856
1999	1.200		0.027	9.509	36.926	27.132	63.597	11.234	1.292
2000	1.387		0.053	9.020	36.201	28.008	65.335	14.480	1.724
2001	1.723		0.098	8.664	35.736	28.997	66.534	18.464	2.041
2002	1.897		0.370	8.403	35.470	29.857	67.329	22.783	2.421
2003	2.112		0.634	8.181	35.570	31.540	67.180	26.475	2.805

2004	2.450		0.970	8.004	35.627	33.354	67.371	30.167	3.237
2005	2.574		1.424	7.854	36.160	34.665	68.152	37.401	3.867
2006	2.317		1.740	7.756	36.946	35.683	68.844	41.496	4.780
2007	2.738		2.204	7.869	36.731	36.594	69.577	45.559	6.220
2008	3.179	5.867	2.654	8.032	36.713	37.321	70.094	49.653	7.820
2009	3.525	7.310	3.163	8.550	36.641	37.811	70.635	54.416	9.756
2010	3.914	9.171	3.970	9.272	36.879	37.363	70.454	59.629	11.666
2011	4.402	11.462	4.862	10.427	37.750	37.086	70.453	63.852	13.364
2012	4.779	14.302	5.805	12.166	39.243	37.103	70.573	67.821	15.457
2013	5.262	17.764	6.676	14.748	40.397	37.211	70.595	72.061	18.309
2014	5.756	21.070	7.198	18.214	41.483	36.951	69.877	76.349	21.963
2015	6.076	25.471	7.913	22.941	41.924	34.663	68.783	81.052	25.703
2016	6.369	32.418	9.065	29.301	42.290	32.475	67.534	85.870	29.023
2017	6.665	41.170	9.994	37.038	43.091		66.861	90.013	31.590
2018	6.966	50.556	10.946	45.404	43.133		66.001	94.599	34.148
2019	7.426	60.260	11.437	55.348	42.293		64.873	100.122	36.456
2020	8.028	73.077	12.089	66.030	41.179		64.375	106.985	38.209

Source: Authors' calculations. The values of R&D expenditures for Chinese and US enterprises are collected from Osiris Publicly Listed Companies Worldwide Database.

Table A9.2: The number of USPTO patent grants, selected Chinese and US enterprises

	Chinese Enterprises			US Enterprises					
	China Petroleum and Chemical Corporation	Huawei Technologies Co., LTD.	ZTE Corporation	Apple Inc.	General Electric Company	Hewlett-Packard Corporation	International Business Machines Corporation	Microsoft Corporation	Qualcomm
1995				107	758	470	1,383	46	
1996				169	819	501	1,867	97	48
1997				206	664	530	1,724	199	45
1998				256	729	805	2,657	334	82
1999				169	699	850	2,756	352	110
2000				85	787	901	2,886	344	110
2001				97	1,107	978	3,411	396	173
2002				76	1,416	1,061	3,288	499	196
2003				80	1,139	1,292	3,415	499	178
2004				94	976	1,775	3,248	629	283
2005				85	904	1,790	2,941	746	200
2006				106	1,051	2,099	3,621	1,463	399
2007				118	911	1,466	3,125	1,637	278
2008		48		185	911	1,422	4,169	2,026	286

2009		82		289	976	1,269	4,887	2,901	356
2010		251		563	1,222	1,480	5,866	3,086	657
2011		356		676	1,444	1,307	6,148	2,309	923
2012		532	101	1,136	1,650	1,393	6,457	2,610	1,292
2013		685	273	1,775	1,737	1,358	6,788	2,659	2,103
2014		773	705	2,003	1,858	1,573	7,481	2,829	2,586
2015	40	799	416	1,937	1,756	1,304	7,309	2,408	2,900
2016	44	1,198	472	2,101	1,644		8,023	2,398	2,897
2017	48	1,472	407	2,225	1,575		8,996	2,440	2,626
2018		1,680	389	2,147	1,584		9,088	2,353	2,300
2019		2,417	263	2,483	1,816		9,253	3,080	2,348

Source: USPTO (https://www.uspto.gov/web/offices/ac/ido/oeip/taf/reports_topo.htm).

Table A9.3: The number of CNIPA patent grants, selected Chinese and US enterprises

	Chinese Enterprises			US Enterprises					
	China Petroleum and Chemical Corporation	**Huawei Technologies Co., LTD.**	**ZTE Corporation**	**Apple Inc.**	**General Electric Company**	**Hewlett-Packard Corporation**	**International Business Machines Corporation**	**Microsoft Corporation**	**Qualcomm**
1987							1		
1988	1						4		
1989	5				18	1	18		
1990	4			1	24	4	21		
1991	4			0	11	4	18		
1992	12			3	28	8	28		
1993	12			0	16	6	39		
1994	26			1	7	0	30		1
1995	28			0	9	0	30		0
1996	21			0	8	1	18		1
1997	22			0	8	1	11		3
1998	19	1		0	10	1	19		1
1999	58	0		0	14	0	30		0
2000	167	8	1	0	25	1	59		5
2001	202	10	1	0	27	5	31		16

2002	179	16	6	3	29	24	119		37
2003	480	126	87	16	53	42	273	11	105
2004	546	501	82	20	52	61	385	20	206
2005	547	487	39	17	74	84	243	24	152
2006	458	448	250	25	64	66	299	28	132
2007	363	935	289	22	118	77	407	70	136
2008	425	2,342	581	45	165	117	674	154	190
2009	**474**	**3,400**	**1,359**	**59**	**219**	**202**	**912**	**342**	**300**
2010	**519**	**2,503**	**2,004**	**53**	**205**	**172**	**699**	**422**	**340**
2011	548	2,475	2,657	70	275	162	470	339	306
2012	992	2,469	2,276	130	396	239	492	496	603
2013	1,772	2,177	1,286	209	510	175	319	542	1,040
2014	1,958	2,149	1,832	287	489	164	277	437	1,029
2015	2,767	2,172	1,978	410	693	172	392	690	1,305
2016	2,910	2,704	1,609	502	1,013	272	736	840	1,596
2017	2,809	3,092	1,634	510	634	210	788	520	1,228
2018	3,013	3,318	1,797	656	450	254	458	589	1,651
2019	3,012	4,530	1,459	834	496	328	269	815	1,586
2020	2,954	6,413	1,348	581	515	400	105	733	1,158

Source: Patsnap database (https://analytics.zhihuiya.com/search/input#/simple).

Part Four

Are There Laws of Innovation?

Chapter 10

The Econometric Models

The annual numbers of patent applications submitted and patent grants received by an economy is a useful indicator of its degree of success in Research and Development (R&D) activities because a patent application or grant must have been based on some underlying original discovery or invention. We begin with the assumption that there exist functions, possibly specific to each individual economy, relating the annual numbers of patent applications to the annual quantities of real R&D capital stock, which may be taken to be a measure of the capacity of each economy for conducting R&D and achieving successful outcomes at any given time. In turn, the annual numbers of patent grants awarded to each economy may depend on its annual numbers of patent applications, appropriately lagged (the average lag will be assumed to be 1 year in this study). These functions will be referred to as the "patent application production functions" and the "patent grant production functions" respectively. Indirectly, the annual numbers of patent grants are also functions of the lagged annual quantities of real R&D capital stock.

There is of course no *a priori* reason why the same functional relationships should apply to both domestic and foreign patent applications and grants across all the economies included in our study. This is especially true for domestic patent applications and grants because the domestic propensities to apply for as well as to grant patents may depend very much on the domestic conditions, cultures, customs, markets, policies, practices, procedures and standards, in addition to the domestic capacities for R&D, proxied by the quantities of their respective real R&D capital stocks. For a variety of reasons that are discussed in Chapter 3, the domestic patent application behaviour and the United States Patent and Trademark Office (USPTO) patent application behaviour can be quite different in some economies, especially in the ones with relatively small home markets, and often do not depend solely on the qualities and quantities of the outcomes of their respective R&D activities. However, for the USPTO patent applications and grants, it is more plausible for the same functional relationships to hold across economies since the United States (US) market itself is important for almost all economies and the same procedures and standards have been and are used by the USPTO to assess the quality of the patent applications received from applicants in different parts of the world.

As a result of these considerations, we shall focus our econometric analysis on only USPTO patent applications and grants and not the respective domestic patent applications and grants. Even then, the propensity to apply for a USPTO patent, given an original discovery or invention of a certain quality, may still vary significantly across economies and change over time for different reasons. In particular, this is especially likely to be true for economies in which the annual numbers of domestic patent applications are smaller than their annual numbers of USPTO patent applications. It is reasonable to assume that if a discovery or invention is good enough for a USPTO patent application, it should be good enough, in terms of quality, for a domestic patent application. Moreover, the cost of application, and subsequent maintenance if granted, of a USPTO patent is in general much more expensive than that of a domestic patent, which should bias the application in favour of a domestic patent. However, as Figure 5.4 of Chapter 5 shows, for six of the 12 economies included in our study — Canada, Hong Kong, China, Italy, Singapore, Taiwan, China, and the United Kingdom (UK), the annual number of USPTO patent applications has exceeded the annual number of domestic applications quite regularly. Thus, the patent applications of these economies, both domestic and foreign, must have been subject to considerations extraneous to the intrinsic quality of their discoveries or inventions, and their annual numbers are therefore potentially biased indicators of their degrees of R&D success. Our econometric analysis will therefore be restricted to USPTO patent applications and grants of the six economies in which the annual numbers of domestic patent applications exceed the annual numbers of USPTO patent applications, that is, Mainland China, France, Germany, Japan, South Korea, and the US. Moreover, in order to assure comparability and consistency of the data over time and across economies, we have used only the data between certain years for the different economies in the analyses in this chapter and Chapter 11. The beginning and ending years of the data used for each economy in these two chapters are presented in Table A10.1.

10.1 A Model for USPTO Patent Applications

First, we formulate a model for USPTO patent applications. In Figure 10.1, the natural logarithm of the annual number of USPTO patent applications of each of the six economies is plotted against the natural logarithm of the

Figure 10.1: The natural logarithm of the annual number of USPTO patent applications versus the natural logarithm of the quantity of real R&D capital stock

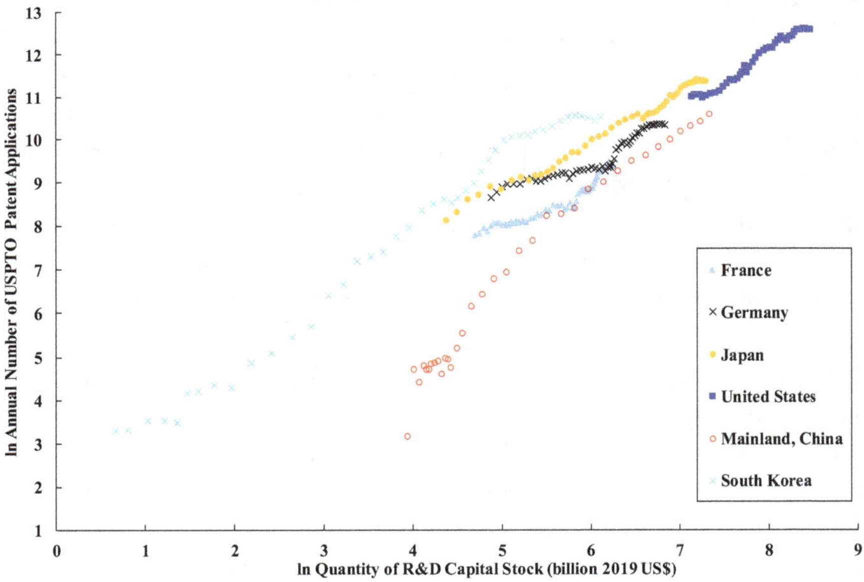

Source: Authors' calculations. Data on the numbers of USPTO patent applications are from Table A5.1 of Chapter 5 and data on the quantity of real R&D capital stocks from Table A3.2 of Chapter 3.

respective quantity of real R&D capital stock in each year. Figure 10.1 provides prima facie evidence that there exists a stable, positive relationship between the annual number of USPTO patent applications and the quantity of real R&D capital stock across the six economies and over time. However, there appears to be some divergence among the economies, especially between the developed economies on the one hand and the developing and newly industrialised economies of East Asia on the other.

In general, the number of USPTO patent applications in the *i*th economy in year t, YA_{USit}, may be taken to be a measure of the outcome resulting from R&D activities in that year. It may be expressed as a function of K_{it}, the quantity of real R&D capital stock in the *i*th economy in year t. Thus,

$$YA_{USit} = F_i(K_{it}), \tag{10.1}$$

where $F_i(K_{it})$ is the "patent application production function" that relates the annual number of USPTO patent applications to the quantity of real R&D capital stock in the *i*th economy in that year. Note that the function $F_i(.)$, subscripted by *i*, may vary with the particular economy, but is assumed not to vary over time.

We assume, however, that after an economy-specific and time-varying transformation, YA_{USit}, the measured annual number of USPTO patent applications, may be converted into an "efficiency-equivalent" or "quality-equivalent" number of USPTO patent applications, YA^*_{USit}, that is comparable across economies. Thus, for example, it is possible that one USPTO patent application submitted by a US resident is equivalent to two USPTO patent applications submitted by a Chinese resident in terms of quality or vice versa. However, YA^*_{USit} is not directly observable. It is assumed that YA^*_{USit} is related to the directly observable YA_{USit} by an economy- and time-specific augmentation factor A_{AUSi} (t):

$$YA^*_{USit} = A_{AUSi}(t) YA_{USit}. \tag{10.2}$$

More specifically, $A_{AUSi}(t)$, the patent application augmentation factor of the *i*th economy, is assumed to take the constant exponential form, so that

$$YA^*_{USit} = A_{AUSi}\exp(c_{USi}t)\ YA_{USit}, \tag{10.3}$$

where A_{AUSi} and c_{USi} are constants that may vary with i, that is, they depend on the specific economy. A_{AUSi} may be identified as the augmentation level parameter and c_{USi} as the augmentation rate parameter of the patent application augmentation factor of the ith economy. A_{AUSi} is a positive constant that may be greater than, equal to, or less than one, and is the "efficiency-equivalent" conversion ratio of the USPTO patent applications of the ith economy at t = 0, and c_{USi} is a constant that may be greater than, equal to, or less than zero, and is the rate of change of the "efficiency-equivalent" conversion ratio of the ith economy per unit time. We note that, without loss of generality, for one economy, A_{AUSi} can be taken to be unity; this is equivalent to choosing that economy's number of patent applications at t = 0 to be the numeraire.

Similarly, the measured quantity of real R&D capital stock of the ith economy, K_{it}, may also be converted into an "efficiency-equivalent" or "quality-equivalent" quantity of real R&D capital stock, K^*_{it}, that is also comparable across economies. Specifically, it is assumed that

$$K^*_{it} = A_{Ki}(t)K_{it} = A_{Ki}\exp(c_{Ki}t)\ K_{it}, \tag{10.4}$$

where A_{Ki} and c_{Ki} are constants that may be identified as respectively the constant capital augmentation level and rate parameters that may vary with the particular economy. We also note that, without loss of generality, for one economy, A_{Ki} can be taken to be unity (so that $\ln A_{Ki} = 0$); this is equivalent to choosing that economy's quantity of real R&D capital stock at t = 0 to be the numeraire.

Since both the "efficiency-equivalent" quantities of patent applications, YA^*_{USit}'s, and real R&D capital stocks, K^{**}_{it}'s, are supposedly comparable across economies, we can assume that they are related by a common production function $F(.)$ that applies across economies:

$$YA^*_{USit} = F(K^*_{it}), \tag{10.5}$$

where $F(.)$ is the so-called "meta-production function".[1] What this means is that if we can measure the outputs and the inputs of each economy appropriately, so that they are "efficiency-equivalent" or "quality-equivalent", they can be related by the same functional relationship across economies. In our empirical implementation, it is assumed that the function $F(.)$ in Eq. (10.5) takes the transcendental logarithmic form, introduced by Christensen, Jorgenson and Lau (1971, 1973), so that

$$\ln YA^{*}_{USit} = \ln A_0 + \alpha_K \ln K^{*}_{it} + \frac{1}{2}\mathrm{B}_{KK}(\ln K^{*}_{it})^2. \tag{10.6}$$

By substituting Eq. (10.3) into Eq. (10.6), we obtain

$$\ln YA_{USit} + \ln A_{AUSi} + c_{USi}\mathrm{t} = \ln A_0 + \alpha_K \ln K^{*}_{it} + \frac{1}{2}\mathrm{B}_{KK}(\ln K^{*}_{it})^2. \tag{10.7}$$

By substituting Eq. (10.4) into Eq. (10.7), and rearranging, we obtain

$$\begin{aligned}\ln YA_{USit} &= -\ln A_{AUSi} - c_{USi}\mathrm{t} + \ln A_0 + \alpha_K(\ln A_{Ki} + c_{Ki}\mathrm{t} + \ln K_{it}) \\ &\quad + \frac{1}{2}\mathrm{B}_{KK}(\ln A_{Ki} + c_{Ki}\mathrm{t} + \ln K_{it})^2 \end{aligned} \tag{10.8}$$

$$\begin{aligned} &= (-\ln A_{AUSi} + \ln A_0 + \alpha_K \ln A_{Ki} + \frac{1}{2}\mathrm{B}_{KK}(\ln A_{Ki})^2) \\ &\quad + (\alpha_K + \mathrm{B}_{KK}\ln A_{Ki})\ln K_{it} \\ &\quad + (-c_{USi} + (\alpha_K + \mathrm{B}_{KK}\ln A_{Ki})c_{Ki})\mathrm{t} + \mathrm{B}_{KK}c_{Ki}\ln K_{it}.\mathrm{t} \\ &\quad + \frac{1}{2}\mathrm{B}_{KK}(\ln K_{it})^2 + \frac{1}{2}\mathrm{B}_{KK}c_{Ki}^2\mathrm{t}^2. \end{aligned} \tag{10.9}$$

Equation (10.9) may be simplified into

$$\begin{aligned}\ln YA_{USit} &= A^{*}_{AUSi} + (\alpha_K + \mathrm{B}_{KK}\ln A_{Ki})\ln K_{it} + c^{*}_{USi}\mathrm{t} \\ &\quad + \mathrm{B}_{KK}c_{Ki}\ln K_{it}.\mathrm{t} + \frac{1}{2}\mathrm{B}_{KK}(\ln K_{it})^2 + \frac{1}{2}\mathrm{B}_{KK}c_{Ki}^2\mathrm{t}^2, \end{aligned} \tag{10.10}$$

[1] However, this assumption of the existence of a meta-production function can and will be explicitly tested statistically.

where

$$A^*_{AUSi} \equiv (-\ln A_{AUSi} + \ln A_0 + \alpha_K \ln A_{Ki} + \frac{1}{2}\mathrm{B}_{KK}(\ln A_{Ki})^2),$$

$$c^*_{USi} \equiv (-c_{USi} + (\alpha_K + \mathrm{B}_{KK} \ln A_{Ki})c_{Ki}). \tag{10.11}$$

We note that the two parameters, A^*_{AUSi} and c^*_{USi}, are unconstrained across economies, since $\mathrm{In}A_{AUSi}$ and c_{USi} are free to assume any value for each economy, but α_K and B_{KK} must be identical across economies.

Equation (10.10) is written entirely in terms of directly observable variables YA_{USit} and K_{it} rather than the unobservable variables YA^*_{USit} and K^*_{it}, and hence can be directly estimated from the empirical data. However, we note that in Eq. (10.10), the square of the coefficient of the fourth term, $\mathrm{ln}K_{it}.\mathrm{t}$, divided by the coefficient of the fifth term, $\frac{1}{2}(\ln K_{it})^2$, must be equal to the coefficient of the sixth term, $\frac{1}{2}\mathrm{t}^2$. This is a direct consequence of the meta-production function model and implies a nonlinear restriction on these parameters for each economy, which will be referred to as the "First Necessary Condition" for the validity of the meta-production function model.

Moreover, Eq. (10.10) further implies that coefficients of the fifth term, $\frac{1}{2}(\ln K_{it})^2$, B_{KK}'s, should be identical across all economies. This is the second necessary condition for the validity of the meta-production function model. These latter cross-economy restrictions will be referred to as the "Equality" restrictions. The "Equality" hypothesis is tested across all economies that satisfy the first necessary condition, with the restrictions implied by the "First Necessary Condition" as the maintained hypothesis. If both the "First Necessary Condition" and the "Equality" restrictions are accepted, the validity of the meta-production function model is confirmed, and these restrictions will be imposed in the further estimation of the model.

In principle, Eq. (10.10) can be directly estimated individually or jointly for all six economies. However, in order to minimise the possibility of serial correlation of the stochastic disturbance terms, Eq. (10.10) is estimated in its first-differenced form in the empirical implementation. Lagging Eq. (10.10) by one period, we have

$$\ln YA_{USi(t-1)} = A^{*}_{AUSi} + (\alpha_K + B_{KK}\ln A_{Ki})\ln K_{i(t-1)} + c^{*}_{USi}(t-1) + B_{KK}c_{Ki}\ln K_{i(t-1)}.(t-1) + \frac{1}{2}B_{KK}(\ln K_{i(t-1)})^2 + \frac{1}{2}B_{KK}c^2_{Ki}(t-1)^2. \quad (10.12)$$

Subtracting Eq. (10.12) from Eq. (10.10), we obtain

$$\begin{aligned}\ln YA_{USit} - \ln YA_{USi(t-1)} &= c^{*}_{USi} + (\alpha_K + B_{KK}\ln A_{Ki})(\ln K_{it} - \ln K_{i(t-1)}) \\ &\quad + B_{KK}c_{Ki}(\ln K_{it}.t - \ln K_{i(t-1)}.(t-1)) + \frac{1}{2}B_{KK}((\ln K_{it})^2 - (\ln K_{i(t-1)}))^2 \\ &\quad + B_{KK}c^2_{Ki}t - \frac{1}{2}B_{KK}c^2_{Ki} \\ &= c^{**}_{USi} + (\alpha_K + B_{KK}\ln A_{Ki})(\ln K_{it} - \ln K_{i(t-1)}) \\ &\quad + B_{KK}c_{Ki}(\ln K_{it}.t - \ln K_{i(t-1)}.(t-1)) \\ &\quad + B_{KK}c^2_{Ki}t + \frac{1}{2}B_{KK}((\ln K_{it})^2 - (\ln K_{i(t-1)})^2),\end{aligned} \quad (10.13)$$

where $c^{**}_{USi} \equiv c^{*}_{USi} - \frac{1}{2}B_{KK}c^2_{Ki} \equiv (-c_{USi} + (\alpha_K + B_{KK}\ln A_{Ki})c_{Ki}) - \frac{1}{2}B_{KK}c^2_{Ki}$. Equation (10.13) is then the actual basic estimating equation for the model of USPTO patent applications. We note that there are five terms on the right-hand side of Eq. (10.13). They are the constant term, ($\ln K_{it} - \ln K_{i(t-1)}$), ($\ln K_{it}.t - \ln K_{i(t-1)}.(t-1)$), t, and $\frac{1}{2}((\ln K_{it})^2 - (\ln K_{i(t-1)})^2)$. However, not all of the coefficients of the different terms are independent. The square of the coefficient of ($\ln K_{it}.t - \ln K_{i(t-1)}.(t-1)$), $B_{KK}c_{Ki}$, divided by the coefficient of $\frac{1}{2}((\ln K_{it})^2 - (\ln K_{i(t-1)})^2)$, B_{KK}, must be equal to the coefficient of the time trend, $B_{KK}c^2_{Ki}$. These nonlinear restrictions are precisely the equivalent of the "First Necessary Condition" in Eq. (10.10) in the first-differenced form.

Equation (10.13) may first be estimated without imposing any restrictions on the parameters. This may be referred to as the "Unconstrained Model". In this unconstrained form, Eq. (10.13) is linear in all its parameters. The "First Necessary Condition", which implies one restriction per economy, may then be individually tested for all of the six included economies. If this restriction is rejected for any economy, that economy cannot be included in the same meta-production function model as the other economies. Equation (10.13) may then be estimated jointly for all six included economies after heteroscedastic adjustments,[2] both with and without the six restrictions implied by the "First Necessary Condition". The difference in the sum of squares of residuals between the unconstrained and the restricted estimation, divided by the relevant degrees of freedom, is asymptotically distributed as a χ^2 variable. A large value of the χ^2 variable implies rejection of the null hypothesis being tested.

Subject to the acceptance of the joint test for the "First Necessary Condition", we proceed to test the "Equality" hypothesis of identical B_{KK}'s across all economies, conditional on this joint hypothesis. If both tests are accepted, the validity of the meta-production function model is confirmed. We then proceed to test whether $B_{KK} = 0$. $B_{KK} = 0$ implies that the elasticity of the annual number of USPTO patent applications with respect to the quantity of real R&D capital stock is a constant that is identical across economies. There is a question of how many restrictions are implied by the hypothesis of $B_{KK} = 0$. In principle, it is only a restriction on a single parameter because only B_{KK} is involved. However, assuming the validity of the meta-production function model, with six economies, there are 19 independent parameters in Eq. (10.13). With the restriction of $B_{KK} = 0$, there are only seven independent parameters left to be estimated, so that the effective number of restrictions is actually 12 (19 – 7). We shall test this hypothesis as if it consists of 12 restrictions.

If the hypothesis of $B_{KK} = 0$ is rejected, we proceed to test the following specific hypotheses on the other parameters: (1) identical c_{Ki}'s across economies; (2) identical A_{Ki}'s across economies (implying $\ln A_{Ki} = 0$, all i, since $A_{Ki} = 1$ for the numeraire economy); and (3) identical c_{USi}'s across economies. However, if the hypothesis of $B_{KK} = 0$ cannot be rejected, the parameters of the USPTO patent application and real R&D capital augmentation factors may not be identifiable, and these additional hypotheses (1)–(3) cannot be tested. Thus, the hypothesis of $B_{KK} = 0$ is pivotal to our further analysis.

---

[2]The heteroskedastic adjustments are made using the estimated standard errors of the stochastic disturbance terms of Eq. (10.13) for the individual economies.

Subject to the outcomes of these tests, the implied restrictions accepted are imposed on the six economies. We can then make use of the restricted parameter estimates of Eq. (10.13) to recover the economy-specific USPTO patent application augmentation rate parameters, c_{USi}'s, for all six economies.[3] However, the recovery of the economy-specific USPTO patent application augmentation level parameters, A_{AUSi}'s, requires the use of the non-first-differenced Eq. (10.10). From Eqs. (10.10) and (10.11), we have

$$\begin{aligned}
&\ln YA_{USit} - (\alpha_K + \mathrm{B}_{KK} \ln A_{Ki}) \ln K_{it} - c^*_{USi}\mathrm{t} - \mathrm{B}_{KK} \mathrm{c}_{Ki} \ln K_{it}.\mathrm{t} \\
&\quad - \frac{1}{2}\mathrm{B}_{KK}(\ln K_{it})^2 - \frac{1}{2}\mathrm{B}_{KK} c^2_{Ki}\mathrm{t}^2 \\
&\quad = A^*_{AUSi}, \\
&\quad = -\ln A_{AUSi} + \ln A_0 + \alpha_K \ln A_{Ki} + \frac{1}{2}\mathrm{B}_{KK}(\ln A_{Ki})^2,
\end{aligned} \tag{10.14}$$

or

$$\begin{aligned}
&\ln YA_{USit} - (\alpha_K + \mathrm{B}_{KK} \ln A_{Ki}) \ln K_{it} - c^*_{USi}\mathrm{t} - \mathrm{B}_{KK} \mathrm{c}_{Ki} \ln K_{it}.\mathrm{t} \\
&\quad - \frac{1}{2}\mathrm{B}_{KK}(\ln K_{it})^2 \\
&\quad - \frac{1}{2}\mathrm{B}_{KK} c^2_{Ki}\mathrm{t}^2 - \alpha_K \ln A_{Ki} - \frac{1}{2}\mathrm{B}_{KK}(\ln A_{Ki})^2 \\
&\quad = -\ln A_{AUSi} + \ln A_0.
\end{aligned} \tag{10.15}$$

Equation (10.15) may be used to generate estimates for the A_{AUSi}'s by substituting the estimated values of the parameters on the left-hand side and then running a regression with only economy-specific constant terms on the right-hand side.[4]

If $\mathrm{B}_{KK} = 0$, then Eq. (10.10) reduces to

$$\begin{aligned}
\ln YA_{USit} &= A^*_{AUSi} + c^*_{USi}\mathrm{t} + \alpha_K \ln K_{it}, \\
&= (-\ln A_{AUSi} + \ln \mathrm{A}_0 + \alpha_K \ln A_{Ki}) + (-c_{USi} + \alpha_K\, c_{Ki})\mathrm{t} \\
&\quad + \alpha_K \ln K_{it},
\end{aligned} \tag{10.16}$$

---

[3] On the assumption that B_{KK} is not equal to zero.

[4] We should bear in mind that $A_{AUSi} = 1$ for the numeraire economy.

in which case it is clearly not possible to separately identify the level and the rate parameters of the USPTO patent application and the real R&D capital augmentation factors for each economy, and our first-differenced estimating Eq. (10.13) reduces to

$$\ln YA_{USit} - \ln YA_{USi(t-1)} = c^{*}_{USi} + \alpha_K (\ln K_{it} - \ln K_{i(t-1)}), \qquad (10.17)$$

from which c^{*}_{USi} $(= -c_{USi} + \alpha_K c_{Ki})$ can be estimated.

10.2 A Model for USPTO Patent Grants

Next, we derive a model for USPTO patent grants. In Figure 10.2, the natural logarithm of the annual number of USPTO patent grants is plotted against the natural logarithm of the annual number of USPTO patent

Figure 10.2: The natural logarithm of the annual number of USPTO patent grants versus the natural logarithm of the annual number of USPTO patent applications, lagged 1 year

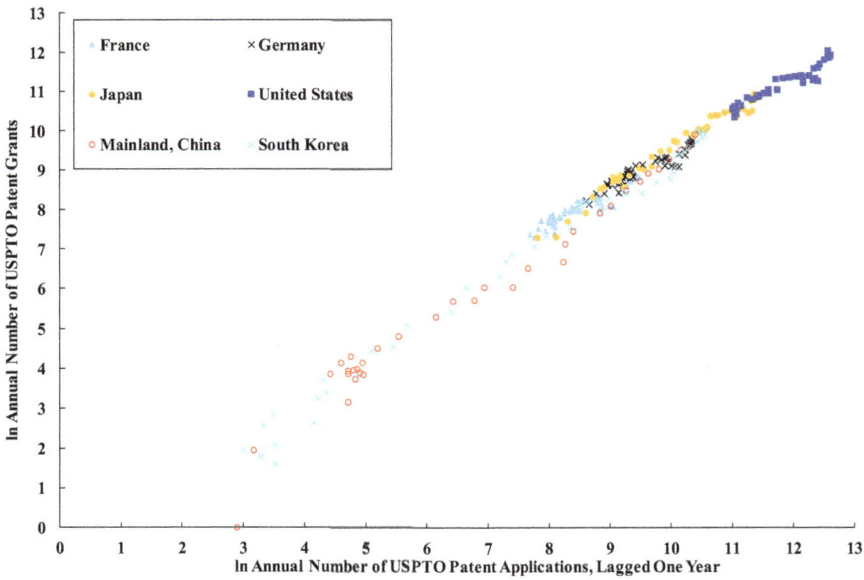

Source: Authors' calculations. Data on the numbers of USPTO patent applications and grants are from Tables A5.1 and A5.2 of Chapter 5, respectively.

applications, lagged 1 year, for all six economies. Figure 10.2 also provides prima facie evidence that there is a stable and positive relationship between the annual number of USPTO patent grants and the annual number of USPTO applications, lagged 1 year, across economies and over time.

We begin with the assumption that the number of USPTO patent grants awarded to the *i*th economy in year t, YG_{USit}, may be expressed as a function of $YA_{USi(t-1)}$, the number of USPTO patent applications from the *i*th economy in year (t – 1). Thus,

$$YG_{USit} = F_i(YA_{USi(t-1)}), \tag{10.18}$$

where $F_i(K_{it})$ is the "patent application production function" that relates the annual number of USPTO patent grants to the annual number of USPTO patent applications in the previous year. Moreover, we assume that there also exist economy-specific and time-varying transformations such that YG_{USit}, the measured annual number of USPTO patent grants, may be converted into an "efficiency-equivalent" or "quality-equivalent" annual number of USPTO patent grants, YG^*_{USit}, that is comparable across economies. More specifically,

$$YG^*_{USit} = A_{GUSi}(\mathrm{t})\, YG_{USit}, \tag{10.19}$$

where $A_{GUSi}(\mathrm{t})$ is the patent grant augmentation factor of the *i*th economy. $A_{GUSi}(\mathrm{t})$ is assumed to take the constant exponential form, so that

$$YG^*_{USit} = A_{GUSi}\exp(c_{GUSi}\mathrm{t})\, YG_{USit}. \tag{10.20}$$

We already have, from Eq. (10.3) above, the conversion factor between the measured number of USPTO patent applications and the "efficiency-equivalent" number of USPTO patent applications:

$$YA^*_{USit} = A_{AUSi}\exp(c_{USi}\mathrm{t})\, YA_{USit}. \tag{10.3}$$

As the "efficiency-equivalent" numbers of both USPTO patent grants and patent applications are available, we assume that there exists a common USPTO patent grant production function linking the "efficiency-equivalent" numbers of patent grants and patent applications, lagged 1 year, for all six economies:

$$YG^{*}_{USit} = F(YA^{*}_{USi(t-1)}). \tag{10.21}$$

In our empirical implementation, it is assumed that the function $F(.)$ in Eq. (10.21) also takes the transcendental logarithmic form, so that

$$\begin{aligned}\ln YG^{*}_{USit} &= \ln G_{US0} + \alpha_{GUSA} \ln YA^{*}_{USi(t-1)} \\ &\quad + \frac{1}{2}\mathrm{B}_{GUSKK}(\ln YA^{*}_{USi(t-1)})^{2}.\end{aligned} \tag{10.22}$$

Substituting Eqs. (10.20) and (10.3) into Eq. (10.22), we obtain

$$\begin{aligned}\ln YG_{USit} &= -\ln A_{GUSi} - c_{GUSi}\mathrm{t} + \ln G_{US0} \\ &\quad + \alpha_{GUSA}(\ln A_{AUSi} + c_{USi}(\mathrm{t}-1) + \ln YA_{USi(t-1)}) \\ &\quad + \frac{1}{2}\mathrm{B}_{GUSKK}(\ln A_{AUSi} + c_{USi}(\mathrm{t}-1) + \ln YA_{USi(t-1)})^{2}\end{aligned} \tag{10.23}$$

$$\begin{aligned}&= (-\ln A_{GUSi} + \ln G_{US0} + \alpha_{GUSA}(\ln A_{AUSi} - c_{USi}) \\ &\quad + \frac{1}{2}\mathrm{B}_{GUSKK}(\ln A_{AUSi} - c_{USi})^{2}) \\ &\quad + (\alpha_{GUSA} + \mathrm{B}_{GUSKK}(\ln A_{AUSi} - c_{USi}))\ln YA_{USi(t-1)} \\ &\quad + (-c_{GUSi} + (\alpha_{GUSA} + \mathrm{B}_{GUSKK}(\ln A_{AUSi} - c_{USi}))c_{USi})\mathrm{t} \\ &\quad + \mathrm{B}_{GUSKK}c_{USi}\ln YA_{USi(t-1)}.\mathrm{t} \\ &\quad + \frac{1}{2}\mathrm{B}_{GUSKK}(\ln YA_{USi(t-1)})^{2} + \frac{1}{2}\mathrm{B}_{GUSKK}c^{2}_{USi}\mathrm{t}^{2}.\end{aligned} \tag{10.24}$$

Equation (10.24) may be simplified into

$$\begin{aligned}\ln YG_{USit} &= A^{*}_{GUSi} + c^{*}_{GUSi}\mathrm{t} + (\alpha_{GUSA} + \mathrm{B}_{GUSKK}(\ln A_{AUSi} - c_{USi})) \\ &\quad \times \ln YA_{USi(t-1)} + \mathrm{B}_{GUSKK}c_{USi}\ln YA_{USi(t-1)}.\mathrm{t} \\ &\quad + \frac{1}{2}\mathrm{B}_{GUSKK}(\ln YA_{USi(t-1)})^{2} + \frac{1}{2}\mathrm{B}_{GUSKK}c^{2}_{USi}\mathrm{t}^{2},\end{aligned} \tag{10.25}$$

where

$$A^*_{GUSi} \equiv (-\ln A_{GUSi} + \ln G_{US0} + \alpha_{GUSA}(\ln A_{AUSi} - c_{USi})$$
$$+ \frac{1}{2}\mathrm{B}_{GUSKK}(\ln A_{AUSi} - c_{USi})^2); \text{ and}$$
$$c^*_{GUSi} \equiv (-c_{GUSi} + (\alpha_{GUSA} + \mathrm{B}_{GUSKK}(\ln A_{AUSi} - c_{USi}))c_{USi}). \qquad (10.26)$$

As before, for one economy, A_{GUSi} can be chosen to be unity, and hence $\ln A_{GUSi} = 0$ for that economy. This is equivalent to measuring all the USPTO patent grants using this economy's number of USPTO patent grants at $t = 0$ as the numeraire.

However, Eq. (10.25) should not be estimated solely on its own because the annual number of USPTO patents granted to each economy also depends on the total patent grant rate of the USPTO, g_t, which fluctuates over time. There are two possible ways to measure the USPTO total patent grant rate: the first is the total number of patents granted divided by the total number of applications submitted, appropriately lagged, and the second is the total number of patents granted to non-US applicants, divided by the total number of applications submitted by non-US applicants, also appropriately lagged. This variable controls for the changes in the behaviour and practices, if any, of the USPTO over time. In Chapter 5, we have found that the USPTO grant rate fluctuates significantly over time, thus affecting the number of patent grants awarded to the applicants independently of their numbers of patent applications (see Figure 5.10 of Chapter 5). However, Figure 5.11 of Chapter 5, which presents the same intertemporal fluctuations in the USPTO grant rates, also shows that there is virtually no difference between the two alternative measures of the USPTO total patent grant rate since 1977. We shall therefore use only the total success rate for all economies in our empirical analysis. The model of USPTO patent grants in Eq. (10.25), with the addition of the USPTO total grant rate variable in its natural logarithmic form, $\ln g_t$, is jointly estimated for all six economies in our study. Thus,

$$\begin{aligned}\ln YG_{USit} &= A^{*}_{GUSi} + c^{*}_{GUSi}\mathrm{t} + (\alpha_{GUSA} + \mathrm{B}_{GUSKK}(\ln A_{AUSi} - c_{USi}))\\&\quad\times \ln YA_{USi(t-1)} + \mathrm{B}_{GUSKK}c_{USi}\ln YA_{USi(t-1)}.\mathrm{t}\\&\quad+\frac{1}{2}\mathrm{B}_{GUSKK}(\ln YA_{USi(t-1)})^2 + \frac{1}{2}\mathrm{B}_{GUSKK}c^2_{USi}\mathrm{t}^2\\&\quad+\delta_i \ln g_t.\end{aligned} \tag{10.27}$$

Equation (10.27) is then the basic estimating equation. As before, for one economy, A_{GUSi} can be chosen to be unity, and hence $\ln A_{GUSi} = 0$. This is equivalent to measuring all the USPTO patent grants using this economy's number of USPTO patent grants at $t = 0$ as the numeraire. However, we should also note that if both the USPTO patent application and grant production functions are estimated for the same economy, there are potentially additional restrictions between the parameters of the USPTO patent application production function in Eq. (10.9) and the USPTO patent grant production function in Eq. (10.24) as the parameters $\ln A_{AUSi}$ and c_{USi} should be identical between the two equations for each economy.

In order to minimise the possibility of serial correlation of the stochastic disturbance terms, Eq. (10.27) is estimated in its first-differenced form. Lagging Eq. (10.27) by one period, we have

$$\begin{aligned}\ln YG_{USi(t-1)} &= A^{*}_{GUSi} + c^{*}_{GUSi}(\mathrm{t}-1)\\&\quad+(\alpha_{GUSA} + \mathrm{B}_{GUSKK}(\ln A_{AUSi} - c_{USi}))\ln YA_{USi(t-2)}\\&\quad+\mathrm{B}_{GUSKK}c_{USi}\ln YA_{USi(t-2)}.(\mathrm{t}-1)\\&\quad+\frac{1}{2}\mathrm{B}_{GUSKK}(\ln YA_{USi(t-2)})^2 + \frac{1}{2}\mathrm{B}_{GUSKK}c^2_{USi}(\mathrm{t}-1)^2\\&\quad+\delta_i \ln g_{(t-1)}.\end{aligned} \tag{10.28}$$

Subtracting Eq. (10.28) from Eq. (10.27), we obtain

$$\begin{aligned}
&\ln YG_{USit} - \ln YG_{USi(t-1)} \\
&\quad = c^{*}_{GUSi} + (\alpha_{GUSA} + \mathrm{B}_{GUSKK}(\ln A_{AUSi} - c_{USi})) \\
&\qquad \times (\ln YA_{USi(t-1)} - \ln YA_{USi(t-2)}) \\
&\qquad + \mathrm{B}_{GUSKK} c_{USi} (\ln YA_{USi(t-1)} . \mathrm{t} - \ln YA_{USi(t-2)} . (\mathrm{t}-1)) \\
&\qquad + \frac{1}{2}\mathrm{B}_{GUSKK}((\ln YA_{USi(t-1)})^2 - (\ln YA_{USi(t-2)})^2) + \mathrm{B}_{GUSKK} c^2_{USi} \mathrm{t} \\
&\qquad - \frac{1}{2}\mathrm{B}_{GUSKK} c^2_{USi} + \delta_i\ (\ln g_t - \ln g_{(t-1)}) \\
&\quad = c^{**}_{GUSi} + (\alpha_{GUSA} + \mathrm{B}_{GUSKK}(\ln A_{AUSi} - c_{USi})) \\
&\qquad (\ln YA_{USi(t-1)} - \ln YA_{USi(t-2)}) \\
&\qquad + \mathrm{B}_{GUSKK} c_{USi} (\ln YA_{USi(t-1)} . \mathrm{t} - \ln YA_{USi(t-2)} . (\mathrm{t}-1)) \\
&\qquad + \frac{1}{2}\mathrm{B}_{GUSKK}((\ln YA_{USi(t-1)})^2 - (\ln YA_{USi(t-2)})^2) \\
&\qquad + \mathrm{B}_{GUSKK} c^2_{USi} \mathrm{t} + \delta_i (\ln g_t - \ln g_{(t-1)}),
\end{aligned} \tag{10.29}$$

where $c^{**}_{GUSi} \equiv (-c_{GUSi} + (\alpha_{GUSA} + \mathrm{B}_{GUSKK}(\ln A_{AUSi} - c_{USi}))c_{USi}) - \frac{1}{2}\mathrm{B}_{GUSKK} c^2_{USi}$. Equation (10.29) is then the actual estimating equation for the model of USPTO patent grants.

Again, the first step is to test jointly the nonlinear restrictions implied by the "First Necessary Condition" of the meta-production function model, followed by a test for the "Equality" restrictions across the six economies, conditional on the "First Necessary Condition". If both tests are accepted, the validity of the meta-production function model is confirmed. We then proceed to test whether $\mathrm{B}_{GUSKK} = 0$. $\mathrm{B}_{GUSKK} = 0$ implies that the elasticity of the annual number of USPTO patent grants with respect to the annual number of USPTO patent applications is a constant that is identical across economies. There is a question of how many restrictions are implied by the hypothesis of $\mathrm{B}_{GUSKK} = 0$. In principle, it is only a restriction on a single parameter; however, assuming the validity of the meta-production function model, with six economies, there are 25 independent parameters in Eq. (10.29). With the restriction of $\mathrm{B}_{GUSKK} = 0$, there are only 13 independent parameters left to be estimated, so that the effective number of restrictions is actually 12 (25–13). We shall test this hypothesis as if it consists of 12 restrictions.

Conditional on the validity of the meta-production function model, we also test the hypothesis of identical δ_i's across economies. This hypothesis implies that fluctuations in the USPTO total grant rate affect the degree of success of the patent applications of all economies equally.

If the hypothesis of $\mathrm{B}_{GUSKK} = 0$ is rejected, we proceed to test the following specific hypotheses on the other parameters: (1) identical c_{USi}'s across economies; (2) identical A_{AUSi}'s across economies (implying $\ln A_{AUSi} = 0$, all i, since $A_{AUSi} = 1$ for the numeraire economy); and (3) identical c_{GUSi}'s across economies. However, if the hypothesis of $\mathrm{B}_{GUSKK} = 0$ cannot be rejected, the USPTO patent application and patent grant augmentation factors may not be identifiable, and these additional hypotheses (1)–(3) cannot be tested. Thus, the hypothesis of $\mathrm{B}_{GUSKK} = 0$ is also pivotal to our further analysis.

Subject to the outcomes of these tests, the implied restrictions accepted are imposed on the six economies. We can then make use of the restricted parameter estimates of Eq. (10.29) to recover the economy-specific USPTO patent grant augmentation rate parameters, c_{GUSi}'s, for all the economies.[5] However, the recovery of the economy-specific USPTO patent grant augmentation level parameters, A_{GUSi}'s, requires the use of the non-first-differenced Eq. (10.27). From Eqs. (10.27) and (10.26), we have

$$\begin{aligned}
&\ln YG_{USit} - c^*_{GUSi}\mathrm{t} - (\alpha_{GUSA} + \mathrm{B}_{GUSKK}(\ln A_{AUSi} - c_{USi}))\ln YA_{USi(t-1)} \\
&\quad - \mathrm{B}_{GUSKK}c_{USi}\ln YA_{USi(t-1)}.\mathrm{t} - \frac{1}{2}\mathrm{B}_{GUSKK}(\ln YA_{USi(t-1)})^2 \\
&\quad - \frac{1}{2}\mathrm{B}_{GUSKK}c^2_{USi}\mathrm{t}^2 - \delta_i \ln g_t. \\
&= A^*_{GUSi} \\
&= -\ln A_{GUSi} + \ln G_{US0} + \alpha_{GUSA}(\ln A_{AUSi} - c_{USi}) \\
&\quad + \frac{1}{2}\mathrm{B}_{GUSKK}(\ln A_{AUSi} - c_{USi})^2,
\end{aligned} \tag{10.30}$$

[5]On the assumption that B_{GUSKK} is not equal to zero.

or

$$
\begin{aligned}
&\ln YG_{USit} - c^*_{GUSi}\mathrm{t} - (\alpha_{GUSA} + \mathrm{B}_{GUSKK}(\ln A_{AUSi} - c_{USi}))\ln YA_{USi(t-1)} \\
&\quad - \mathrm{B}_{GUSKK}c_{USi}\ln YA_{USi(t-1)}.\mathrm{t} - \frac{1}{2}\mathrm{B}_{GUSKK}(\ln YA_{USi(t-1)})^2 \\
&\quad - \frac{1}{2}\mathrm{B}_{GUSKK}c^2_{USi}\mathrm{t}^2 - \delta_i \ln g_t \\
&\quad - \alpha_{GUSA}(\ln A_{AUSi} - c_{USi}) - \frac{1}{2}\mathrm{B}_{GUSKK}(\ln A_{AUSi} - c_{USi})^2 \\
&\quad = -\ln A_{GUSi} + \ln G_{US0}.
\end{aligned}
\tag{10.31}
$$

Equation (10.31) may be used to generate estimates for the A_{GUSi}'s by substituting the estimated values of the parameters on the left-hand side and then running a regression with only economy-specific constant terms on the right-hand side.[6]

Finally, it is also worth noting that if $\mathrm{B}_{GUSKK} = 0$, then Eq. (10.27) reduces to

$$
\ln YG_{USit} = A^*_{GUSi} + c^*_{GUSi}\,\mathrm{t} + \alpha_{GUSA}\ln YA_{USi(t-1)} + \delta_i \ln g_t, \tag{10.32}
$$

$$
\begin{aligned}
&= (-\ln A_{GUSi} + \ln G_{US0} + \alpha_{GUSA}(\ln A_{AUSi} - c_{USi})) + (-c_{GUSi} + \alpha_{GUSA}c_{USi})\mathrm{t} \\
&\quad + \alpha_{GUSA}\ln YA_{USi(t-1)} + \delta_i \ln g_t.
\end{aligned}
\tag{10.33}
$$

Equation (10.33) shows clearly that the level and rate parameters of the patent application and patent grant augmentation factors, A_{GUSi}, A_{AUSi}, c_{GUSi} and c_{USi}, cannot be uniquely identified. Our first-differenced estimating Eq. (10.29) reduces to

$$
\begin{aligned}
&\ln YG_{USit} - \ln YG_{USi(t-1)} = c^*_{GUSi} + \alpha_{GUSA}(\ln YA_{USi(t-1)} - \ln YA_{USi(t-2)}) \\
&\quad + \delta_i(\ln g_t - \ln g_{(t-1)}).
\end{aligned}
\tag{10.34}
$$

However, Eq. (10.34) can be used to generate estimates of the c^*_{GUSi}'s and to test whether they are equal across economies. Once estimates of the

[6]We should bear in mind that $A_{GUSi} = 1$ for the numeraire economy.

c^*_{GUSi}'s are available, Eq. (10.32) can be used to generate estimates of the A^*_{GUSi}'s and to test whether they are equal across economies.

10.3 The Empirical Implementation

In the empirical implementation, the US is always chosen to be the numeraire economy, so that the numbers of USPTO patent applications and grants and the quantities of the real R&D capital stocks are all measured relative to the US quantities at t = 0. Thus, for the US, $A_{AUSi} = A_{GUSi} = A_{Ki} = 1$, and hence $\ln A_{AUSi} = \ln A_{GUSi} = \ln A_{Ki} = 0$.

First, we must test whether the meta-production function model is suitable for the analysis of USPTO patent applications and patent grants. This is done in two steps. In step one, we test the nonlinear restrictions referred to as the "First Necessary Condition". The joint hypothesis that all of these nonlinear restrictions on the coefficients hold for all included economies is directly tested for both USPTO patent applications and patent grants.[7] If the test for the "First Necessary Condition" is accepted, then we proceed to step two, to test the hypothesis of "Equality" of the B_{KK}'s (and similarly that of the B_{GUSKK}'s), across all economies, conditional on the "First Necessary Condition", separately for patent applications and patent grants. If this "Equality" hypothesis is also accepted for a model, then the validity of the meta-production function assumption is confirmed for that model.

Subject to the acceptance of the validity of the meta-production function model, the hypotheses of a zero coefficient for the second-order term in the translog production functions (B_{KK} and B_{GUSKK}) are separately tested. In addition, if the hypothesis of a zero second-order term is rejected, we proceed to test respectively the hypotheses that the rate and level parameters of the real R&D capital augmentation factors, the USPTO patent application augmentation factors, and the USPTO patent grant augmentation factors are

[7] To carry out this joint test, we need to estimate the coefficients of all selected economies in the form of a pooled regression. For the pooled regression, the data of the different economies are adjusted for heteroscedasticity, using the estimated standard errors of the unrestricted regression of the basic estimating equation of each model for each individual economy.

identical across economies.[8] For the model of USPTO patent grants, we also test the equality of the δ_i's, the effects of the USPTO total grant rate, across economies.

For the hypotheses testing, we set an overall level of significance of 0.1 (10%) each for the tests of the USPTO patent application and patent grant models, which means that the probability of our falsely rejecting a hypothesis when it is true is less than or equal to 10%. Because of the central importance of the meta-production function model within our analysis, within the 10%, we assign a level of significance of 0.05 (5%) to the tests of its validity, divided equally between the two hypotheses necessary for its validity, the "First Necessary Condition" and the "Equality" restrictions. The remaining 0.05 (5%) is allocated over specific hypotheses on the parameters at 0.01 (1%) each.

Conditional on the validity of the meta-production function model, the first specific hypothesis to be tested is whether the second-order coefficient of the translog production function is zero. This is an important hypothesis because, depending on its outcome, it will determine how our analysis should proceed. We assign a level of significance of 0.01 (1%) to this hypothesis. If this hypothesis cannot be rejected, then it is not possible to identify the parameters of the augmentation factors and we shall have to terminate the sequence of tests. If this hypothesis is rejected, then for the patent applications model, we proceed to test the following additional hypotheses: (1) identical capital augmentation rates; (2) identical capital augmentation levels; and (3) identical patent application augmentation rates. Each of these hypotheses is tested, conditional on the validity of the meta-production function model. For the model of USPTO patent grants, we proceed to test the following additional hypotheses: (1) identical patent application augmentation rates; (2) identical patent application augmentation levels; and (3) identical patent grant augmentation rates. In addition, we also test the hypothesis of the equality of the coefficients of the USPTO total grant rate across economies. The levels of significance

[8] Note that in the event of a zero coefficient for the second-order term in the translog production function (B_{KK} or B_{GUSKK}), the parameters of the real R&D capital, patent application and patent grant augmentation factors cannot be separately identified, and consequently hypotheses on these parameters cannot be tested.

for each of the specific tests on the parameters are set at a uniform 0.01 (1%) each. We proceed to estimate the parameters and separately test the hypotheses for each of the two models in succession in the following sections.

10.3.1 *The model for USPTO patent applications*

First, we estimate the model for USPTO patent applications in Eq. (10.13) for the six economies. We begin our analysis by testing the implied nonlinear restrictions of the joint hypothesis of the "First Necessary Condition" for the six economies. There are six restrictions, one per economy. This joint hypothesis cannot be rejected at a level of significance of 0.025. (We also test this hypothesis for each of the six economies individually. It turns out that none of these individual tests of the "First Necessary Condition" can be rejected at any reasonable level of significance. The detailed results are presented in Table A10.2.) Conditional on the acceptance of the joint test of "First Necessary Condition", the hypothesis of "Equality", that is, identical B_{KK}'s across all economies, is also tested. With six economies, there are five restrictions. The hypothesis of "Equality" also cannot be rejected at a level of significance of 0.025, thus confirming the validity of the meta-production function model for USPTO patent applications. The test results are reported in Table 10.1.

Given the validity of the meta-production function model for USPTO patent applications, we proceed to test whether $B_{KK} = 0$, conditional on the meta-production function model. The hypothesis of $B_{KK} = 0$, with its implied 12 restrictions, cannot be rejected at the 0.01 level of significance. But $B_{KK} = 0$ implies that the level and rate parameters of the USPTO patent application and the real R&D capital stock augmentation factors, A_{AUSi}, c_{USi}, A_{Ki}, and c_{Ki} cannot be uniquely identified and therefore hypotheses about them cannot be tested.

With $B_{KK} = 0$, we proceed to estimate Eq. (10.17):

$$\ln YA_{USit} - \ln YA_{USi(t-1)} = c^{*}_{USi} + \alpha_K (\ln K_{it} - \ln K_{i(t-1)}), \qquad (10.17)$$

Table 10.1: Tests of hypotheses, USPTO patent applications

Maintained Hypothesis	Tested Hypothesis	Level of Significance	Critical Value	Test Statistic	p-Value	Accept/ Reject
Unconstrained	First Necessary Condition	0.025	2.4593	1.6230	0.1412	Accept
First Necessarty Condition	Equality of B_{KK}'s	0.025	2.6165	1.7759	0.1182	Accept
Meta-Production Function	$B_{KK} = 0$	0.01	2.2537	2.1972	0.0123	Accept
Meta-Production Function with $B_{KK} = 0$	Equality of c^*_{USi}'s	0.01	3.0851	1.3055	0.2618	Accept
Meta-Production Function with $B_{KK} = 0$ and identical c^*_{USi}'s	c^*_{USi}'s $= 0$	0.01	6.7273	0.5728	0.4498	Accept
Meta-Production Function with $B_{KK} = 0$ and c^*_{USi}'s $= 0$	Equality of A^*_{AUSi}'s	0.01	3.0849	117.3548	0.0000	Reject

Note: $c^*_{USi} \equiv (-c_{USi} + \alpha_K c_{Ki})$; $A^*_{AUSi} \equiv (-\ln A_{AUSi} + \ln A_0 + \alpha_K \ln A_{Ki})$.

where $c^*_{USi} \equiv (-c_{USi} + \alpha_K c_{Ki})$ and test whether the c^*_{USi}'s are equal across economies,[9] and if so, whether they are equal to zero. At a level of significance of 0.01, the hypothesis of equality of the c^*_{USi}'s cannot be rejected. In addition, the hypothesis of a common zero c^*_{US} for all six economies also cannot be rejected at a level of significance of 0.01. With the c^*_{USi}'s being set equal to zero, we can estimate the A^*_{AUSi}'s from a rearranged version of Eq. (10.16):

$$\ln YA_{USit} - c^*_{US}t - \alpha_K \ln K_{it} = \ln YA_{USit} - \alpha_K \ln K_{it} = A^*_{AUSi}, \qquad (10.35)$$

into the left-hand side of which the known estimated values of the parameter α_K is plugged. We also test whether the A^*_{AUSi}'s are equal across

[9] Note that equality of the c^*_{USi}'s does not imply the equality of the c_{USi}'s.

Table 10.2: Estimated parameters of the USPTO patent application production functions

Parameter	Estimate	Standard Error	t-statistic	P-value
c^*_{US}	0.000	N.A.	N.A.	N.A.
α_K	1.132	0.087	13.004	[.000]
A^*_{AUSi}'s				
France	2.217	0.067	33.048	[.000]
Germany	2.717	0.067	40.500	[.000]
Japan	3.156	0.067	47.049	[.000]
United States	2.971	0.076	38.945	[.000]
Mainland, China	1.028	0.083	12.449	[.000]
South Korea	3.325	0.074	45.156	[.000]

economies,[10] and if so, whether they are equal to zero. However, we note that $A^*_{AUSi} \equiv (-\ln A_{AUSi} + \ln A_0 + \alpha_K \ln A_{Ki})$, which means that neither A_{AUSi} nor A_{Ki} can be uniquely identified. At a level of significance of 0.01, the hypothesis of equality of the A^*_{AUSi}'s can be rejected. These test results are also reported in Table 10.1.

We impose all the restrictions implied by the meta-production function model and all the accepted hypotheses and re-estimate all the parameters for the model of USPTO patent applications. The results are presented in Table 10.2. Table 10.2 shows that for a given quantity of real R&D capital stock, South Korea has the highest annual number of USPTO patent applications, followed by Japan, and Mainland, China has the lowest annual number, other things being equal. This may be due, in part, to the significantly lower USPTO patent application rate of Mainland China.

10.3.2 *The model for USPTO patent grants*

For the model of USPTO patent grants, we estimate Eq. (10.29) for all six economies. Again, we first test the "First Necessary Condition" jointly for

[10] Similarly, the equality of the A^*_{AUSi}'s does not imply the equality of the A_{AUSi}'s.

all the included economies. This hypothesis cannot be rejected at a level of significance of 0.025. (We also test this hypothesis for each of the six economies separately. The p-values of these tests indicate that this hypothesis cannot be rejected for all six economies at any reasonable level of significance. The detailed results are presented in Table A10.3.) Conditional on the joint hypothesis of the "First Necessary Condition", the hypothesis of "Equality", that is, identical B_{GUSKK}'s across the six economies, is tested. This hypothesis also cannot be rejected at a level of significance of 0.025, confirming the validity of the meta-production function model for USPTO patent grants. The test results are reported in Table 10.3.

Table 10.3: Tests of hypotheses, USPTO patent grants

Maintained Hypothesis	Tested Hypothesis	Level of Significance	Critical Value	Test Statistic	*p*-Value	Accept/ Reject
Unconstrained	First Necessary Condition	0.025	2.4606	0.2816	0.9453	Accept
First Necessary Condition	Equality of B_{GUSKK}'s	0.025	2.6177	1.4033	0.2236	Accept
Meta-Production Function	$B_{GUSKK} = 0$	0.01	2.2554	1.0567	0.3976	Accept
Meta-Production Function	Equality of δ_i's	0.01	3.0900	0.1513	0.9795	Accept
Meta-Production Function with $B_{GUSKK} = 0$	Equality of c^*_{GUSi}'s	0.01	3.0867	2.2195	0.0527	Accept
Meta-Production Function with $B_{GUSKK} = 0$, and identical c^*_{GUSi}'s	c^*_{GUSi}'s = 0	0.01	6.7293	15.2893	0.0001	Reject
Meta-Production Function with $B_{GUSKK} = 0$, identical δ_i's and identical c^*_{GUSi}'s	Equality of A^*_{GUSi}'s	0.01	3.0849	112.2517	0.0000	Reject

Note: $c^*_{GUSi} \equiv (-c_{GUSi} + \alpha_{GUSA}\, c_{USi})$; $A^*_{GUSi} \equiv (-\ln A_{GUSi} + \ln G_{US0} + \alpha_{GUSA}\, (\ln A_{AUSi} - c_{USi}))$.

Given the validity of the meta-production function model for USPTO patent grants, we proceed to test the hypothesis that $\mathrm{B}_{GUSKK} = 0$.[11] The hypothesis of $\mathrm{B}_{GUSKK} = 0$ cannot be rejected at a level of significance of 0.01. These results are reported in Table 10.3.

Subject to the validity of the meta-production function model, we also test whether the δ_i's are identical across economies. The equality of the δ_i's across economies implies that the effects of changes in the USPTO total grant rates affect the annual numbers of patent grants of all economies equally. This hypothesis cannot be rejected at a level of significance of 0.01.

With $\mathrm{B}_{GUSKK} = 0$, it is not possible to identify the level and rate parameters of the USPTO patent grant and patent application augmentation factors, and hence to test hypotheses on them. We therefore proceed to estimate Eq. (10.34):

$$\ln YG_{USit} - \ln YG_{USi(t-1)} = c^*_{GUSi} + \alpha_{GUSA}\,(\ln YA_{USi(t-1)} - \ln YA_{USi(t-2)}) + \delta_i\,(\ln g_t - \ln g_{(t-1)}), \tag{10.34}$$

where $c^*_{GUSi} \equiv (-c_{GUSi} + \alpha_{GUSA}\, c_{USi})$. We test the hypothesis of the equality of the c^*_{GUSi}'s across economies in Eq. (10.34),[12] and if so, whether they are equal to zero. At a level of significance of 0.01, the hypothesis of equality of the c^*_{GUSi}'s cannot be rejected. However, the hypothesis of a common zero c^*_{GUS} for all six economies can be rejected at a level of significance of 0.01. With the estimated c^*_{GUS}, we estimate the A^*_{GUSi}'s from a rearranged version of Eq. (10.32), in which we have set $\delta_i = \delta$ in accordance with our test results:

$$\ln YG_{USit} - c^*_{GUS}\,\mathrm{t} - \alpha_{GUSA} \ln YA_{USi(t-1)} - \delta \ln g_\mathrm{t} = A^*_{GUSi}. \tag{10.36}$$

We plug into the left-hand side of Eq. (10.36) the known estimated values of the parameters, c^*_{GUS}, α_{GUSA} and δ, and run the regression on economy-specific constant terms. We also test whether the A^*_{GUSi}'s are equal across economies,[13] and if so, whether they are equal to zero. At a

[11] We note that if $\mathrm{B}_{GUSKK} = 0$, the USPTO grant and application augmentation factors are not identifiable, and hypotheses on their level and rate parameters cannot be tested.

[12] Note that equality of the c^*_{GUSi}'s does not imply the equality of the c_{GUSi}'s.

[13] Similarly, the equality of the A^*_{GUSi}'s does not imply the equality of the A_{GUSi}'s.

Table 10.4: Estimated parameters of the USPTO patent grant production functions

Parameter	Estimate	Standard Error	*t*-statistic	*P*-value
C^*_{GUS}	0.032	0.008	3.950	[.000]
α_{GUSA}	0.402	0.087	4.621	[.000]
δ	1.196	0.141	8.496	[.000]
A^*_{GUSi}'s				
France	–1.509	0.105	–14.368	[.000]
Germany	–0.936	0.105	–8.910	[.000]
Jápan	–0.504	0.105	–4.798	[.000]
United States	0.189	0.119	1.580	[.114]
Mainland, China	–3.223	0.129	–24.943	[.000]
South Korea	–2.516	0.115	–21.832	[.000]

level of significance of 0.01, the hypothesis of equality of the A^*_{GUSi}'s can be rejected. These test results are also reported in Table 10.3.

The final estimation is done with all the restrictions on the parameters implied by the meta-production function model and the accepted hypotheses imposed. The results are presented in Table 10.4.

Table 10.4 shows that for a given annual number of USPTO patent applications, lagged 1 year, the United States has the highest annual number of USPTO patent grants, followed by Japan, and Mainland, China has the lowest, other things being equal. This may be due, in part, to the significantly lower USPTO patent application rate of Mainland China.

10.4 Summary of the Estimation Results

From Eq. (10.33), the natural logarithm of the annual number of USPTO patent grants of the *i*th economy in year t is given by

$$\ln YG_{USit} = A^*_{GUSi} + c^*_{GUS}\,\mathrm{t} + \alpha_{GUSA}\ln YA_{USi(t-1)} + \delta \ln g_t. \tag{10.37}$$

From Eq. (10.16), the natural logarithm of the annual number of USPTO applications of the *i*th economy in year t is given by

$$\ln YA_{USit} = A^*_{AUSi} + \alpha_K \ln K_{it}. \tag{10.38}$$

We note that with the exception of the constants A^*_{GUSi}'s and A^*_{AUSi}'s, all the other parameters of Eqs. (10.37) and (10.38) are identical across the economies. Finally, by combining Eqs. (10.37) and (10.38), we have

$$\begin{aligned}\ln YG_{USit} &= A^*_{GUSi} + c^*_{GUS}\,\mathrm{t} + \delta \ln g_t + \alpha_{GUSA} \ln YA_{USi(t-1)} \\ &= A^*_{GUSi} + c^*_{GUS}\,\mathrm{t} + \delta \ln g_t + \alpha_{GUSA}(A^*_{AUSi} + \alpha_K \ln K_{i(t-1)}) \\ &= (A^*_{GUSi} + \alpha_{GUSA}A^*_{AUSi}) + c^*_{GUS}\,\mathrm{t} + \delta \ln g_t + \alpha_{GUSA}\alpha_K \ln K_{i(t-1)}, \quad (10.39)\end{aligned}$$

where all parameters, with the exception of the constants $(A^*_{GUSi} + \alpha_{GUSA} A^*_{AUSi})$'s, are identical across economies. It is interesting to compare the estimated values of $(A^*_{GUSi} + \alpha_{GUSA} A^*_{AUSi})$, which can be calculated from Tables 10.2 and 10.4, across the six economies. This is done in Table 10.5.

The last column of Table 10.5 also shows that for a given quantity of real R&D capital stock of the preceding year, the United States has the highest annual number of USPTO patent grants, followed by Japan, and Mainland, China the lowest, other things being equal. This may also be due, in part, to the significantly lower USPTO patent application rate of Mainland China.

This completes our estimation of the econometric models of USPTO patent applications and patent grants. We note that the final model yields statistically significant estimates of the parameters. The analysis and interpretation of the empirical results will be presented in Chapter 11.

Table 10.5: Estimated values of the economy-specific constants in the USPTO patent grants production functions

Economy	A^*_{GUSi}	α_{GUSA}	A^*_{GUSi}	$A^*_{GUSi} + \alpha_{GUSA} A^*_{GUSi}$
France	–1.509	0.402	2.217	–0.618
Germany	–0.936	0.402	2.717	0.156
Japan	–0.504	0.402	3.156	0.764
United States	0.189	0.402	2.971	1.382
Mainland, China	–3.223	0.402	1.028	–2.810
South Korea	–2.516	0.402	3.325	–1.180

Appendix

Table A10.1: The beginning and ending years of the data for the six economies in chapters 10 and 11

Economy	Beginning Year	Ending Year
France	1967	2019
Germany	1967	2019
Japan	1967	2019
US	1979	2019
Mainland, China	1985	2019
South Korea	1976	2019

Table A10.2: Economy-specific tests of the first necessary condition for the validity of the meta-production function model, USPTO patent applications (six economies)

Economy	Test Statistic	*p*-Value	Accept/Reject
France	1.6022	0.2117	Accept
Germany	0.0492	0.8254	Accept
Japan	0.0612	0.8057	Accept
US	0.7689	0.3864	Accept
Mainland, China	0.0308	0.8618	Accept
South Korea	2.5009	0.1219	Accept

Table A10.3: Economy-specific tests of the first necessary condition for the validity of the meta-production function model, USPTO patent grants (six economies)

Economy	Test Statistic	*p*-Value	Accept/Reject
France	0.3943	0.5331	Accept
Germany	0.5151	0.4765	Accept
Japan	0.5486	0.4626	Accept
US	0.0110	0.9171	Accept
Mainland, China	0.2697	0.6075	Accept
South Korea	0.3485	0.5585	Accept

Chapter 11

The Research Findings

The econometric analysis in Chapter 10 indicates that, at the economy level, there appears to be a "Law of Innovation" that is common to the six economies analysed. Innovation, measured in terms of the annual numbers of United States Patent and Trademark Office (USPTO) patent applications and patent grants, appears to depend on the quantity of real investment in Research and Development (R&D) and in particular on the quantity of the accumulated real R&D capital stock, in a similar and statistically significant, though not completely identical, manner across the six economies in our study — Mainland China, France, Germany, Japan, South Korea, and the United States (US), all economies with their numbers of domestic patent applications exceeding or equal to their numbers of USPTO patent applications.

On the whole, the meta-production function models for the USPTO patent applications and patent grants fit the data of all the included economies reasonably well, except for Mainland China (see the following discussion). We have not attempted to model the domestic patent application and grant behaviour of our selected economies because the diversity in their propensities to apply for and to award patents makes it virtually impossible for a single meta-production function model to capture it adequately.

11.1 Interpretation of the Empirical Findings

From the results of our estimation of the econometric models in Chapter 10, we can calculate the values of the elasticities of the annual number of USPTO patent applications with respect to the quantity of real R&D capital stock as well as the elasticities of the annual number of USPTO patent grants with respect to the lagged annual number of USPTO patent applications, and ultimately the elasticities of the annual number of USPTO patent grants with respect to the lagged quantity of real R&D capital stock of the individual economies. According to Eq. (10.37), the natural logarithm of the annual number of USPTO patent grants of the *i*th economy in year t, $\ln YG_{USit}$, is given by

$$
\begin{aligned}
\ln YG_{USit} &= A^*_{GUSi} + c^*_{GUS}\,\mathrm{t} + \alpha_{GUSA} \ln YA_{USi(t-1)} + \delta \ln g_t \\
&= A^{*\,1}_{GUSi} + \underset{(0.008)^2}{0.032}\,\mathrm{t} + \underset{(0.087)}{0.402} \ln YA_{USi(t-1)} + \underset{(0.141)}{1.196} \ln g_t,
\end{aligned} \tag{11.1}
$$

where the estimated values of the parameters and their standard errors are taken from Table 10.4, which have incorporated all the restrictions implied by the accepted hypotheses. Differentiating Eq. (11.1) partially with respect to $\ln YA_{USi(t-1)}$, we obtain the elasticity of the annual number of USPTO patent grants with respect to the annual number of USPTO patent applications in the previous year of the *i*th economy, holding the year, t, and the USPTO total patent grant rate constant:

$$
\frac{\partial \ln YG_{USit}}{\partial \ln YA_{USi(t-1)}} = \alpha_{GUSA} = 0.402. \tag{11.2}
$$

Thus, all six economies have the same estimated elasticity. Differentiating Eq. (11.1) partially with respect to time, t, we obtain the rate of growth of the annual number of USPTO patent grants, holding the annual number of USPTO patent applications in the previous year of the *i*th economy and the USPTO total patent grant rate constant. The rate of growth also turns out to be the same for all six economies:

$$
\frac{\partial \ln YG_{USit}}{\partial \mathrm{t}} = c^*_{GUS} = 0.032 \quad \text{or} \quad 3.2\%. \tag{11.3}
$$

The natural logarithm of the annual number of USPTO patent applications of the *i*th economy in year t, $\ln YA_{USit}$, is, according to Eq. (10.38), given by

[1]The estimates of the A^*_{GUSi}'s of specific economies are presented in Table 10.4.

[2]Numbers in parentheses are estimated standard errors.

$$\begin{aligned} \ln YA_{USit} &= A^*_{AUSi} + c^*_{US}t + \alpha_k \ln K_{it} \\ &= A^*_{AUSi}{}^3 + \underset{(0.087)}{1.132} \ln K_{it}. \end{aligned} \tag{11.4}$$

Differentiating Eq. (11.4) partially with respect to $\ln K_{it}$, we obtain the elasticity of the annual number of USPTO patent applications with respect to the quantity of real R&D capital stock, holding t constant:

$$\frac{\partial \ln YA_{USit}}{\partial \ln K_{it}} = \alpha_K = 1.132. \tag{11.5}$$

Thus, all six economies also have the same estimated elasticity. Differentiating Eq. (11.4) partially with respect to t, holding the quantity of real R&D capital stock constant, we obtain zero:

$$\frac{\partial \ln YA_{USit}}{\partial t} = 0. \tag{11.6}$$

This implies that there is no autonomous growth in the annual number of USPTO applications without the growth of the quantity of the real R&D capital stock.

It is of interest to see how well Eqs. (11.1) and (11.4) fit the actual data. In Figure 11.1, the actual and fitted values of the annual numbers of USPTO patent grants of both Mainland China and the US (from Eq. (11.1)) are plotted against time. The goodness of fit of the annual number of USPTO patent grants of the US is excellent. However, the goodness of fit of the annual number of USPTO patent grants of Mainland China is quite poor. There is significant over-estimation before 2004 and significant under-estimation since. We believe this is due to the abrupt change in the annual rate of growth of the number of USPTO patent grants awarded to Mainland China, from virtually zero to an average of over 26%, beginning in 1996. Even the addition of an economy-specific time-trend term in Eq. (11.1) would not have been able to reflect this.

[3]The estimates of the A^*_{AUSi}'s of specific economies are taken from Table 10.2.

Figure 11.1: The actual and fitted values of the annual numbers of USPTO patent grants, Mainland China and the US

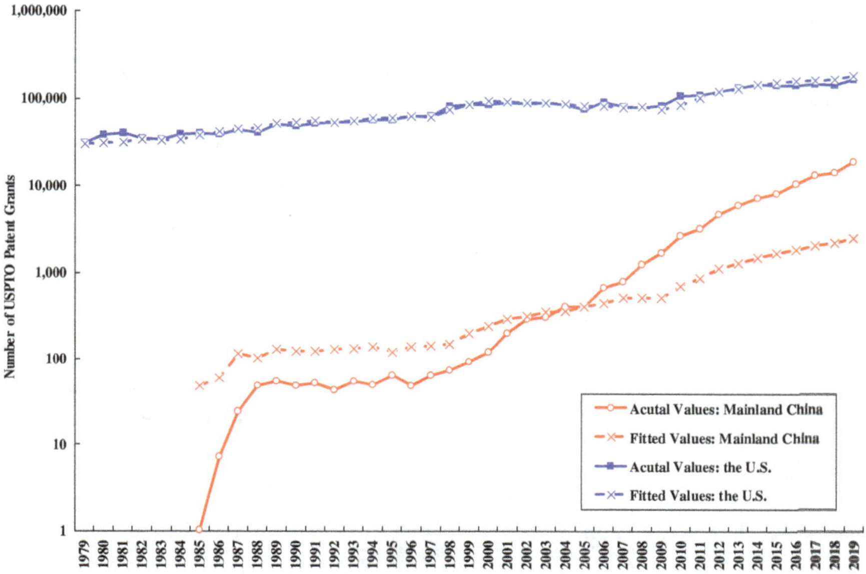

Source: Data on the actual values of annual numbers of USPTO patent grants are from Table 5A.2 of Chapter 5 and the fitted values are based on authors' calculations.

In Figure 11.2, the actual and fitted values of the annual numbers of USPTO patent applications of both Mainland China and the US (from Eq. (11.4)) are plotted against time. The goodness of fit of the annual number of USPTO patent applications of the US is not bad, but there is a systematic bias — over-estimation before 1997 and under-estimation thereafter. The goodness of fit of the annual number of USPTO patent applications of Mainland China is just as poor as its annual number of USPTO patent grants in Figure 11.1. There is significant over-estimation before 2001 and significant under-estimation since. We believe this is also due to the very abrupt and rapid rise in the number of USPTO patent applications from Mainland China beginning in the late 1990s as well as the absence of an economy-specific time-trend term in Eq. (11.4).

Actually, the annual number of USPTO patent grants awarded to the *i*th economy is indirectly a function of the quantity of real R&D capital stock, lagged 1 year. It is, according to Eq. (10.39), given by

Figure 11.2: The actual and fitted values of the annual number of USPTO patent applications, Mainland China and the US

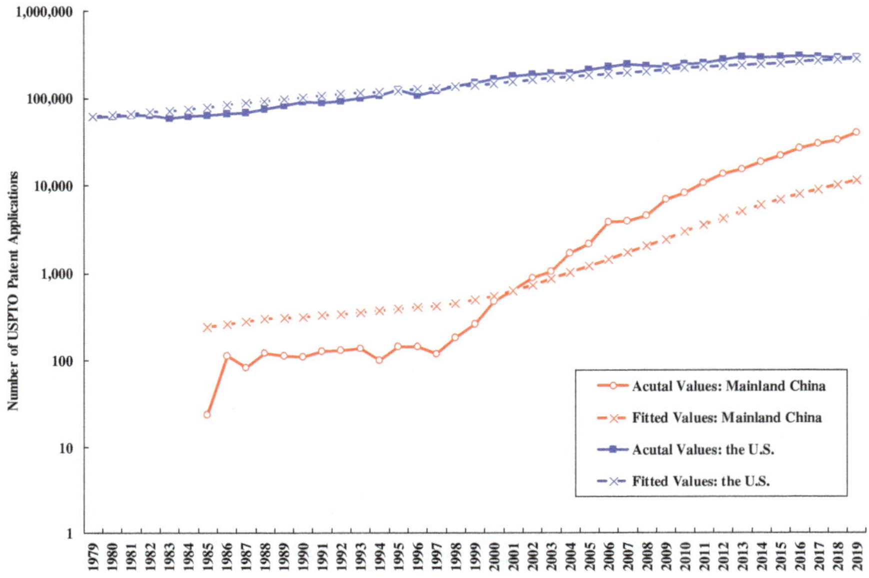

Source: Data on actual values of annual numbers of USPTO patent grants are from Table 5A.1 of Chapter 5 and the fitted values are based on authors' calculations.

$$\ln YG_{USit} = (A^{*}_{GUSi} + \alpha_{GUSA} A^{*}_{AUSi}) + c^{*}_{GUS}\, t + \delta \ln g_t + \alpha_{GUSA}\alpha_k \ln K_{i(t-1)}. \tag{11.7}$$

In Figure 11.3, the natural logarithm of the annual number of USPTO patent grants is plotted against the natural logarithm of the quantity of real R&D capital stock, lagged 1 year. Figure 11.3 provides prima facie evidence that there exists a stable, positive relationship between the annual number of USPTO patent grants of the *i*th economy and its lagged quantity of real R&D capital stock, across economies and over time. However, the relationship appears stronger and more similar for the developed economies than for Mainland China and South Korea.

Differentiating Eq. (11.7) partially with respect to $\ln K_{i(t-1)}$, we obtain the elasticity of the annual number of USPTO patent grants with respect to the quantity of real R&D capital stock of the previous year of the *i*th

Figure 11.3: The natural logarithm of the annual number of USPTO patent grants versus the natural logarithm of the quantity of real R&D capital stock, lagged 1 year

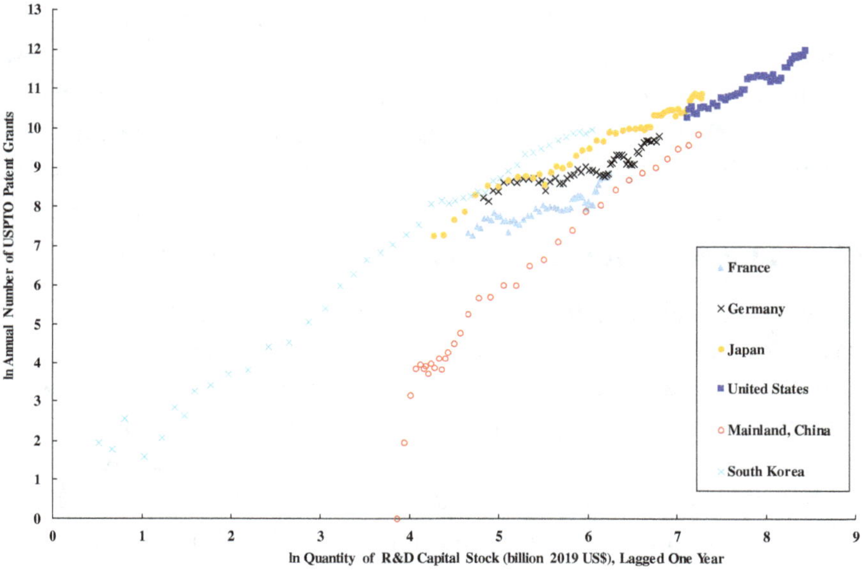

Source: Authors' calculations. Data on the annual numbers of USPTO patent grants are from Table A5.2 of Chapter 5 and data on the quantities of R&D capital stocks are from Table A3.2 of Chapter 3.

economy, holding the year t and the USPTO total patent grant rate constant:

$$\frac{\partial \ln YG_{USit}}{\partial \ln K_{i(t-1)}} = \alpha_{GUSA}\alpha_k = 0.402 \times 1.132 = 0.455. \tag{11.8}$$

Once again, all six economies also have the same estimated elasticity. Differentiating Eq. (11.7) partially with respect to t, we obtain the rate of growth of the annual number of USPTO patent grants of the *i*th economy, holding the quantity of its lagged real R&D capital stock and the USPTO total grant rate constant:

$$\frac{\partial \ln YG_{USit}}{\partial t} = c^*_{GUS} = 0.032 \text{ or } 3.2\%. \tag{11.9}$$

More specifically, we find that, on average, a 10% increase in the quantity of real R&D capital stock of the preceding year increases the annual number of USPTO patent grants by 4.55%, that is, an elasticity of 0.455. In addition, a 10% increase in the quantity of real R&D capital stock increases the annual number of USPTO patent applications grants by 11.32%, that is, an elasticity slightly greater than one. Overall, it confirms the importance of investment in R&D for the occurrence of innovation.

11.2 The Addition of a Second Lagged Variable

However, there is a question on the disparity between these two estimated elasticities, granted that they actually refer to different things. One would have expected that the elasticity of the annual number of patent grants with respect to the annual number of patent applications should be closer to one. One possible explanation for the relatively low estimated elasticity may be due to the fact that in Eq. (10.37) (and Eq. (11.1)), only the annual number of USPTO patent applications lagged 1 year is included on the right-hand side. In actual fact, the number of patent grants in a given year may also depend on the number of patent applications submitted more than 1 year ago. In order to try to address this issue, we augment Eq. (11.1) as

$$\begin{aligned}\ln YG_{USit} &= A^*_{GUSi} + c^*_{GUS}\,\mathrm{t} + \alpha_{GUSA} \ln YA_{USi(t-1)} \\ &\quad + \alpha_{GUSA1} \ln YA_{USi(t-2)} + \delta \ln g_t,\end{aligned} \tag{11.10}$$

adding an independent variable, the number of USPTO patent applications lagged 2 years. Lagging Eq. (11.10) by one period and subtracting it from Eq. (11.10), we obtain

$$\begin{aligned}&\ln YG_{USit} - \ln YG_{USi(t-1)} \\ &\quad = c^*_{GUS} + \alpha_{GUSA}(\ln YA_{USi(t-1)} - \ln YA_{USi(t-2)}) \\ &\qquad + \alpha_{GUSA1}(\ln YA_{USi(t-2)} - \ln YA_{USi(t-3)}) + \delta(\ln g_t - \ln g_{(t-1)}),\end{aligned} \tag{11.11}$$

which is then estimated. Plugging these estimated parameters into Eq. (11.10), and moving everything except the economy-specific constant terms to the left-hand side, we can obtain new estimates of the A^*_{GUSi}'s. The estimated results are presented in Table 11.1.

Table 11.1: The estimated parameters of Eq. (11.11)

Parameter	**Estimate**	**Standard Error**	***t*-statistic**	***P*-value**
c^*_{GUS}	0.016	0.008	1.879	[0.060]
α_{GUSA}	0.296	0.082	3.635	[0.000]
α_{GUSA1}	0.516	0.081	6.337	[0.000]
δ	1.252	0.135	9.260	[0.000]
A^*_{GUSi}'s				
France	–4.558	0.041	–111.180	[0.000]
Germany	–4.391	0.041	–107.112	[0.000]
Japan	–4.223	0.041	–103.012	[0.000]
United States	–4.098	0.047	–87.680	[0.000]
Mainland, China	–5.227	0.051	–103.103	[0.000]
South Korea	–4.984	0.045	–110.556	[0.000]

Substituting the estimated parameters in Table 11.1 into Eq. (11.10), we obtain

$$\ln YG_{USit}$$
$$= A^{*}_{GUSi}{}^{4} + \underset{(0.008)^{5}}{0.016.t} + \underset{(0.082)}{0.296} \ln YA_{USi(t-1)} + \underset{(0.081)}{0.516} \ln YA_{USi(t-2)} + \underset{(0.135)}{1.252} \ln g_t. \quad (11.12)$$

Using Eq. (11.12), we construct Figure 11.4, presenting both the actual and fitted values of the annual numbers of USPTO patent grants for both Mainland China and the US. A comparison of Figures 11.1 and 11.4 shows a much-improved fit of the annual number of USPTO patent grants for Mainland China[6] and the same excellent fit for the US.

Combining Eqs. (11.10) and (11.4), we obtain

[4] The estimates of the A^*_{AUSi}'s of specific economies are taken from Table 11.1.

[5] Numbers in parentheses are estimated standard errors.

[6] Even though there is overestimation before 1998 and underestimation after 2008.

Figure 11.4: The actual and fitted values of the annual numbers of USPTO patent grants, Mainland China and the US, with estimated parameters from Table 11.1

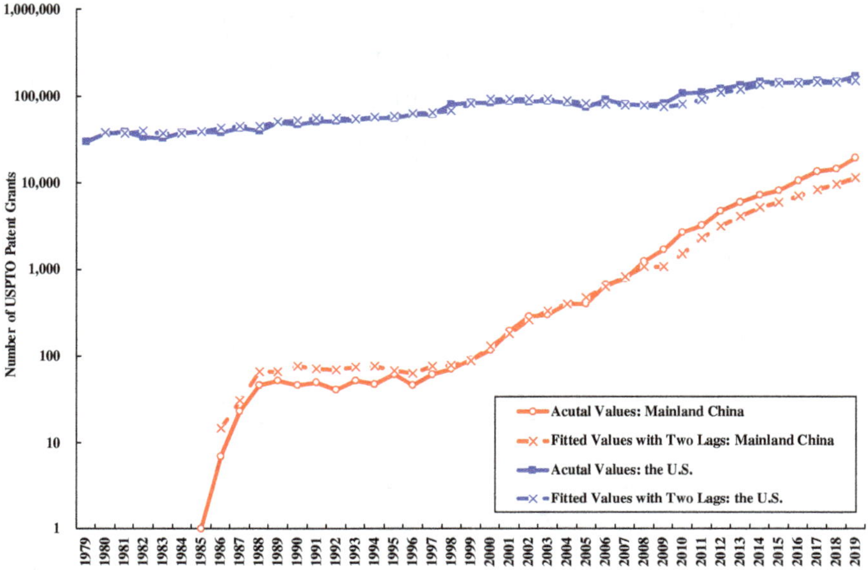

$$\begin{aligned}
\ln YG_{USit} &= A^{*}_{GUSi} + c^{*}_{GUS}\,\mathrm{t} + \alpha_{GUSA}\ln YA_{USi(t-1)} + \alpha_{GUSA1}\ln YA_{USi(t-2)} \\
&\quad + \delta\,\ln g_t, \\
&= A^{*}_{GUSi} + c^{*}_{GUS}\,\mathrm{t} + \alpha_{GUSA}(A^{*}_{AUSi} + 1.132\ln K_{i(t-1)}) \\
&\quad + \alpha_{GUSA1}(A^{*}_{AUSi} + 1.132\ln K_{i(t-2)}) + \delta\,\ln g_t \\
&= (A^{*}_{GUSi}{}^{7} + (\alpha_{GUSA} + \alpha_{GUSA1})A^{*}_{AUSi}{}^{8}) + \underset{(0.008)^{9}}{0.016}.\mathrm{t} \\
&\quad + \underset{(0.087)}{1.132} \times (\underset{(0.082)}{0.296}\ln K_{i(t-1)} + \underset{(0.081)}{0.516}\ln K_{i(t-2)}) + \underset{(0.135)}{1.252}\ln g_t. \qquad (11.13)
\end{aligned}$$

In the steady state, $K_{i(t-1)} = K_{i(t-2)} = K_i$, so that the partial derivative of $\ln YG_{USit}$ with respect to K_i, that is, the elasticity of the annual number of

---

[7]The estimates of the A^{*}_{GUSi}'s of specific economies are taken from Table 11.1.
[8]The estimates of the A^{*}_{AUSi}'s of specific economies are taken from Table 10.2.
[9]Numbers in parentheses are estimated standard errors.

USPTO patent grants with respect to the real R&D capital stock, is given by $(\alpha_{GUSA} + \alpha_{GUSA1}) \times 1.132 = (0.296 + 0.516) \times 1.132 = 0.919$, slightly less than one.[10] Differentiating Eq. (11.13) with respect to t, we obtain

$$\frac{\partial \ln YG_{USit}}{\partial t} = c^{*}_{GUS} = 0.016 \text{ or } 1.6\%. \tag{11.14}$$

This is the autonomous rate of growth of the number of USPTO patent grants, holding all other variables constant. However, we believe this reflects the residual effects of patent applications submitted more than 2 years ago.

11.3 The Economies of Scale of R&D

R&D is an activity that is believed to exhibit inherent economies of scale. Doubling the R&D resources is believed to more than double the probability of a discovery or invention, since it is then possible to pursue the same objective from two or more different directions. However, it may also create competition for the scarce R&D resources, such as R&D manpower and critical equipment, which may in some cases lower the probability of a discovery or invention. We estimate the degree of local returns to scale in real R&D capital stock among the economies in our study. Given a production function Y = F(X), where Y is the quantity of output and X is a vector of quantities of inputs, the existence of economies of scale implies that $F(\lambda X) > \lambda F(X)$, for any positive scalar λ, $\lambda > 1$; that is, any expansion of the quantities of inputs will result in a more than proportionate increase in the quantity of output. The degree of local returns to scale at X is given by $\left.\frac{\partial \ln F(\lambda X)}{\partial \ln \lambda}\right|_{\lambda=1}$. If X is a scalar variable, then $\left.\frac{\partial \ln F(\lambda X)}{\partial \ln \lambda}\right|_{\lambda=1} = \left.\frac{\partial \ln F(\lambda X)}{\partial \ln X}\right|_{\lambda=1} = \frac{d \ln F(X)}{d \ln X}$.

Thus, the degree of local returns to scale in the production of USPTO patent applications from real R&D capital stock is given by the elasticity in Eq. (11.5), 1.132, indicating slightly increasing returns to scale. The

---

[10] We believe this number would be even closer to one if we had included a third lagged number of USPTO patent applications in Eq. (11.10).

degree of local returns to scale in the production of USPTO patent grants from real R&D capital stock from Eq. (11.8), is given by the elasticity, 0.455. Taken by itself, there appear to be significantly decreasing returns to scale. However, using the estimation results in Table 11.1, the annual number of USPTO patent grants is indirectly a function of the quantities of the real R&D capital stocks, lagged 1 and 2 years respectively, as in Eq. (11.13). In the steady state, the elasticity of the annual number of USPTO patent grants with respect to the quantity of real R&D capital stock is estimated to be 0.919, indicating slightly decreasing returns to scale. There does not appear to be any evidence of significant increasing returns to scale to investment in R&D at the economy-wide level.

Part Five

Beyond R&D and Patents

Chapter 12

Complementary Inputs to R&D Capital

In addition to real Research and Development (R&D) capital, complementary inputs, such as R&D researchers, are needed to produce innovation. Complementary inputs are also needed, in addition to real R&D capital, in order to produce real Gross Domestic Product (GDP) in an economy. What are some complementary inputs to real R&D capital? At the microeconomic level, there are, of course, the R&D researchers and the physical R&D infrastructure, such as structures and equipment. However, we should note that R&D expenditure *per se* already includes the total cost of the human resources employed in the R&D activities as well as the investment in R&D-related structures and equipment. Thus, only the current-period R&D manpower input should be considered a complementary input in R&D activities to avoid double-counting.

At the macroeconomic level, within an aggregate production function framework, there are of course the conventional inputs of production: tangible capital, labour, and human capital. Human capital, in particular, should be complementary to R&D capital, since R&D activities must be carried out and its results applied and implemented by educated (including some highly educated), experienced, and skilled workers. In Figure 12.1, the quantity of human capital of each economy in our study, measured as the total number of person-years of schooling (including tertiary education) among the working-age population, defined as those aged between 15 and 64, are presented. However, as comparable data on the mean years

Figure 12.1: The quantity of human capital (total person-years of education), G-7 countries, Mainland China, and four EANIEs

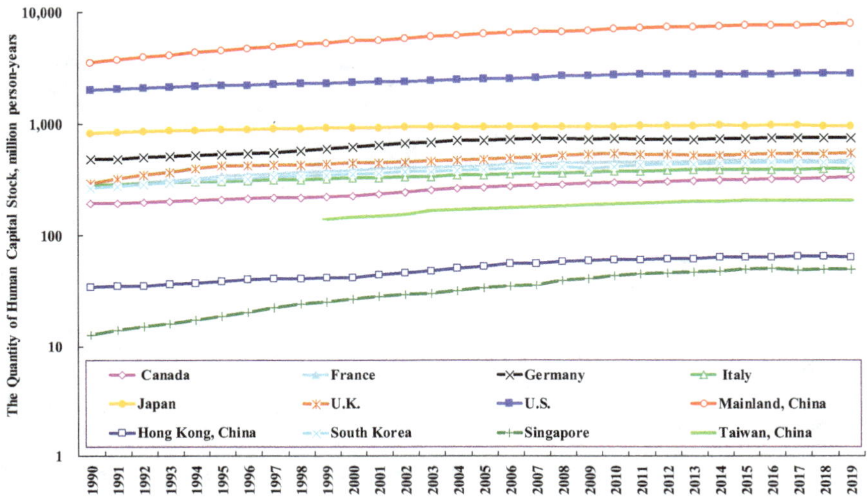

Source: Data are collected from Human Development Reports, United Nations Development Programme, and the Directorate General of Budget, Accounting and Statistics, Taiwan, China.

of schooling of the working-age population are not readily available across economies, instead, we use the mean years of schooling achieved by people aged 25 and above and multiply it to the total working-age population. This is likely to result in a downward bias in our estimates of the total quantity of human capital, especially for economies with a rapidly expanding educational system at the primary and secondary levels.[1] Figure 12.1 shows that Mainland China has the highest total quantity of human capital, primarily on the basis of its large population, followed by the United States (US) and Japan.

In Figure 12.2, we compare the quantities of human capital across the economies in our study on a per capita basis. Figure 12.2 shows that the US was the leader in terms of human capital per capita until 2003 when it was overtaken by Germany. As of 2019, Germany remained the leader, followed by Canada, South Korea and Taiwan, China. The US fell to fifth

[1] Typically, the number of years of schooling changes very little over time for an individual aged 25 and above.

Figure 12.2: The quantity of human capital per capita, G-7 countries, Mainland China, and four EANIEs (person-years per person)

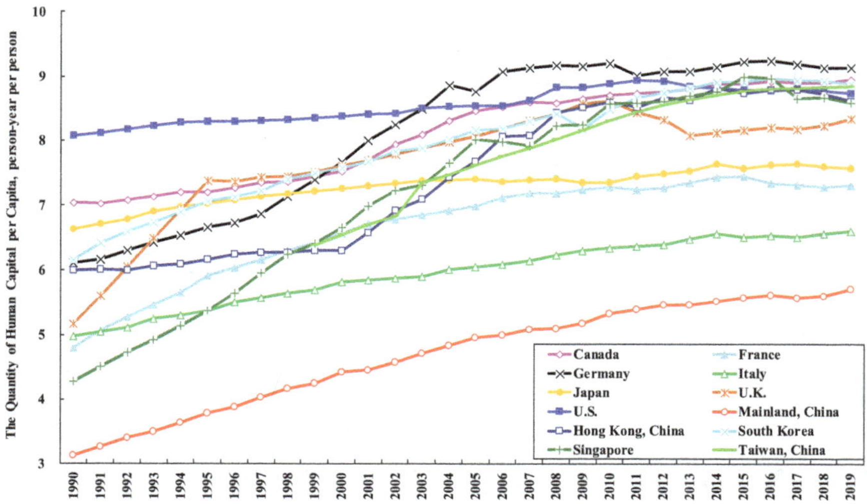

Source: Data are collected from Human Development Reports, United Nations Development Programme, and the Directorate General of Budget, Accounting and Statistics, Taiwan, China.

place. Mainland China is in the last place among our economies. Despite significant increases in the total number of person-years of education for Mainland China in recent decades, the quantity of Chinese human capital in per capita terms is still relatively low, especially because our measurement includes only the school-years of those aged 25 and above and hence cannot reflect the huge expansion of the tertiary education sector in Mainland China in the past decade or so. It will take another couple of decades before the quantity of Mainland Chinese human capital per capita can catch up to the level of the G-7 economies.

In Figure 12.3, we plot a scatter diagram between the total quantity of human capital, measured in terms of person-years of education, and the quantity of real R&D capital stock in the same year. Figure 12.3 shows a very diverse scatter. The ratio of human capital to real R&D capital varies greatly across economies and over time. If they were constant across economies, the scatter points should all lie on the same straight line. However, Figure 12.3 clearly shows that, overall, the quantities of human capital and real R&D capital are positively correlated — the more real

Figure 12.3: A scatter diagram between the quantity of human capital and the quantity of real R&D capital stock, G-7 countries, Mainland China, and four EANIEs

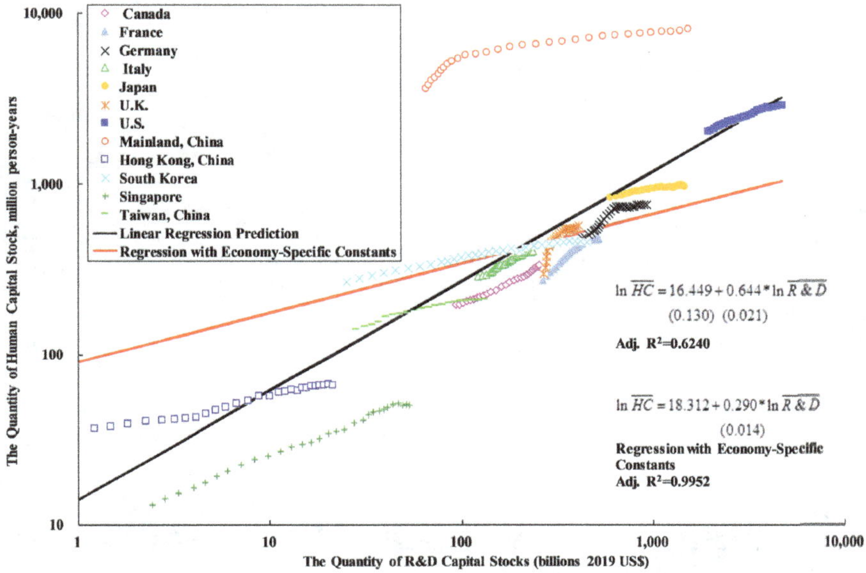

Source: Data are collected from Human Development Reports, United Nations Development Programme, and the Directorate General of Budget, Accounting and Statistics, Taiwan, China. The quantities of R&D capital stocks are from Table A3.2 of Chapter 3.

R&D capital, the more human capital, and vice versa. The G-7 economies as a group do appear to have similar elasticities of human capital with respect to R&D capital. Among the East Asian economies other than Japan, there is a wide spread, with Mainland China having the highest ratio of human capital to R&D capital and Singapore the lowest. The goodness of fit of the simple linear regression of the natural logarithm of the quantity of human capital on the natural logarithm of the quantity of real R&D capital is relatively poor (the black line), reflecting the significant diversity among the economies, but the linear regression with economy-specific constants has a much better fit (the red line).[2] The elasticity

[2]The red line in Figure 12.3 is drawn with a constant term set equal to the weighted average of all the economy-specific constants with the shares of the number of observations of each economy in the total number of observations as weights.

Figure 12.4: The number of R&D researchers, G-7 countries, Mainland China, and three EANIEs

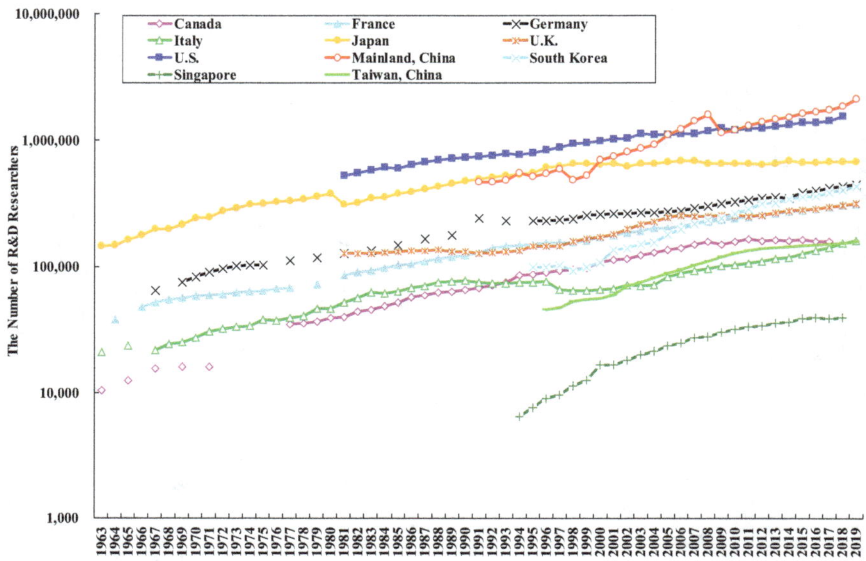

Source: The number of R&D researchers is collected from Main Science and Technology Indicators, OECD.

of human capital with respect to R&D capital does not seem to vary significantly across economies, and a 10% increase in the real R&D capital of an economy is associated with an approximately 3% increase in its human capital.

At a more microeconomic level, the number of R&D researchers in an economy is important because these are the actual people who have to carry out the R&D activities. However, R&D researchers *per se* constitute only a small proportion of the scientists and engineers in an economy. In Figure 12.4, the total numbers of R&D researchers, including researchers in (1) natural sciences and engineering,[3] (2) social science, humanities, and the arts, and (3) not elsewhere classified, are presented and compared across economies.[4] The number of R&D researchers does not include other R&D personnel such as technicians

[3] Data for ONLY the number of natural scientists and engineers are not readily available.

[4] Data for Hong Kong, China are not readily available.

Figure 12.5: The number of R&D researchers per capita, G-7 countries, Mainland China, and three EANIEs

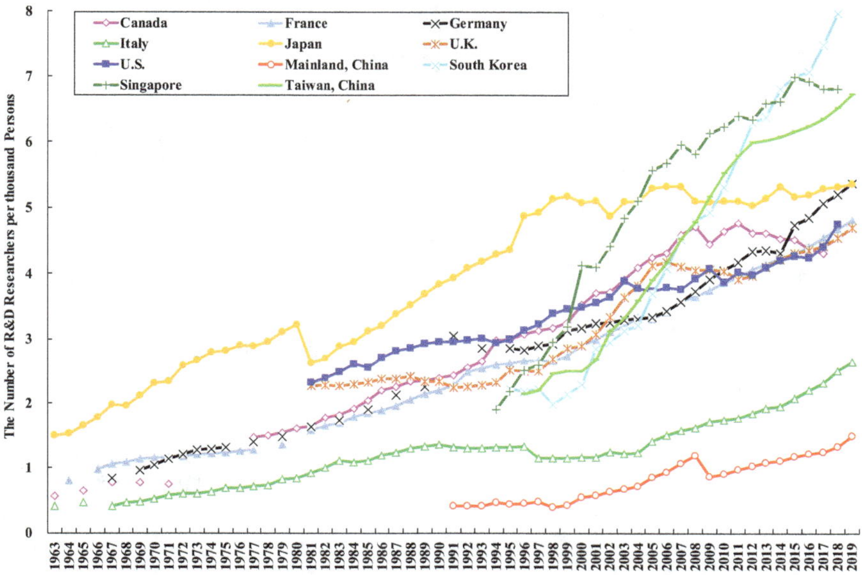

Source: Authors' calculations. The number of R&D researchers is collected from Main Science and Technology Indicators, OECD. The population data are from International Financial Statistics (Canada, France, Germany, Italy, Japan, South Korea, Singapore, and US), World Development Indicators (US), and the local statistical agencies (Mainland China and Taiwan, China).

and other support staff. Traditionally, the US had the highest number of R&D researchers. However, Mainland China has been catching up very fast and has overtaken the US in 2010.

In Figure 12.5, we compare the number of R&D researchers of the economies in our study on a per capita basis. Figure 12.5 shows that despite significant increases in the total number of R&D researchers in Mainland China, the number of Mainland Chinese R&D researchers is still low in per capita terms. In fact, it is the lowest in our sample of economies, due, in part, to its large population. It will probably take decades before the number of Chinese R&D researchers per capita can catch up to the level of the G-7 economies.

In Figure 12.6, we plot a scatter diagram between the total number of R&D researchers and the quantity of real R&D capital stock in the same

Figure 12.6: A scatter diagram between the number of R&D researchers and the quantity of real R&D capital stock, G-7 countries, Mainland China, and three EANIEs

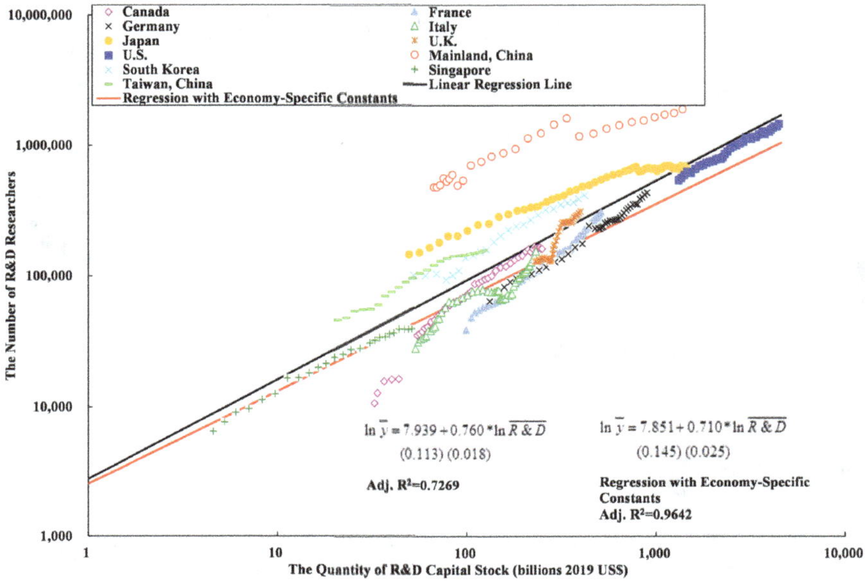

Source: The number of R&D researchers is collected from Main Science and Technology Indicators, OECD. The quantities of R&D capital stocks are from Table A3.2 of Chapter 3.

year. Figure 12.6 shows that overall, the number of R&D researchers and the quantity of real R&D capital stock are positively correlated. Moreover, the correlation appears to be tighter than that between human capital and real R&D capital in Figure 12.3, which is what should be expected. The elasticity of the number of R&D researchers with respect to the quantity of real R&D capital is approximately greater than 0.7, that is, a 10% increase in real R&D capital is likely to result in a more than 7% increase in the number of R&D researchers. However, Mainland China appears to have a lower real R&D capital to R&D researcher ratio than all the other economies. This may perhaps be due in part to the lower cost of R&D labour relative to real R&D capital in Mainland China.

An important determinant of whether innovation can enhance the actual rate of technical progress of an economy is its total number of scientists and engineers because these are the people who have to implement the discoveries and inventions in actual manufacturing and other

Figure 12.7: The number of scientists and engineers, selected economies

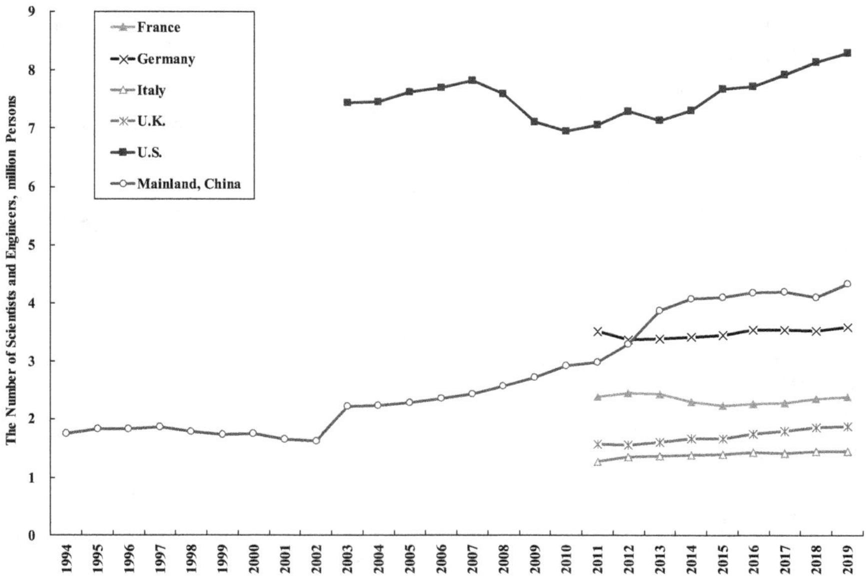

Source: Labour Statistics (ISCO level 2), International Labour Organisation; Chinese Labour Statistical Yearbook.

productive activities downstream from R&D. In fact, the proportion of scientists and engineers directly engaged in R&D activities is probably a small percentage of the total. In Figure 12.7, the total numbers of scientists and engineers of selected economies in our sample are compared.[5] Figure 12.7 shows that the US has by far the highest number of scientists and engineers, followed by Mainland China and Germany.[6]

In Figure 12.8, we compare the number of scientists and engineers of selected economies in our sample on a per capita basis. Figure 12.8 shows that Germany has the highest number of scientists and engineers per

[5] Unfortunately, it is not possible to compare the number of scientists and engineers across all the economies in our sample because the data are not readily available for some of them.

[6] The definition of "scientists and engineers" in Chinese statistics may not be exactly the same as that used by the International Labour Organisation. However, we believe they are broadly comparable.

Figure 12.8: The number of scientists and engineers per capita, selected economies

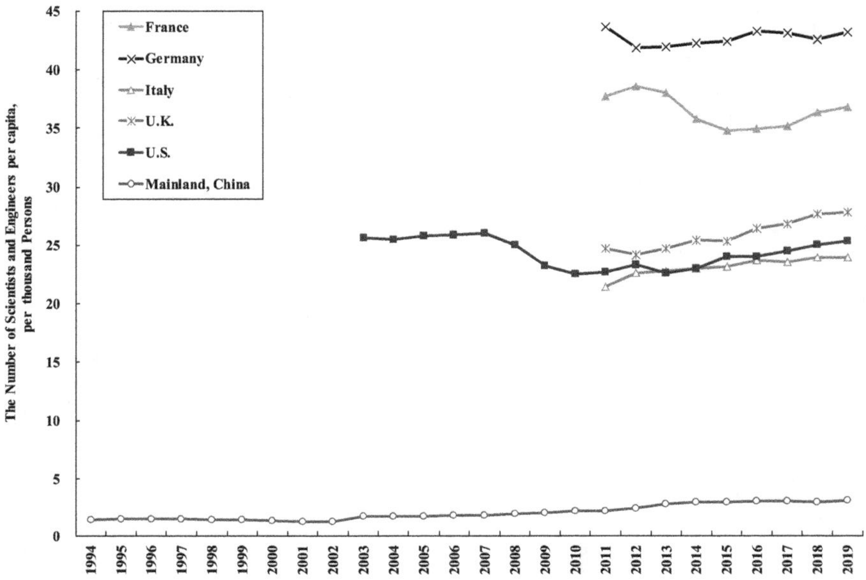

Source: Labour Statistics (ISCO level 2), International Labour Organisation; Chinese Labour Statistical Yearbook.

capita, followed by France. We believe that the US has a relatively low number of scientists and engineers per capita among the developed economies mainly because of its relatively smaller manufacturing sector. The number of Mainland Chinese scientists and engineers in per capita terms is still low despite significant increases in the total number of scientists and engineers in the recent decade. It will take decades before the number of Chinese scientists and engineers per capita can catch up to the levels of the developed economies.

Chapter 13

Other Indicators of Innovation Success

In Chapters 3–7, we have examined two major indicators of the innovation output of an economy at the macroeconomic level — the total numbers of patent applications to and patent grants from domestic and foreign patent offices — and shown that they depend positively and monotonically on the quantities of real Research and Development (R&D) capital stock, defined as the cumulative total real R&D expenditures less the depreciation of an assumed 10% per year. In Chapter 8, we have also developed several other indicators of relative success in innovation, again at the macroeconomic level.

There are of course other possible indicators of innovation output at the economy-wide level, for example, the total number of articles published in professional and scientific journals, the number of frequently cited published journal articles, the frequency of major scientific awards such as the Nobel Prize, and the annual value of income from licence fees and royalties. It is not possible to undertake an exhaustive examination of all of these alternative indicators of innovation output, but some of them will be briefly discussed in turn in the following sections.

13.1 The Number of Published Articles in Professional Journals

When a new and original discovery or invention is made, it is likely that the first public disclosure is through a research paper authored by the discoverer(s) or inventor(s). The research paper, after being peer-reviewed and confirmed to be valid, is then published as an article in a professional journal. Thus, the publication of such an article should also be considered as an output of R&D activities and an indicator of innovation success. In Figure 13.1, the time series of the number of scientific and engineering articles published in professional journals by authors who are residents of a given economy included in our study between 2000 and 2018 are presented.[1,2] These articles include those published in the following fields:

Figure 13.1: The number of scientific and engineering articles in professional journals, G-7 countries, Mainland China, and three EANIEs

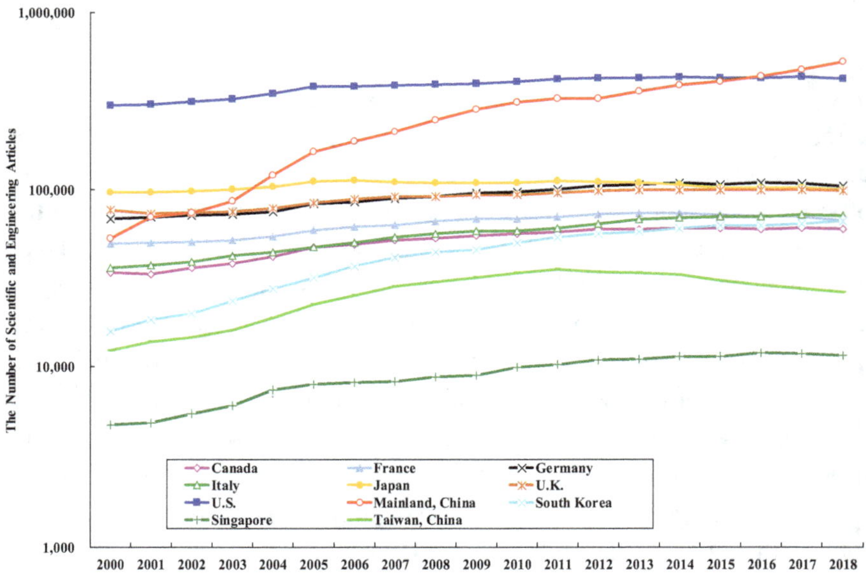

Source: World Development Indicators and Science & Engineering Indicators, US National Science Foundation.

[1]The numbers of scientific and engineering articles for G-7 countries, Mainland China, Singapore, and South Korea are taken from the World Development Indicators (WDI) database of the World Bank. Data for Taiwan, China are collected from Science & Engineering Indicators, US National Science Foundation. Data on Hong Kong, China are not readily available.

[2]Counts are based on fractional assignments; articles with authors from different economies are allocated proportionately to each economy.

physics, biology, chemistry, mathematics, clinical medicine, biomedical research, engineering and technology, and earth and space sciences. The journals are limited to those that are abstracted in the Institute for Scientific Information's Science Citation Index (SCI) and Social Sciences Citation Index (SSCI).

Figure 13.1 shows that in 2000, the United States was far and away the leader in the annual number of published scientific and engineering articles, with more than 300,000. In contrast, Mainland China had only 53,000 articles. Japan, the United Kingdom (UK), and Germany were in the second, third and fourth places, respectively. However, the number of articles authored by Mainland Chinese residents began to increase rapidly, and Mainland China overtook first Japan in 2004 and then the United States (US) in 2016 to take the lead in the total number of published scientific and engineering articles. In 2018, Chinese authors published 530,000 articles compared to the 420,000 of the US authors, with Germany in a distant third place with 104,000 articles. Japan used to be the second most prolific publisher of scientific and engineering articles until it was overtaken by Mainland China in 2004 and Germany in 2014. In last place in 2018 was Singapore.[3] Over the period 2000–2018, the number of scientific and engineering articles grew in every economy in our study at rates ranging from 0.1% per annum for Japan to 12.8% per annum for Mainland China, with an average of 4.0%. The number of articles from the US grew at 1.8% per annum. For the world as a whole, the number of articles grew at 4.8% per annum. The rapid growth of the number of articles from Mainland China inevitably crowded out potential articles from the rest of the world. In fact, between 2014 and 2018, the number of articles from Canada, France, Germany, Japan, the UK, the US, and Taiwan, China all declined.

In Figure 13.2, the numbers of scientific and engineering articles in professional journals published by authors resident in a given economy per thousand persons each year are compared across the economies in our study. Surprisingly, Singapore is the leader among the economies included in our study, followed by Canada and the UK. The US falls into the middle

[3]Comparable figures on the number of articles published by residents of Hong Kong, China are not readily available.

Figure 13.2: The number of scientific and engineering articles in professional journals per thousand persons, G-7 countries, Mainland China, and three EANIEs

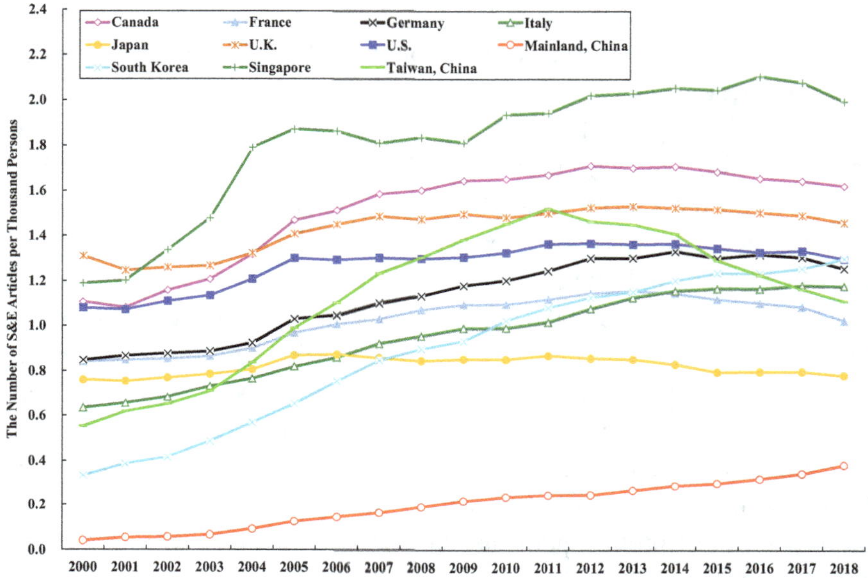

Source: The numbers of scientific and engineering articles are from World Development Indicators and Science & Engineering Indicators, US National Science Foundation. The population data are from International Financial Statistics (Canada, France, Germany, Italy, Japan, South Korea, Singapore, and UK), World Development Indicators (US) and the local statistical agencies (Mainland China, Hong Kong, China and Taiwan, China).

of the group. Equally surprisingly, Japan is in the next to the last place. Mainland China, with only one-third of the number of articles per capita as the US, is in the last place in part because of its large population.

In Figure 13.3, the number of scientific and engineering articles in professional journals published by authors resident in a given economy each year is plotted against the quantity of its real R&D capital stock. Not surprisingly, the number of articles also bears a positive relationship to the quantity of real R&D capital stock. The higher the quantity of real R&D capital stock, the higher is the number of scientific and engineering articles published in professional journals. However, as pointed out above, since the mid-2010s, the numbers of published articles have been declining for Canada, France, Germany, Japan, the UK, the US, and Taiwan, China, even as the total for the world has continued to increase. This may be explained in part by the large

Figure 13.3: A scatter diagram between the numbers of scientific and engineering articles and the quantities of real R&D capital stock, G-7 countries, Mainland China, and three EANIEs

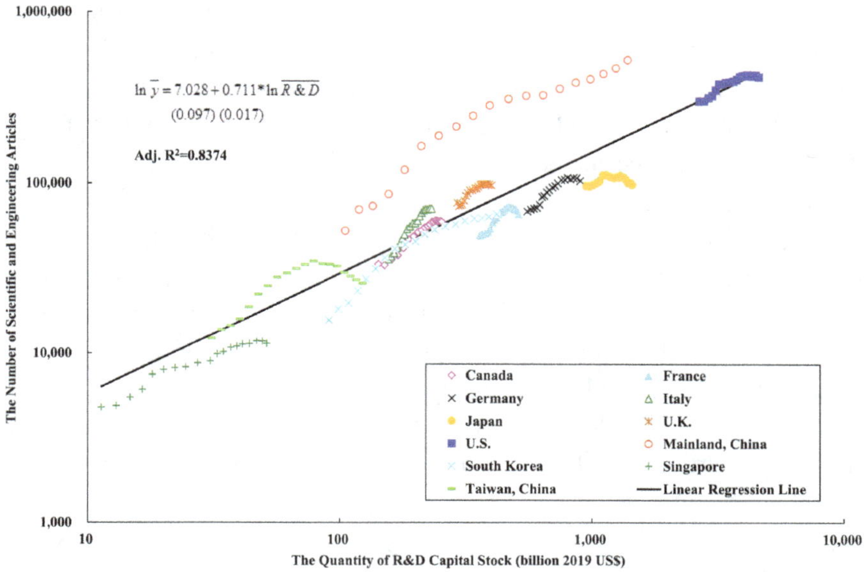

Source: World Development Indicators; Science & Engineering Indicators, US National Science Foundation; and Table A3.1 of Chapter 3.

increases in the number of article submissions and publications by authors from Mainland China, which have in effect crowded out those authors from other economies. This is evidenced by the dips at the ends of the economy-specific number of articles quantity of real capital stock lines. Nevertheless, the overall positive relationship between the number of published articles and the quantity of real R&D capital stock is unmistakable. The linear regression yields a statistically highly significant coefficient of 0.711, which can be interpreted as the elasticity of the annual number of articles with respect to the quantity of real R&D capital. We believe the relatively low estimate of the elasticity may have been caused by the decline in the number of articles in most of the economies beginning in the mid-2010s. Mainland China does appear to be an over-achiever in Figure 13.3.[4]

[4] In some Chinese universities, there is a publication requirement for the completion of master and Ph.D. degrees. Having high-quality publications which are cited in SSCI and SCI is also a requirement for obtaining tenured academic positions in most Chinese universities and research institutes. This may explain, in part, the surge in the number of Chinese published articles.

13.2 The Number of Frequently Cited Articles

However, not all published articles are of equal quality or importance. The highest-quality articles are often the most frequently cited. In Figure 13.4, we present time-series data on the number of "top 1% most cited science and engineering articles" published by the residents of each economy in our study. The US has been and continues to be the leader in the number of "top 1% most cited science and engineering articles". However, Mainland China has made great progress since 2000, overtaking Italy in 2003, France in 2004, Japan and Canada in 2005, Germany in 2008 and the UK in 2010, to reach the second place with just below 5,000 articles, compared to the just above 8,000 for the US. It is of interest to note that with the exception of Mainland China, the numbers of frequently cited articles of the other East Asian economies, including Japan, are relatively low.

In Figure 13.5, the number of top 1% most cited Science and Engineering articles published in professional journals written by authors

Figure 13.4: The number of top 1% most cited S&E articles in the scopus database, G-7 countries, Mainland China, and three EANIEs

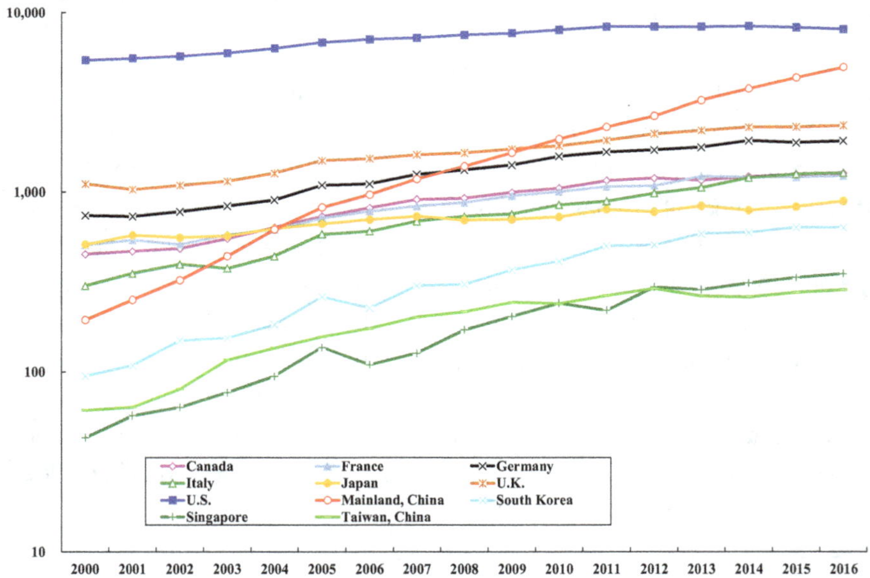

Source: Authors' Calculations. Data are collected from Table S5a-2 and Table S5a-35, Science & Engineering Indicators, US National Science Foundation.

Figure 13.5: A scatter diagram between the number of top 1% most-cited S&E articles and the quantity of real R&D capital stock, G-7 countries, Mainland China, and three EANIEs

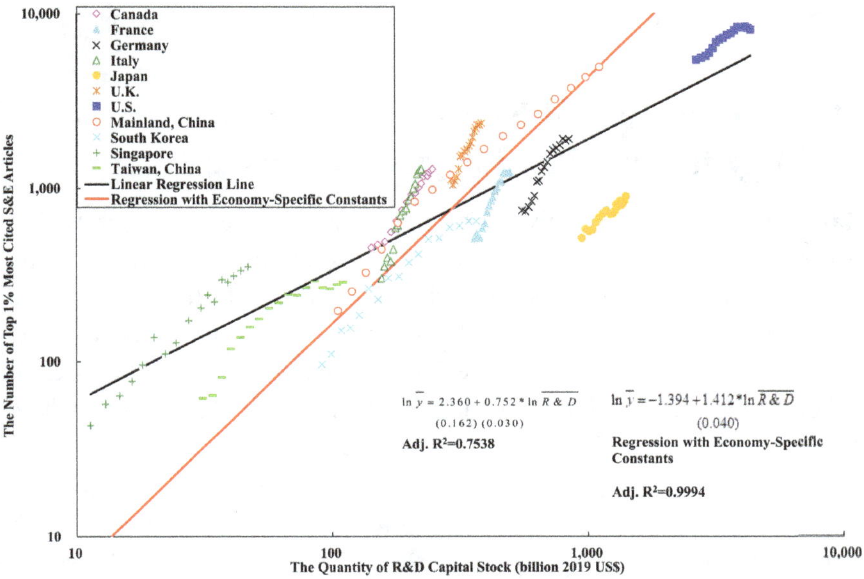

Source: Data on the number of top 1% most cited S&E articles are the same as Figure 13.4. Data on the quantity of R&D capital stock are from Table A3.2.

resident in each economy each year is plotted against the quantity of its real R&D capital stock. Once again, the number of top 1% most cited S&E articles also has a positive relationship to the quantity of real R&D capital stock. The higher the quantity of real R&D capital stock, the higher is the number of top 1% most cited S&E articles. Two separate linear regression lines, one with economy-specific constant terms (the red line)[5] and one without (the black line), are plotted in Figure 13.5. They both show a significant positive relationship between the number of top 1% most cited articles and the quantity of real R&D capital stock. However, the linear regression with economy-specific constants (the red

[5]The red line in Figure 13.5 is drawn with a constant term set equal to the weighted average of all the economy-specific constants with the shares of the number of observations of each economy in the total number of observations as weights.

line) has a much better overall fit (Adjusted R^2 of 0.9994) and an estimated elasticity of the number of most cited articles with respect to the real R&D capital stock of 1.41, indicating that substantial economies of scale once economy-specific factors are controlled.

13.3 The Number of Nobel Prizes in Chemistry, Physics, and Physiology or Medicine

Major scientific awards given for important original discoveries and inventions are also good indicators of innovation output. There are many such awards. We choose to look at the Nobel Prizes in the physical and life sciences, that is, the Nobel Prizes in Chemistry, Physics, and Physiology or Medicine. In Figure 13.6, the cumulative total number of Nobel Prizes received by the nationals of the G-7 countries and China

Figure 13.6: The cumulative number of Nobel Prizes in Chemistry, Physics and Physiology or Medicine, G-7 countries and China

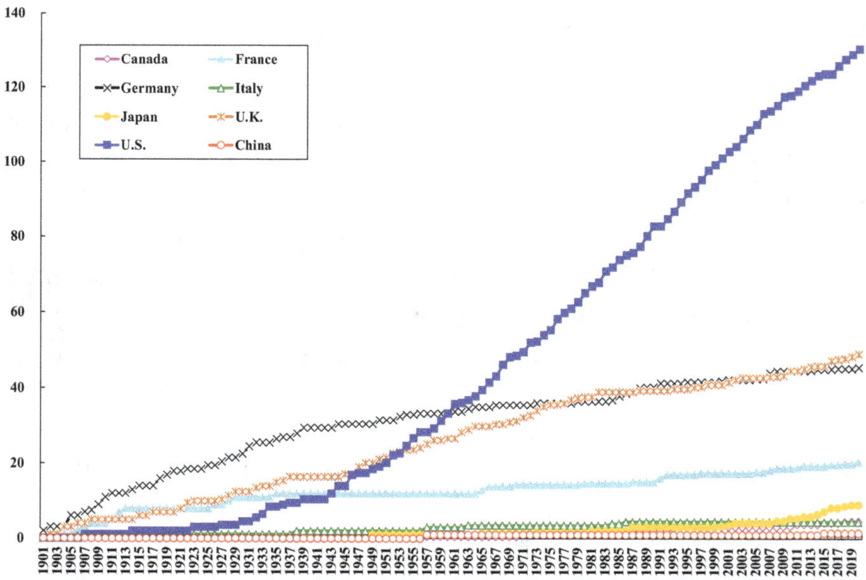

Source: Derived from Nobel Prize website.

Figure 13.7: A scatter diagram between the cumulative number of Nobel Prizes in Physical Sciences and the quantity of real R&D capital stock, G-7 countries and China

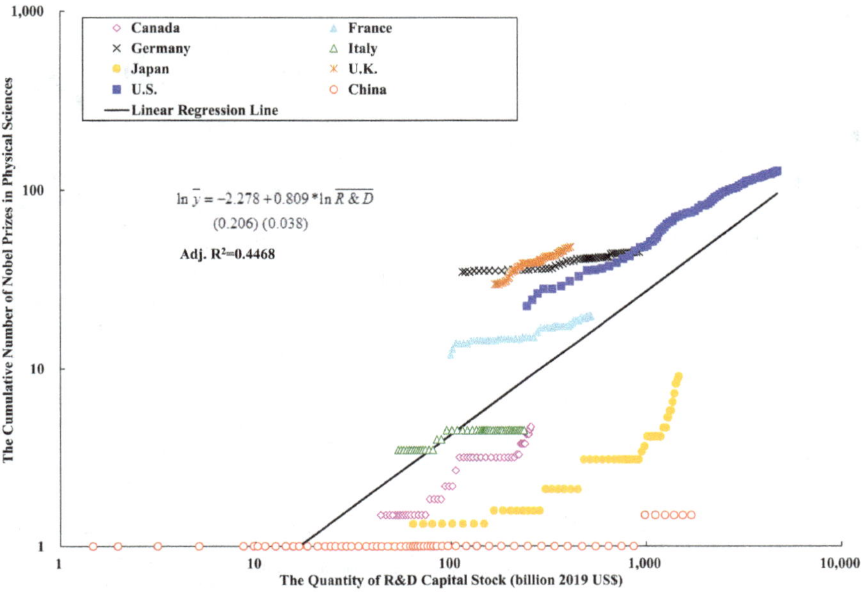

Source: Figure 13.6 and Table A3.1 of Chapter 3.

(Mainland only) is presented. (There has been no Nobel Prize in the physical and life sciences awarded to the residents of the four EANIEs.)

Figure 13.6 shows that as of 2020, the United States has the highest cumulative number of Nobel Laureates, 130.4, in the physical and life sciences.[6] In fact, it has had a commanding lead since 1961. It is followed by the UK, with 49.1 Laureates, and Germany, with 45.6 laureates. China has only 1.5 Laureates. The gap between the US and the other G-7 countries plus China is large. In fact, the cumulative number of US Nobel Laureates is just shy of the combined total of the other G-7 countries and China, 135.

In Figure 13.7, the cumulative total number of Nobel Prizes in the physical and life sciences received by the nationals of the G-7 countries

[6]The number of prizes are fractional because each Nobel Prize can be shared by as many as three laureates each year.

Figure 13.8: A scatter diagram between the cumulative number of Nobel Prizes in Physical Sciences and the quantity of real basic R&D capital stock, G-7 countries and China

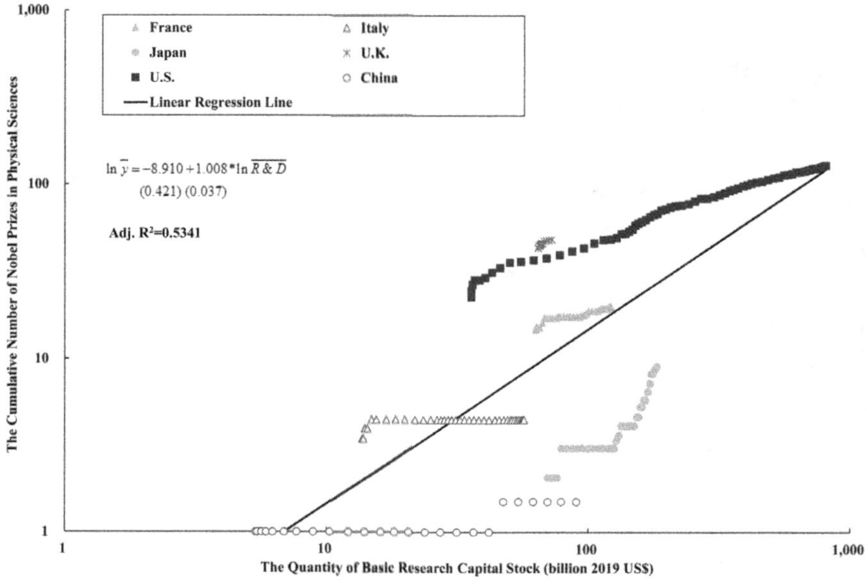

Sources: Figure 13.6 and Table A3.4 of Chapter 3.

and China each year is plotted against the quantity of its real R&D capital stock. The relationship is also positive: the higher the quantity of real R&D capital stock of an economy, the higher is its cumulative number of Nobel Laureates. The linear regression line is also statistically significant. However, there appears to be a large gap between the "over-achievers" of the US, the UK, Germany, and France on the one hand and the "under-achievers" of Canada, Italy, Japan, and China on the other.

Alternatively, we can also draw a scatter diagram between the cumulative number of Nobel Prizes and the quantity of real basic research capital stock each year. This is presented in Figure 13.8. (Unfortunately, data on basic research expenditures are not readily available for Canada and Germany.) The relationship is also positive: the higher the quantity of real basic research capital stock of an economy, the higher is its cumulative number of Nobel Laureates. In fact, the goodness of fit of the linear regression of the number of Laureates on the quantity of real basic research capital stock (Adjusted $R^2 = 0.5341$) is better than the one on the quantity of real R&D capital stock (Adjusted $R^2 = 0.4468$), which shows that basic research is probably a more important determinant of breakthrough scientific discoveries.

On the basis of this cursory examination of other indicators of innovation success, we can conclude that they are all positively and monotonically related to the quantity of real R&D capital stock. The connection between innovation and R&D is always present, no matter how innovation is measured.

Finally, while in principle, the value of licence fees and royalties received is also a good indicator of innovation success, it is in practice quite difficult to collect such data in a comprehensive way. In addition to domestic revenue from licence fees and royalties, there can also be significant foreign revenue from license fees and royalties. However, these fees and royalties are sometimes booked to tax havens for tax avoidance reasons. Furthermore, whatever data available are often not disaggregated to the level of the individual economies by either origin or destination. It will have to await a further study in itself.

Part Six

Concluding Remarks

Chapter 14

Conclusions and Directions for Further Research

Are There Laws of Innovation? Our investigations, as reported in Chapters 1–13, allow us to answer unequivocally: Yes, there are "Laws of Innovation"! This is certainly true at the economy-wide level. Innovation is found not to be accidental or fortuitous. It is also not manna from heaven. It is basically the outcome of Research and Development (R&D) activities conducted in an economy over a long period of time. The more an economy invests in R&D, the more innovation success it will be able to generate over time, and the more sustainable its economic growth will become.

We have established that the numbers of patent applications and grants are useful measures of innovation output. We have also established that the quantity of real R&D capital stock is a useful measure of innovation input. Moreover, a positive and monotonic relationship between innovation output and innovation input has also been consistently and repeatedly identified and confirmed with empirical data. Specifically, the positive relationship between the number of patent applications submitted by and patent grants awarded to the residents of an economy and the quantity of its real R&D capital stock has been empirically established for different economies and different patent granting agencies (including the United States Patent and Trademark Office (USPTO), European Patent Office (EPO) and China National Intellectual Property Administration (CNIPA)), and at both the macroeconomic and microeconomic levels.

Our investigations also show that the number of patent grants by a foreign patent authority (for example, USPTO, EPO, and CNIPA), as opposed to the number of domestic patent grants, is a more reliable indicator of the relative success in innovation across economies. However, on balance, it also appears that the number of USPTO patent grants is probably a more reliable indicator to use because its economy-specific grant rates appear to be quite consistent and uniform across different economies and exhibit no obvious biases.

Through our econometric analysis of USPTO patent applications and grants in Chapters 10 and 11 for the six economies with more domestic patent applications than USPTO patent applications,[1] consisting of Mainland China, France, Germany, Japan, South Korea and the United States (US), we have also rigorously established that the positive relationship between the number of patent applications and patent grants and the quantity of real R&D capital stock is actually quite similar across the different economies. In fact, one cannot reject the hypothesis that they are identical. Thus, the common "Laws of Innovation" appear to apply across economies. The estimated elasticity of the number of USPTO patent grants awarded to an economy with respect to the quantity of its lagged real R&D capital stock is 0.92.[2] It means, on average, a 1% increase in the quantity of the real R&D capital stock of an economy increases its annual number of USPTO patent grants by 0.92%, indicating the existence of some slight decreasing returns to scale.[3] However, we believe that the R&D enterprise on balance exhibits approximately constant returns to scale. In any case, we should bear in mind that the quantity of real R&D capital stock is the cumulative total of a decade of R&D investments and cannot be changed significantly either upwards or downwards overnight.

---

[1] It is reasonable to assume that if a discovery or invention is good enough for a USPTO patent application, it should be good enough, in terms of quality, for a domestic patent application. Moreover, the cost of application, and subsequent maintenance if granted, of a USPTO patent is, in general, much more expensive than that of a domestic patent. Thus, when a USPTO patent application is submitted without concurrently submitting a domestic patent application, considerations extraneous to the quality of the discovery or invention must have been involved. In this case, the number of patent applications is a biased indicator of innovation success.

[2] See Chapter 11.

[3] An elasticity of one indicates constant returns to scale.

Other indicators of innovation success, such as publications in professional journals and frequency of citations, also show a similar relationship with the quantity of real R&D capital stock. In particular, our analysis of the Nobel Prizes in the physical and life sciences identifies investment in basic research as an important determinant of cumulative success in Nobel Prizes in the long run.

It would be interesting to extend our econometric model for the analysis of USPTO patent applications and grants to include EPO patent applications and grants and CNIPA patent applications and grants. Like the USPTO, the EPO and the CNIPA are likely to maintain more consistent and uniform standards and procedures in their assessment of the quality of the patent applications, at least insofar as foreign applicants are concerned.

Another interesting question is whether there exist cross-economy externalities in R&D. What we have in mind is whether a higher quantity of real R&D capital stock in one economy can raise the R&D output, for example, patent grants, in another economy. We believe this is not only possible but also quite likely, given the large volume of published professional and scholarly articles and educational exchanges. However, this effect may be difficult to identify and quantify empirically. Perhaps one can begin with a study of cross-economy collaboration in R&D as revealed in publications in professional and scientific journals.

Yet another interesting question is the relative distribution of the stocks of working USPTO patents across the economies included in our study.[4] A patent grant is typically valid for 20 years from the date of application (not the date of the patent grant). Thus, at any given time, the stock of working patents may be approximately estimated by the cumulative total number of patent grants over the previous 19 years, on the assumption that it takes, on average, 1 year from the date of application for a patent grant to be approved. The estimated time series of the stocks of working USPTO patents of each economy in our study between 2000 and 2019 are presented in Figure 14.1. Figure 14.1 shows that the US has consistently had the largest stock of working USPTO patents. Japan is in second place. Even though the other East Asian economies, including

[4] It is also possible to look at patents granted by other patent offices. However, judging from the economy-specific USPTO patent application success rates, it appears that the USPTO has maintained uniform standards for all economies, including the US itself.

Figure 14.1: The stock of working USPTO patent grants, the G-7 countries, Mainland China, and four EANIEs

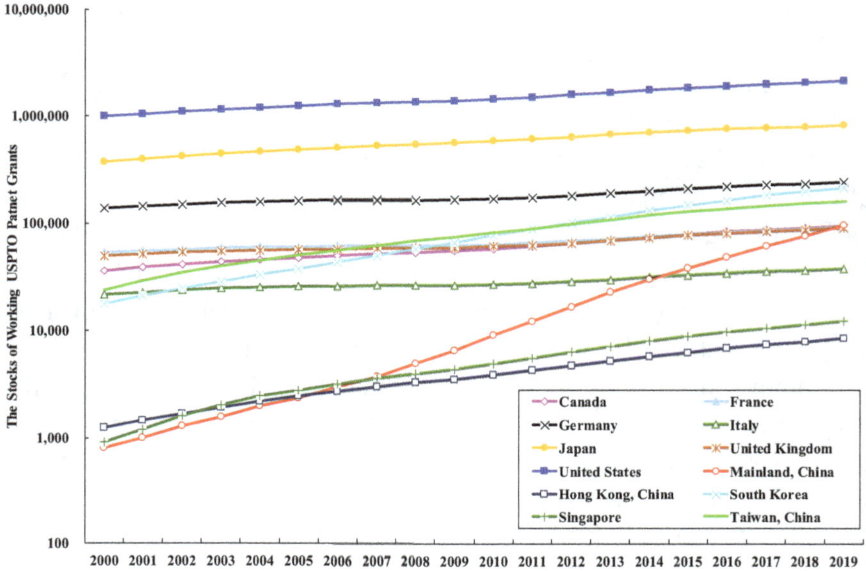

Source: Authors' calculations. The number of USPTO patent grants are from Table A5.2 of Chapter 5.

Mainland China, have been catching up fast, but it is likely to take a while before they reach the same level as the developed economies.

Our investigations also reveal the rising importance of East Asian economies other than Japan, especially Mainland China, in the creation of patents worldwide. In Figure 14.2, we compare the share of the total number of USPTO patent grants accounted for by the G-7 countries without Japan and those of Mainland China and the EANIEs with Japan.[5] We refer to the group of G-7 countries without Japan as "G-7 Countries ex Japan" and Mainland China and the EANIEs with Japan as "East Asian economies". The share of G-7 Countries ex Japan has fallen from a peak of almost 95% in 1963 to just below 60% in 2019, while the share of East Asian economies has risen from less than 1% in 1963 to almost 31% in 2019. It is clear that, over time, the centre of gravity of innovation has

[5] Japan may also be considered an East Asian economy, along with Mainland China and the four EANIEs.

Figure 14.2: The distribution of USPTO patent grants, G-7 countries ex Japan, Japan, Mainland China, and four EANIEs

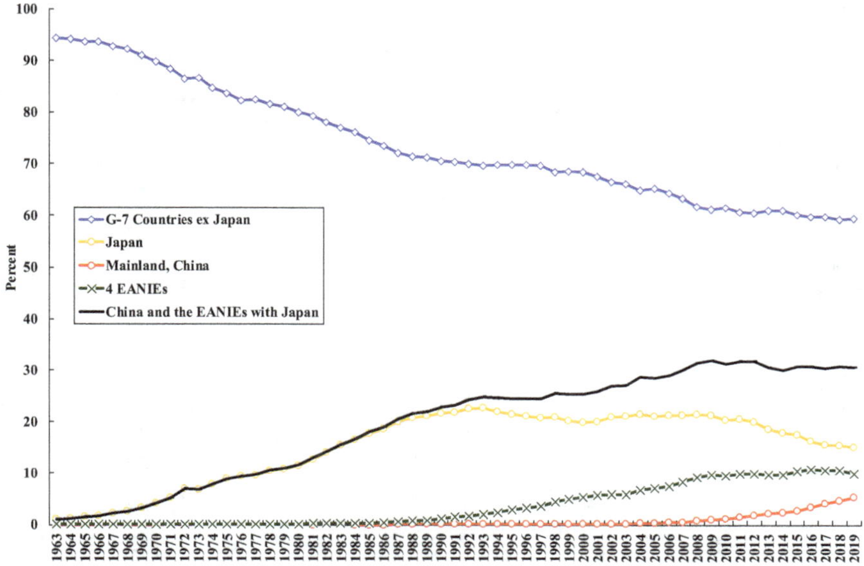

Source: Table A5.2 of Chapter 5.

been gradually shifting from the developed to the developing economies and also from European and North American economies to East Asian economies. It is, however, noteworthy that the share of Japan has also been declining since the early 1990s and the rate of increase of the share of the four EANIEs seems to have plateaued. It will probably take another couple of decades before the share of East Asian economies in USPTO patent grants can rise above 40%, but it will likely do so on the strength of USPTO patent applications from Mainland China.

For the sake of comparison, we also look at the distribution of CNIPA patent grants between the "G-7 Countries ex Japan" and the East Asian economies, consisting of Mainland China, Japan and the four EANIEs. In Figure 14.3, we compare the shares of the total number of CNIPA patent grants accounted for by these two groups of economies. Figure 14.3 shows that, in 2019, G-7 Countries ex Japan accounted for less than 10% of CNIPA patent grants and East Asian economies accounted for almost 90%, with 78% from Mainland China itself. We believe this is due, in part,

Figure 14.3: The distribution of CNIPA patent grants, G-7 countries ex Japan, Japan, Mainland China, and four EANIEs

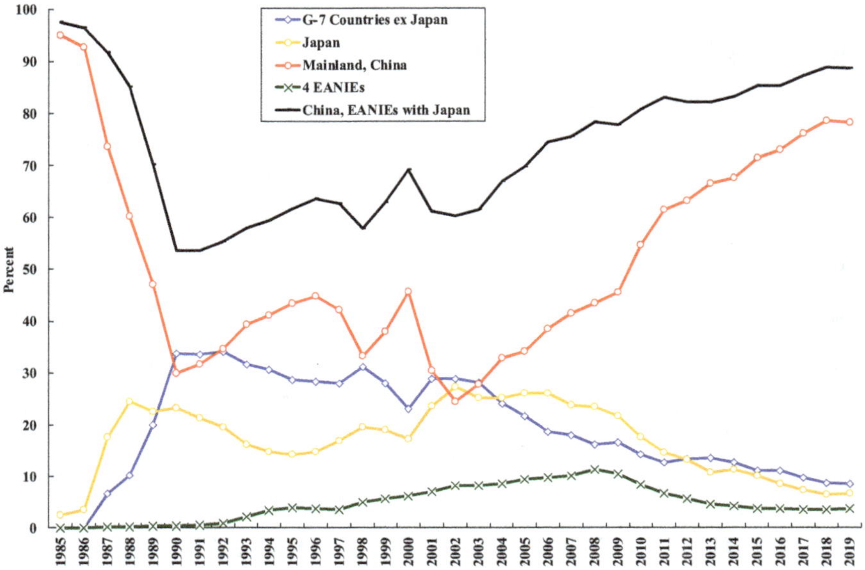

Source: China Statistical Yearbook, various years.

to the low CNIPA patent application rates from economies outside of Mainland China. As the patent application rates from other economies rise, the share of G-7 Countries ex Japan should also begin to rise, perhaps ultimately to 30%. This is not inconsistent with the hypothesis that the centre of gravity of innovation will continue to shift from European and North American economies to East Asian economies.

Finally, it remains to be established that the quantity of the working stock of patent grants of an economy can have a positive effect on its rate of technical progress or equivalently the rate of growth of its total factor productivity, perhaps with a time lag. One possible alternative approach is to use our estimated time series of quantities of real R&D capital stocks as a variable input in the estimation of aggregate production functions in addition to the conventional inputs of tangible capital, labour and human capital. While these are all worthwhile research initiatives, they are beyond the scope of this study and will have to be taken up in other studies in the future.

References

Beneito P. 2006. The innovative performance of in-house and contracted R&D in terms of patents and utility models. *Research Policy*, **35**: 502–517.

Boskin MJ and Lau LJ. 1992. International and intertemporal comparison of productive efficiency: An application of the meta-production function approach to the group-of-five (G-5) countries. *Economic Studies Quarterly*, **43**: 298–312.

Christensen LR, Jorgenson DW and Lau LJ. 1971. Conjugate duality and the transcendental logarithmic function. *Econometrica*, **39**: 255–256.

Christensen LR, Jorgenson, DW and Lau, LJ. 1973. Transcendental logarithmic production frontiers. *The Review of Economics and Statistics*, **55**: 28–45.

Cincera M. 1997. Patent, R&D, and technologyical spillovers at the firm level: Some evidence from econometric count models for panel data. *Journal of Applied Econometrics*, **12**: 265–280.

Crépon B and Duguet E. 1997. Estimating the innovation function from patent numbers: GMM on count panel data. *Journal of Applied Econometrics*, **12**: 243–263.

Deolalikar AB and Röller L-H. 1989. Patenting by manufacturing firms in India: Its production and impact. *The Journal of Industrial Economics*, **37**: 303–314.

Griffith R, Huergo E, Mairesse J and Peters B. 2006. Innovation and productivity across four European countries. *Oxford Review of Economic Policy*, **22**: 483–493.

Hall BH, Griliches Z and Hausman JA. 1986. Patents and R and D: Is there a lag? *International Economic Review*, **27**: 265–283.

Hausman JA, Hall BH and Griliches Z. 1984. Econometric models for count data with an application to the patents-R&D relationship. *Econometrica*, **52**: 909–938.

Hayami Y and Ruttan VW. 1970. Agricultural productivity differences among countries. *American Economic Review*, **60**: 895–911.

Hu JL, Yang CH and Chen CP. 2014. R&D efficiency and the national innovation system: An international comparison using the distance function approach. *Bulletin of Economic Research*, **66**: 55–71.

Kanwar S and Singh S. 2018. The innovation-R&D nexus in an emerging economy: Evidence from the Indian manufacturing sector. *Australian Economic Papers*, **57**: 35–54.

Kim JI and Lau LJ. 1994. The sources of economic growth of the East Asian newly industrialized countries. *Journal of the Japanese and International Economies*, **8**: 235–271.

Kim JI and Lau LJ. 1995. The role of human capital in the economic growth of the East Asian newly industrialised countries. *Asia-Pacific Economic Review*, **1**: 3–22.

Kim JI and Lau LJ. 1996. The sources of Asian Pacific economic growth. *Canadian Journal of Economics*, **29**: S448–S454.

Krugman P. 1994. The myth of Asia's miracle. *Foreign Affairs*, **73**: 62–78.

Lau LJ and Park JS. 2002. Sources of East Asian economic growth revisited. Working Paper, Department of Economics, Stanford University, Stanford, CA, December.

Lau LJ and Yotopoulos PA. 1989. The meta-production function approach to technological change in world agriculture. *Journal of Development Economics*, **31**: 241–269.

Ministry of Science and Technology, The People's Republic of China. 2006. *Guojia Zhongchangqi Kexue he Jishu Fazhan Guihua Gangyao (2006–2020) (Outline of the National Medium- and Long-Term Scientific and Technological Development Plan (2006–2020))*, Beijing. Available at http://www.most.gov.cn/kjgh/kjghzcq/.

Park J. 2004. International and intersectoral R&D spillovers in the OECD and East Asian economies. *Economic Inquiry*, **42**: 739–757.

Potužáková Z and Öhm J. 2018. R&D investments, EPO patent applications and the economic heterogeneity within the EU. *Review of Economic Perspectives (Národohospodářský Obzor)*, **18**: 177–191.

Rousseau S and Rousseau R. 1997. Data envelopment analysis as a tool for constructing scientometric indicators. *Scientometrics*, **40**: 45–56.

Sharma S and Thomas VJ. 2008. Inter-country R&D efficiency analysis: An application of data envelopment analysis. *Scientometrics*, **76**: 483–501.

Teitel S. 1994. Patents, R&D expenditures, country size, and per capita income: An International comparison. *Scientometrics*, **29**: 137–159.

Voutsinas I, Tsamadias C, Carayannis E and Staikouras C. 2018. Does research and development expenditure impact innovation? theory, policy and practice insights from the Greek experience. *The Journal of Technology Transfer*, **43**: 159–171.

Young A. 1992. A tale of two cities: Factor accumulation and technical change in Hong Kong and Singapore. In Blanchard OJ and Fischer S (eds.), *National Bureau of Economic Research Macroeconomics Annual.* Cambridge, MA: The MIT Press, 13–54.

Index

www.ingramcontent.com/pod-product-compliance
Lightning Source LLC
LaVergne TN
LVHW010335220926
848484LV00004BB/903